The Design of Education

Second Edition

Jossey-Bass Publishers
San Francisco

Substantial discounts on bulk quantities of Jossey-Bass books are available to corporations, professional associations, and other organizations. For details and discount information, contact the special sales department at Jossey-Bass Inc., Publishers (415) 433–1740; Fax (800) 605–2665.

For sales outside the United States, please contact your local Simon & Schuster International office.

 Manufactured in the United States of America on Lyons Falls Pathfinder Tradebook. This paper is acid-free and 100 percent totally chlorine-free.

Library of Congress Cataloging-in-Publication Data

Houle, Cyril O., date.
    The design of education / Cyril O. Houle. — 2nd ed.
    p. cm. — (The Jossey-Bass higher and adult education series)
    Includes bibliographical references and indexes.
    ISBN 0-7879-0209-8
    1. Adult education. 2. Evening and continuation schools.
  I. Title. II. Series
  LC5215.H69   1996
  374—dc20   95-44776

SECOND EDITION
HB Printing 10 9 8 7 6 5 4 3 2 1

The Jossey-Bass
Higher and Adult Education Series

• •

Consulting Editor
Adult and Continuing Education

Alan B. Knox
University of Wisconsin, Madison

Contents

· ·

Preface

Systematic learning by men and women now permeates our culture. Formal institutions—universities, community colleges, public schools, libraries, museums, and others—offer varied programs, many of great size. Personal and social ills are prevented or remedied by education. Occupational skills are maintained, refined, or advanced by study. Organizations and associations with special purposes use instruction to help achieve them: one thinks at once of churches, hospitals, welfare centers, resort hotels and public parks, industrial and commercial organizations, labor unions, and all sorts of special interest groups, great and small. In addition to these formal and structured efforts are countless personal ventures of independent study, "twelve-step" group meetings, tutoring, mentoring, atelier instruction, and other forms of inquiry and accomplishment.

For almost a century now, the collective term for all these ventures has been *adult education,* and people have studied its nature and processes, producing a voluminous literature and creating research and training centers, graduate programs of study, professionalizing associations, and other evidences of an established field of thought and work. But a generalized concept of that field has not been fully established in the popular consciousness, not even among those engaged in learning or in offering educational opportunities. Rather than educators, many individuals consider themselves to be county agricultural agents, conference coordinators, industrial or military trainers, therapists, extension professors, literacy teachers, librarians, social workers, curators, or people engaged in other specialized categories. The nature of adult education and its potential relevance or value are unknown to them, either as central to their work or as a resource to aid their understanding or performance.

Those who believe that adult education has generalized ideas, principles, and practices that would be useful to people in all or most specialized learning programs must define and describe such elements clearly and forcefully if they are to win widespread support. Such advocacy has often occurred in the past and still continues, being especially strong in the advancement of such special formats of learning as: discussion as a complex method, forums and panels, the processes growing from the study of the dynamics of groups, the use of the mass media for education, the conduct of residential conferences, the assessment of experiential learning, and community development. Today the concepts of distance education and transformational learning are powerful ideas that are likely to encourage many new formats. Innovations usually begin in one program and spread to others as they prove to be valuable, sometimes having only limited applications but occasionally (as with discussion or group dynamics) reaching out to the farthest limits of organized adult learning.

Beginning in the 1960s, a growing number of writers on adult education have sought to go beyond the development of formats to demonstrate that all of the countless episodes of adult learning, however diverse their form, follow a similar pattern of behavior. For many years (and continuing to the present), the core idea of adult education has been identified in many ways: as shared history; as the achievement of some special goal, such as religious salvation, universal literacy, liberal education, informed citizenship, or economic advancement; as the application of an academic field such as psychology, sociology, or cultural history; or as a cluster of like-minded colleagues sharing fraternally in a movement. To such ideas, the writers on program development have added another. They have asserted that since adult education is essentially a practical field, its core endeavor must be the analysis and improvement of basic systems of planning and operation.

Such is the theme of the present book, and it makes its case by developing two lines of argument. First, eleven basic educational situations will be described; it will be demonstrated that virtually every learning act, episode, or institution can be fitted into one of them. As in the natural sciences, the creation of a taxonomy is but a first step in controlled inquiry, but it is essential to all the later ones. To illustrate, two basic situations may be designated (for quick reference purposes) as a group-designed activity and a teacher-designed one. These two are profoundly different, and all who participate in either one are aware of that fact. A group leader who tries to be a teacher or a teacher who acts only as a leader will soon run afoul of the learners' expectations. Similarly a learner who seeks instruction will be frustrated by its denial as will a learner who desires participation but gets lectures instead.

The second line of argument in this book is that the same basic elements of design are present in all educational situations, though the way that those elements are implied or improved is distinctive for each category. Thus the sequencing of activities is an important component of all eleven categories but is applied in a unique fashion in each one. A group-planned discussion can follow the inclinations of its members; they devise and shift the schedule as they see fit. The schedule for a teacher-planned activity, by contrast, must be governed, at least in part, by the nature and volume of the content to be taught.

It is assumed here that educators of adults grow in competence as they gain the ability to perform well in the first situation in which they serve. Many will move on to another, where the process of gaining mastery is repeated though made easier by the fact that the two share the same basic pattern. At some point, those who seek to improve their competence will encounter a basic system of program development and adopt it as a general guide to action. Continuing growth occurs when other systems are encountered and reconciled with the first. At no point should any system (including the one presented in this book) be accepted as dogma, since that approach will freeze or limit the improvement of competence.

The Evolution of the System

The first edition of this book, published in 1972, was the result of a quarter-century's active practice in teaching, research, reading, administration, and reflection. In the years since 1972, during which I have continued to work full time in adult education on an even broader basis than before, the need for a systematic approach to program planning and implementation has become ever more apparent. During the last ten years, moreover, it has been evident that the book needed revision if it was to continue to be useful, and I have been accumulating notes to be used in such a revision. During most of that time, I was also reading widely in order to be able to write *The Literature of Adult Education*, published in 1992. Virtually all of the 1,241 references cited in that book deal in some way with the themes of this one. In preparing this second edition, I have therefore been able to use the raw material of almost twenty-five years of additional experience and reflection.

Most of the readers of this second edition will come to it fresh and will not be interested in how it compares to the first. For the few who are mindful of such matters, a quick enumeration of the basic changes and similarities may be helpful. Much more stress is now given to the importance of a systematic approach to program planning and implementation as a central unifying feature of adult education in both theory and practice. This edition's analysis of the ways by which people can internalize such a system replaces a chapter that was no more than a commentary. A chapter dealing with the revision of organizational systems has been omitted since its scope now appears too detailed and special. Similarly a lengthy bibliography is no longer necessary. The case studies and illustrations represent modern practice, and the literature of the past quarter-century is included. The almost universal modern acceptance of adult learning as a way of achieving goals or meeting needs underlies the discussion throughout. Finally, many new terms or ideas are used to replace or add to earlier ones, and the unintended sexist language of the first edition has been replaced.

This last change proved to be hard to make. Education is here often addressed in terms of the uniqueness of its episodes, each with a learner and often a leader, in either case a *he* or *she*. Always to use the plural *they* or to avoid singular pronouns altogether dulls the sharpness of decision making and leads to blandness and impersonality. My chief solution to the problem is to use he or she as interchangeable terms.

The taxonomy and the basic pattern of practice are the same in both editions, though the terms used may now be clearer than before. I have found no useful way of improving these formulations, perhaps because they are so deeply etched in my mind and practice as to be ineradicable. When one tries to discover essences, one arrives at fundamentals not easily changed. The eleven program situations were initially derived out of much reading and thought as well as hundreds of discussions with individuals and groups in which the formulation was on trial. A large number of later presentations by myself and others have not led to the addition or subtraction of any categories, though illustrations have been given of examples very near the boundaries of each one. A few authors have chosen the taxonomy as a basis for their own writings. All other references to it, favorable or unfavorable, have accepted it as a whole. The basic pattern of practice has also survived close scrutiny by many people who have studied and used it.

As already noted, the first edition was one of a group of early works on the same theme that received substantial immediate attention in both academic and operational quarters. Each was subjected to widespread analysis and gained followers in both literature and practice. This group of books, whose number is steadily growing, has been subjected to searching comparative studies that highlighted similarities, differences, and varied frames of reference. In Chapter One, some of these basic formulations will be identified, as will some of the better-known comparative studies.

Audience

This book is intended not merely for those who are already specialists in the field but also for everyone deeply interested in the nature or improvement of adult learning. In an effort to reach out to all such people, the language I have used is as lucid as possible. As already suggested, however, the central target audience is made up of people who want to improve their performance and need a general frame of reference to help them do so. Such people may be beginners, or they may be seasoned veterans at the pinnacle of success. No matter how eminent, people in the performing arts—acting, singing, dancing, playing musical instruments—never escape the need for analyzing their work and refining their habits; sometimes they even feel they must return to the fundamentals of their craft. Adult educators have the same need throughout their careers. Perhaps this book will help them meet it.

Anyone primarily interested in understanding or mastering the system presented here might well turn at once to Chapter Six and follow any of the procedures it suggests.

Overview of the Contents

This book presents an extended view of the two central formulations already mentioned. Chapter One deals with the ways by which other systems of program planning and implementation have helped shape the field of adult education. Chapter Two offers a brief overview of the proposed design, and Chapter Three describes case studies to show how the system here proposed can be used to interpret practice, even in highly unusual situations. Chapter Four deals in depth with the categories of educational situations, and Chapter Five does the same thing for the elements of program design; these two chapters are amplifications of the briefer accounts given in Chapter Two. Chapter Six indicates the ways that basic design patterns may be used by an individual to create and master a personal system of practice.

The Glossary defines the important terms of the book for the use of analytical readers. It is presented in two different ways: in the customary alphabetical form and in an exposition that uses the key words in context and thereby provides a brief statement of the whole argument of the book.

The References identify some of the major published sources on which that argument relies and suggest additional readings on the topics with which it deals.

Acknowledgments

My obligation to many people for the ideas in this book is so great that I could not fully acknowledge it without providing a list of tedious length. Therefore only a few names will be mentioned. In the preparation of this second edition, Professor Alan B. Knox, the editor of this series of books, has provided great support and assistance. Several years ago, the publisher requested an appraisal of the feasibility of a second edition from three professors of adult education: Stephen Brookfield, Ronald M. Cervero, and Thomas J. Sork; the resulting work has profited from their suggestions. For indispensable help with the cases presented in Chapter Three, I am indebted to Professor Knox, Roger Heylin, Terry Gibson, and Mary Lou Proch.

My chief debt—both emotional and intellectual—is to one who needs no special mention here since everybody who knows me has long been aware of my reliance on her. During all of the time that

I have been at work on both editions, the W. K. Kellogg Foundation has supported my research and writing activities, and I am grateful to it for doing so. My other chief source of help and inspiration has been my colleagues and students at the University of Chicago during my years of residence there, and it is to them that both editions of the book are dedicated.

Sarasota, Florida   Cyril O. Houle
December 1995

The Author

· ·

Cyril O. Houle is professor emeritus of education at the University of Chicago and senior program consultant at the W. K. Kellogg Foundation. He received his B.A. and M.A. degrees (both in 1934) from the University of Florida and his Ph.D. degree (1940) from the University of Chicago; all three degrees were in education.

From 1939 to 1978, Houle was employed at the University of Chicago. There he served on the faculty and also in numerous other capacities, notably as dean of University College, the university's extension division. During his time at the University of Chicago, he was engaged in research and teaching at the graduate level in the fields of adult and higher education. From 1938 onward, he had occasional contacts with the W. K. Kellogg Foundation; in 1976, his association with it became his central interest. He has also been a visiting faculty member at other universities, including the University of California, Berkeley; Leeds University; the University of Washington; the University of Wisconsin, Milwaukee; and Oxford University. He has been heavily engaged in community service at all levels of government and has worked in thirty-five foreign countries. His many honors and awards include the Tolley medal, membership in the National Academy of Education, and honorary doctorates from eleven universities.

Houle has been contributing to the literature of adult education since the mid 1930s and has published books in every decade from that one to the present. He is also a specialist on the operation of nonprofit and governmental boards, and his latest book on the subject is *Governing Boards* (1989).

The Design of Education

1

Credos and Systems

There are nine and sixty ways of constructing tribal lays,
And every single one of them is right.
— Rudyard Kipling, *In the Neolithic Age*

When an episode of learning or teaching is analyzed, either while it is occurring or afterward, it is seen to be an intricate meshing of countless aims and actions. The teacher, if there is one, has general purposes, specific ends, and personal reasons for undertaking his work. Similarly, each learner has broad aspirations, immediate goals, and private motives. Some evidence of objectives may be made manifest by formal statements, but beneath this visible tip of the iceberg lie all the desires and dreams unexpressed by either teacher or learner and sometimes hidden deep in their subconsciousness.

The efforts made to achieve desired ends are also diverse and complexly interwoven. If a class is discussing the novels of Patrick O'Brian, for example, any thoughtful person can readily identify such customary components of education as leadership, teaching technique, content, social interaction, and evaluation. However, the full reality of what occurs in the mind, emotions, and body of each participant and the nature of its effect are so intricate that they defy complete analysis, particularly since close scrutiny makes both teacher and learners self-conscious, thereby altering the nature of the educative experience.

Yet the process of education can be neither understood nor improved unless the realities of learning and teaching are examined in either a natural setting where an individual or group embarks on a personally guided quest for knowledge or in some managed setting, such as a formal classroom. One approach to studying the learning process focuses on a component of instruction that is separated from the others for detailed analysis. While every such investigator is likely to overestimate the significance of his or her topic, each usually understands very well that it is but one part of a total educational process. Another approach is to focus on the learning process as a whole and try to combine its components into an overall system that can serve both as a tool of analysis for understanding what happens in an educational activity and as an instrument of program planning to guide future actions. This second approach is the one used in this book.

Its central purpose is to present a system of educational design that may have relevance to education at any age of life but that has grown specifically out of an analysis of the organized and purposeful learning activities of men and women. In one way or another, adult education has been discernible in all historical periods, but the first effective expression of the term itself did not appear until after World War I. Since then, many people have sought to identify its essence as a field of endeavor and perhaps eventually as a profession. The system proposed here owes much to the growth of thought in adult education and the credos and systems that have been widely espoused as guides to practice. Against this background, the rest of the book describes and illustrates the system of educational design suggested here.

Growth of Systematic Thought in Adult Education

Adult education has emerged as a distinctive field of study and application, giving coherence to many activities that formerly were not thought to be related to one another. As has been true in such other comprehensive areas of human aspiration as health, welfare, safety, and recreation, those who first perceived the vast scope of adult education did so with a spirit of exaltation. They believed that men and women who understood the limitlessness of learning as a way of developing human potential would seize every educational opportunity offered them to advance both themselves and society. The early period of the field was therefore a time of defining goals and exhorting everyone to achieve them.

After a first surge of growth and interest, which occurred in the United States in the 1920s, it became clear to the leaders of the emerging field that enunciation by writers and lecturers of the values of adult education is not sufficient to make most men and women seek to achieve them. Learning experiences that embody those values must be so organized and conducted that a gradually increasing number of learners can discover the rewards of greater skill, understanding, and sensitiveness. The experiences must then be analyzed to discover their principles of success, which can be applied creatively in other situations. As these truths were realized, there began a period of preoccupation with process, either as a generalized technique (such as discussion, demonstration, or sensitivity training) or as a form of service performed by such institutions as a university, an industry, or a voluntary association. The field itself, as a synthesis of many such processes, developed slowly as methods and activities were perfected and their use broadened and as the leaders of various programs established and maintained contact with one another.

As time went on, it became increasingly evident that no substantial unity could be built upon such casual approaches and fortuitous contacts. The people involved in what was essentially a field of practical operation rather than of abstract thought had no deep sense that they were all engaged in the same fundamental activity. A community-centered school, a public library, and a social settlement might be located in the same neighborhood, they might all serve adults, their directors might be good friends, they might occasionally use one another's facilities and services, and they might be guided by the same aims of community involvement. Yet the staff members of each agency would regard themselves as representatives of a distinctive institution employing a way of work different from that of the others.

Their view was reinforced by the traditional conception that education is an institution-centered activity. Adult education emerged late on the scene at a time when egalitarian influences were reinforcing the rapid advancement of schools, colleges, and universities. Both analysts and administrators of education for children and youth centered their attention almost entirely on the classroom setting with only occasional glances at other learning and teaching activities undertaken in individual, group, or institutional settings.

But the points of service and the areas of application of adult education are multiform. Its practice is more like that of the engineer, social worker, architect, or therapist—indeed, like that of most professions—than it is like that of the school or college teacher or administrator. Since adulthood stretches out for many years and the diversity of life-styles is great, the education of men and women occurs in many different settings and takes countless forms. Any effort to build a system of educational process on the work of a specific goal, method of practice, or institution is limited. For example, the attempt to make universal generalizations on the basis of community development, group discussion, or the procedures of a university extension division are repudiated by many educators of adults because those generalizations do not conform to the reality they experience.

Many efforts have been made to find better and deeper ways of conceptualizing programs. Plans and methodologies, such as group dynamics, change theory, community development, and systems analysis, have been proposed (all of them will be described later in this chapter). Each was accepted by some people and rejected by others. At least a few of the latter, restive at being called conservative or traditional because they would not espouse the new techniques, looked more deeply than before at their work and developed theories of process that made explicit what had hitherto been implicit in, for example, independent study, tutorial teaching, and the creative use of the classroom. As a result of the advancement of new systems and the better understanding of old ones, the level of discussion deepened, and a more mature, thoughtful sense of common identity began to emerge.

As yet, however, it cannot be said that most of the work in the field is guided by any of these systems or even by the desire to follow a systematic theory. As Knox (1991, p. 228) has pointed out, educators "tend to develop programs quite intuitively." The typical career worker in adult education is still concerned only with an institutional pattern of service or a methodology, seldom or never catching a glimpse of the total terrain of which he or she is cultivating one corner, and content to be, for example, a farm or home adviser, museum curator, public librarian, or industrial trainer. While such people are adult educators, they do not know or do not wish to believe that they are. The winning of their attention and support must be a major aim of anyone who hopes to enlarge and strengthen the field.

Those who do identify themselves with adult education hold widely varying views about its essential nature. Most such people have worked out a guiding credo—a simple statement of belief— that channels and directs their ordinary practices. Others have put forward organized systems to achieve a basic coherence of process that the field does not at present possess. A few such model builders are doctrinaire and even evangelistic, but the field has not been polarized by rigid and opposing systems of belief. Instead, much fluidity and inconsistency of opinion exist. A healthy safeguard against dogmatism is the fact that most people who build careers in the field must constantly meet the test of the market; they must attract and retain the attention of men and women who are free to do things other than learn.

The following review of credos and systems is therefore not a way of sorting everybody in the field into neat categories based on dominant conceptions of practice but a summary of widely held and used views from which a given individual may shift back and forth as necessity dictates. About each credo or system, only enough is said here to identify it, not to provide a complete description.

Credos

One credo that has been consistently avowed since the earliest days of the organized field and is still staunchly supported by many people is the belief that adult education should be a movement unified by a common effort to achieve a single, all-encompassing goal. The first major delineation of the field was published in 1919 by the Adult Education Committee of the British Ministry of Reconstruction in a document that had a powerful impact on both British and American thought. Its authors were almost wholly oriented to what they variously called general, humanistic, nonutilitarian, or liberal education. The force and persuasiveness with which they expressed its values consolidated a point of view that was written into law and governmental regulations and has affected British adult education ever since. In the 1920s and the 1950s, heavily financed efforts were made to center American practice on liberal education (Stubblefield and Keane, 1994). Other examples of mission-oriented adult education are abundant in the cultural histories of various nations, where efforts have been centered on such objectives as economic growth, religious evangelism, the winning of a war, or the conversion of a people to a political or economic theory. In any such case, it has been argued that if all people who consider themselves adult educators believe deeply in the same broad mission, they will create a movement built on its achievement.

A second credo is based on the belief that since men and women are mature and know what they need to learn, the task of the educator of adults is to discover what that is and provide it for them. Among those who hold this view, a branch public librarian should want a balanced collection that can meet any request for a book; the evening school director should offer to provide any course desired by ten or more people; and the community college dean should use advisory committees to discover the desires of her constituency. The educators' methodological task is to devise, perfect, and use the techniques and instruments that reveal the apparent interests and the felt or ascribed needs of the individuals or groups they serve. The field gains coherence from a common concern with this task, a sharing of the ways by which it is undertaken, and a collective use of its results.

A third credo is centered on the idea that the educator of adults should adapt the aims and methods of other forms of schooling to fit the requirements of men and women. Sometimes this adaptation is merely one of time or place, as when a high school equivalency program is offered in the evening or a university extension course is given off campus. Sometimes it is creative in approach, as when the elementary school curriculum is redesigned to suit the needs of adult illiterates or a special program is created to lead to the baccalaureate degree. The central idea in any such case is that certain standards for mastery of content or skill have already been established, and it is the task of educators of adults to achieve these standards with their own clientele. This common concern gives unity of approach to the whole field and is thought to elevate its stature since the central focus of effort is upon the achievement of goals that are already well established in any literate society.

A fourth credo emphasizes the importance of powerful and creative leaders in various roles. Teachers should be masters operating in an individualistic fashion, their teaching an expression of basic character tempered by thought, study, and experience; they transform abstract knowledge by the use of what the Danes call the living word. The creator of an institution or a movement—such as Bishop Grundtvig, Albert Mansbridge, or Seaman Knapp—uses the force of personality to achieve the ends sought. The administrator infuses the program with his own ideas and policies; the head of a Danish folk high school is called a *vorstander,* a particularly apt term since such a person usually stands very much at the forefront of the institution.

The field of adult education may be given unity by this conception in three general ways. First, all those concerned chiefly with leadership find community in discussing and fostering it. Second, the leaders of various institutions interact with one another in dealing with common interests and concerns; in the United States, this activity has provided most of the unity achieved. Third, the idea of adult education itself may become the central concern of a leader—such as Eduard Lindeman, Frederick Keppel, or E. A. Corbett—who uses the resources of his or her personality to knit its several components together.

A fifth credo is based on the improvement of generalized institutional processes. The most evident fact about adult education is its multiple sponsorship, and all who administer programs have common concerns arising from an effort to master the fundamentals of management but also from a desire to know how to handle such specifics of adult learning as the provision of resources, the charging of fees, the scheduling of activities, and the recruitment and compensation of teachers. Much of the shop talk of adult educators and much of the training in the field deal with such matters as these. Efforts are also constantly being made to define the proper roles and interrelationships of institutions. For example, what service should an industrial human resources department offer on its own, and what service should it request of outside organizations? Should the museum be concerned solely with displaying its own resources, or should it also lend them to other institutions? What is the level of subject matter appropriate to the public school, the community college, and the university? The effort expended in dealing with such questions tends to knit the field together.

A sixth credo, not widely held perhaps but expressed often enough to deserve mention, is given its impetus by a desire to subvert formalism so that energies may be creatively released. Those who hold this view usually do not seek to replace present structures with others more personally desirable. They argue only that institutionalization of either structure or thought creates undesirable rigidity and that adult educators should stress informality, improvisation, and new and unconventional ways of thought. The goal of adult education should be the freeing of the human spirit; the means used should be unusual, provocative, and challenging to those who take part. This contrarian view can range all the way from a mild posture of independence to a determined nihilism and from a general impatience with the status quo to a dedicated seeking of the avant-garde. The field itself is defined in personal terms as a communion of fellow spirits.

While the thoughts of at least a few people seem to be wholly encompassed by each of these credos or others like them, most educators of adults are not thus confined. They may express one belief at one time, another at another. They may accept one credo as dominant, subordinating one or more of the others to it. They may even espouse several at the same time. But some of the credos directly contradict one another; for example, the first is inconsistent with the second and the fifth with the sixth. Therefore while each credo has provided some unifying force in the field, none of them is stable or profound enough to synthesize all practice.

Systems

The need for a deeper conception of the field than can be provided by any of these credos has been the chief reason why so many systems of thought have been proposed, each designed to provide a theoretical basis for educational programming. Some were simple. Their proponents announced, often in an exalted fashion, that a teaching method such as the creative use of problem solving or a teaching technique such as computerized instruction was so important or so suited to the requirements of adults that it reduced all other approaches to insignificance. Other systems provided undergirding for one of the credos, pushing its analysis to a deeper level of thought. For example, the work of Sir Richard Livingstone on the Danish folk schools was powerfully influential in reinforcing the all-encompassing goal of liberal adult education, and many books have dealt with group behavior or institutional theory in terms that suggested they were universal to adult education.

The need for broader and more systematic approaches to programming did not become apparent until the 1940s. In an exhaustive survey of the literature of the field published in 1941, Beals and Brody report no writings on general adult educational design and few that analyzed the basic processes followed in the various areas of concern of the field. (A similar disinterest in the topic in the British literature is suggested by its scant treatment by Davies and Thomas in their 1988 bibliography.) But following World War II, some American educators began to focus on programming much more sharply than before. Some of their approaches overlap, but each has a distinctive thrust and each is considered separately in the following account of them.

Systems Based on Dewey's Thought

The early major development of adult education in the United States in the 1920s and 1930s occurred at the same time the educational theories of John Dewey were finding their fullest expression in practice. His thought was centered on the child in the school, but—perhaps as a result of his experiences in such institutions as Hull House and the extension programs of the University of Chicago—his theories of teaching and learning had a universal quality that strongly appealed to the founding fathers of adult education. Many of them felt that their own work was a protest against what they regarded as the rigid, formal, and involuntary servitude of the schools; therefore they applauded Dewey's attacks on traditionalism and made enthusiastic common cause with the leaders of the progressive education movement that carried out his ideas in schools and colleges.

In a summary of his educational thought made late in his career, Dewey established the dichotomies between his own approach and that of "educational reactionaries, who [were then] gaining force." He said, "To imposition from above is opposed expression and cultivation of individuality; to external discipline is opposed free activity; to learning from tests and teachers, learning through experience; to acquisition of isolated skills and techniques by drill is opposed acquisition of them as means of attaining ends which make direct vital appeal; to preparation for a more or less remote future is opposed making the most of the opportunities of present life; to static aims and materials is opposed acquaintance with a changing world" (Dewey, 1938, pp. 5–6, 22). While such language as this has relevance to learning at any age, some educators of adults took it as almost a direct message to themselves since it expressed so clearly their own feelings about the nature of their field and the mission it was called upon to perform.

More important, they found underpinning for programming in the pragmatic approach that Dewey suggested. His insistence that education be related to all experience made it possible to consider the work not merely of established institutions of formal schooling but also of such other organizations as libraries and museums and of such forms of activity as community development, independent study, supervision, and travel. The specific goals of learning, he argued, were constantly changing and evolving; the sole principles of process were the continuity of experience and the interaction of the learner with his environment; and the central distinction between education and miseducation was that the former enlarged the capacity of the individual or society for richer experiences in the future while the latter arrested, diminished, or distorted it. The very openness of the system of programming thus suggested gave a sense of exhilarating progressiveness and forward motion to many people as they set about the reconstruction of the learning or teaching experiences with which they were concerned.

While their method rested fundamentally on Dewey's conception of the nature of education, it was reinforced by the breadth of his thought on other topics and issues of concern to the early leaders of adult education. The very act of thinking, he believed, was a process of solving problems: a difficulty arises, the specific nature of the problem is defined, possible solutions are formulated and tested, and finally the most adequate one is chosen. When this process is used to guide education, it becomes a constant quest for competence and enlightenment as an individual or group seeks continuously to solve problems encountered in the effort to reach defined goals. Such an approach is equally applicable in the classroom and in the world outside it and can therefore provide unity for the great array of structured experiences which make up the field of adult education. This sense of coherence was also fostered by other aspects of Dewey's thought as he turned his attention to the advancement of democracy, to ethics, to art, to creation of groups and communities, to growth of the individual, and to countless other matters.

Articulate exponents of his method and thought soon interpreted them to educators of adults. As early as 1926, Eduard C. Lindeman published a series of essays that applied Dewey's approach in various ways, suggesting, for example:

> The approach to adult education will be via the route of *situations*, not subjects. Our academic system has grown in reverse order: subjects and teachers constitute the starting point, students are secondary. In conventional education the student is required to adjust himself to an established curriculum; in adult education the curriculum is built around the student's needs and interests. Every adult person finds himself in specific situations with respect to his work, his recreation, his family life, his community life, et cetera—situations which call for adjustments. Adult education begins at this point. Subject matter is brought into the situation, is put to work, when needed. Texts and teachers play a new and secondary role in this type of education; they must give way to the primary importance of the learner [pp. 8–9].

An even more systematic exposition of Dewey's thought as it applied to adult education was published by Ruth Kotinsky in 1933. Such books were supplemented by countless essays dealing firsthand or derivatively with Dewey's approach. Gradually his influence came to permeate the methodological thought of the emerging field.

In a broad sense, it still does, for some of its central ideas are deeply embedded in the subsequent systems that are described later. Each sets forth a more explicit process of program development than that formulated by Dewey and has thereby in some measure violated the openness and fluidity of approach characteristic of his work. His thought was a point of departure for all of them, however—a fact that can be demonstrated by both analytical comparison and study of historical relationships. Even those theorists who depart radically from his views in some respects (holding, for example, that the central aims of education are enduring and universal and do not grow out of the interaction of the individual with his environment) tend to follow program-development systems based on Dewey's theories. When some of the detailed conceptualizations of process (such as change theory and systems analysis) grow tedious and mechanical, it is refreshing to return to their wellsprings in Dewey's writing to gain the vast perspective it provides.

Systems Based on Tyler's Thought

The educational reactionaries of whom Dewey spoke did not give way readily before the onslaught of the new forms of education based upon his work. The major lines of battle were drawn within the schools themselves as conservatives confronted progressives. Conflict also arose at the points where one level of institution intersected with another. For example, universities required entering students to have completed an established pattern of courses based on the mastery of prescribed subject matter. Secondary school staffs who wished to be innovative found themselves unable to make very many changes without penalizing their college-bound students. In cases of direct confrontation between defenders of traditional values and proponents of radical change, victory went now to one side, now to another, but it soon became clear that some new conception of curriculum building would have to be devised to serve as a synthesis between old and new. Many leaders of education turned their attention to this task, but the major contribution proved to be that made by Ralph W. Tyler.

His work was essentially comparative and collaborative. He directed major national studies of secondary schools and colleges, undertook countless surveys of institutions and areas of work, and became a continuing consultant to the staffs of many agencies. He accepted adult education as an essential part of the instructional establishment, paying particular attention to the Cooperative Extension Service and to continuing occupational and professional training. Thus he examined, led in establishing, or guided many forms of educational innovation and derived his fundamental methodology from the study and comparison of a large and broadly based variety of cases. He involved in this work not only members of the staffs of the programs he aided but also many colleagues, some of whom became outstanding leaders of American educational thought. He wrote few seminal works; his major impact was felt directly on the field itself as institutions put into effect his ideas on the fundamental strategy of program building.

That strategy is now so well understood and established that it undergirds most modern educational theory and practice. Its essence can be summarized briefly. In any program, the first task is to define purposes by considering studies of the learners, of contemporary life, and of the suggestions of subject specialists. Such data as may be derived from these studies should be screened by the educational and social philosophy of the curriculum builder and by the findings of the psychology of learning in order to produce specific objectives that should guide instruction. These objectives should be stated in a fashion that makes them useful in selecting learning experiences and guiding teaching. Such experiences are then chosen according to certain principles and to conform to various categories of goals and are organized in such a way as to produce desired results. The processes of evaluation should be so designed as to measure the degree to which identified objectives have been achieved, and that knowledge should be used in future planning.

This brief summary suggests only the bare outline of the Tyler rationale as first presented in 1950. Since then, its various aspects have been enormously enlarged and enriched. The sources and nature of objectives have been extensively and variously analyzed and taxonomized. Program building in countless situations has vastly increased knowledge of how that process should be used even as central reliance on a single fundamental rationale has given coherence to work undertaken at every level of education. As scientific knowledge has grown concerning the sources and screens (such as the nature of the learner, the suggestions of subject specialists, or the psychology of learning), it has been put to use within the established system. Expertise in the evaluation of learning has been carried to a high degree of competence.

Even as Tyler's thought evolved through the years, so did that of his followers. A number of variant program-development systems have been proposed, and sharp disagreements exist over the proper way to consider various components of the rationale, most particularly the sources or method of statement of objectives and the validity of various forms of evaluation. But even with all this amplification and disagreement, the fundamental way of thought that Tyler suggested still remains intact, underlying the discussion and practice of most education today. In this process, the old debates between the progressives and the reactionaries have been lessened as both parties have found an acceptable method of designing and conducting education.

The reinforcement of the rationale in the field of adult education has come about in three major ways. First, many institutions have found it necessary to reconstruct their programs and have used all or part of Tyler's rationale in doing so, often with his direct guidance or that of one of his followers. Thus the staff members involved have come to have firsthand experience with the application of his ideas. Second, almost all of those who hold advanced degrees in adult education have secured them in graduate departments or schools of education where they have been extensively exposed to Tyler's ideas. Finally, many of the program-planning models devised by theoreticians of adult education have flowed directly or indirectly from his rationale. Certainly that fact is true of the framework suggested in this book.

Systems Based on Lewin's Thought

The educational ideas of both Dewey and Tyler grew out of their observation of the processes of education. And while both were aware of learning as a universal and lifelong activity, they tended to center their attention on its most highly developed form: the work of schools and colleges for children and young people. The two clusters of systems that are now to be considered reversed that emphasis since they were first used extensively in program building for adults and were only later applied in the schooling of youth. Moreover, both clusters were borrowed from social psychology, not education. They were inspired by the conceptions of many people but most significantly of Kurt Lewin, a European who migrated to the United States in the 1930s and whose early death prevented him from working out the program patterns suggested by his ideas. A group of his students and followers found in the burgeoning growth of adult education an opportunity to develop and systematize his thought, however.

The first set of systems was originally known by the umbrella term *group dynamics*. This designation was always inappropriate, for if the term had a literal meaning at all, it referred to the subfield of social psychology that deals with the objective study of the nature of small groups and their influence on the actions of their members. To those engaged in such study, however, it soon became clear that

the theoretical knowledge they discovered could have major practical consequences. Many new concepts and techniques were devised (among them feedback, role playing, body language, buzz
groups, hidden agenda, special forms of nondirective leadership,
reactor panels, listening teams, problem census, and involvement)
that were to become part of the colloquial speech of educators of
adults. Somehow *group dynamics* came to be used as a collective
term to describe such practices and their theoretical foundations.

Back of this language lay the deeply serious belief of those who
identified themselves with the group dynamics movement that the
group and the larger human associations of which it is the cellular
unit have a powerfully educative potential for man and society.
Since several leaders of the movement were also key figures in adult
education, it was natural that the field should be used to explore
means for channeling and using the power inherent in the group.
It seemed likely that the central methodological purpose of adult
education could be found in group dynamics. Leland Bradford suggested as much in 1947:

> Perhaps the basic problem of adult education is that of
> educating adults for group work. We have educated
> people as individuals and expected them to perform suc-
> cessfully in a society that is primarily one of group com-
> plexity. . . . The most difficult problems we face today are
> essentially group problems. They are major problems pri-
> marily because we have not been taught the skills of
> working as groups toward the solution of group prob-
> lems. . . . The education of adults demands different
> methods than do other educational fields. . . . The basic
> method of adult education is rapidly becoming the dis-
> cussion method. . . . It is obviously incumbent upon
> those in adult education to strengthen discussion method
> and group work as the process of democracy. . . . We
> must, in adult education, go deeply into an exploration

into methods and technics of group discussion and group growth. Only as we become really skilled in these areas will we be of important service to others [pp. 167–170].

As these ideas were worked out in the late 1940s and the 1950s, group dynamics came to have a powerful impact on adult education. People who believed strongly in the group approach served as officers, executives, or editors for national associations and journals and used their positions to put forward their ideas in publications and speeches and to structure meetings according to their theories. Strong opposition to this alleged effort to capture the field quickly grew up, with the result that opinion became polarized.

Yet as time went on, efforts to study or enhance the educativeness of the group began to change. Attention shifted from means to ends, to finding out what people could learn about themselves and their relationships with others and how they could use that knowledge creatively in primary social associations. Instead of being called the group dynamics approach, the movement began to be known as sensitivity training or human relations education. Methods of analysis also grew more subtle and applications more profound. The formalized training group (T-group) and the encounter group were devised and began to take many forms, some elaborate, some bizarre. These complex formulations could not be as readily transplanted to all fields of practice as could such simple techniques as feedback and nondirective leadership. Sensitivity training gradually became a special program area of adult education, cutting across all institutional lines in its application but no longer being advocated as a universal system of planning and analysis.

But group dynamics did make a significant positive contribution to adult education by stressing the importance of treating every socialized learning situation as a group. Teachers, leaders, and administrators of even the most formal kinds of activities strive much harder than they did in earlier days to take advantage of the important reinforcement that fellow learners can offer one another. And learners themselves are likely to suggest or even insist upon a group approach, for an awareness of sensitivity training in one or another of its countless forms has now entered into the common culture and become an accepted part of human association.

The second cluster of program-design theories that grew out of Lewin's ideas came to be called *change theory*. While highly complex in its formulations and applications, it rests on the idea that in any defined social situation the present level of accomplishment is supported by some forces and held back by others. The amount of goods produced in a factory, the incidence of disease in a community, the ability of a woman to read and write her mother tongue, the stability and social integrity of a nation—all such conceptualized levels of practice can be analyzed in the same basic way by asking two questions: What forces are at work to increase the level of performance? What forces operate to keep it from rising higher?

Anyone seeking to improve practice in any situation must begin by answering these questions and then go on to ask two others. How can the positive forces be reinforced? How can the negative ones be weakened? The operative task becomes one of identifying a present performance level, "unfreezing" it by strengthening positive influences and weakening negative ones, establishing as high a new level of operation as desirable, and then "refreezing" it so that it will not slip back again. In this process, two major roles are involved: the client or client system that is helped to improve and that may be an individual, group, institution, community, or society; and the change agent, a single person or group who uses both technical expertise and skill in human interaction to bring about the desired change by entering into a helping relationship. For example, if increased production in a factory is desired, its supervisory group is the client system, and a specialist in industrial management is the change agent. To be effective fully, the agent must be an expert in both production techniques and the handling of human relationships.

This concept of method has been widely used in many fields of social action and is not distinctive to adult education. Indeed, the analysis of forces in a situation usually reveals that they take complex forms, some unrelated to education. Industrial production, for instance, may be held back by a low level of work skills but also by poor wage incentive systems, weak management, bad working conditions, and ineffective collective-bargaining practices. Change agents must take account of all such conditions, or they are effective neither as analysts nor as instruments of reform. But in the search for an integrative theory of program design, some educators of adults have been so attracted by the change theory concept that they have adopted it as their central strategy. Its influence is clearly seen, for example, in Coolie Verner's definition of adult education as "a relationship between an educational agent and a learner in which the agent selects, arranges, and continuously directs a sequence of progressive tasks that provide systematic experiences to achieve learning for those whose participation in such activities is subsidiary and supplemental to a primary productive role in society" (1964, p. 32).

The processes through which a change agent and client interact are infinitely complex, but the bare outlines of at least one strategy may be sketched. A sequence begins when a client becomes aware of the existence of a problem; sometimes this awareness appears independently, sometimes it results from stimulation by the agent. The agent assesses the motivation and capacity of the client to change, thereby diagnosing the forces that either favor or resist growth. The agent also assesses his or her own motivations and resources in helping the client. As a result, appropriate change objectives and targets are worked out, and the helping role of the change agent is more precisely defined than it was before. Suitable strategies are identified and applied. Throughout this process but particularly at its conclusion, attention is devoted to the ways changes will be stabilized and maintained. Finally, the helping relationship is terminated.

Many alternate strategies of application of change theory have been devised, growing out of both theoretical considerations and applications to special types of situations. Also, several terms, particularly *change agent*, have proved to be attractive and are used either by themselves or as parts of strategies that have different theoretical bases. The term *change* has itself been given many interpretations. To some people, it signifies broad social advance toward new conceptions of personal or social order; it is progressive, liberal, or radical in connotation. But other people adopt a less value-laden approach. Desired change may equally as well, they say, be directed toward the strengthening of conservative or reactionary values.

Change theory is particularly useful when education must be undertaken in natural situations, not those formally established for the sake of learning. Its milieu is the factory, the community, the labor union, or some similar setting, particularly one in which changes must be brought about by the use of several kinds of activity. For example, a safety specialist acting as a change agent may reduce the highway accident rate by better law enforcement, improved engineering, and more effective education. She may apply this third remedy in many ways: mass campaigns to inform drivers of the rules of the road, stringent training programs for those who want drivers' licenses, instruction of engineers on appropriate standards of highway construction and of law enforcement officers on how to carry out their duties, and special courses required of habitual breakers of traffic laws. For her, education is not a separate approach but is intimately intertwined with enforcement and engineering.

The application of change theory is less useful in other situations. Its reliance upon the distinction between the change agent and the client means that it cannot serve very well to guide the self-educative activities of the individual. Verner recognizes this difficulty and eliminates such activities from consideration. Other theorists suggest that the same individual can play the roles of change agent and client simultaneously, but in practice this conception is hard to apply. Nor does change theory easily fit other categories of situations, such as the voluntary group, the classroom, or the educative use of the mass media. And its general design has to do with the handling of a specific act or episode and therefore does not provide for either a series or an aggregate of episodes.

Systems Based on Community Development

The attempt to use community improvement as a basic strategy of program design in adult education has had many different starting points. The focal idea is that residents in a community (which may be variously defined in geographic or social terms) should be helped to act collectively to solve some problem that affects the lives of all of them. In planning and undertaking this task, they achieve tangible results. But if the process is skillfully handled, they also learn how to attack other problems and are motivated to do so by their feeling of success in their initial efforts. Thus a community may be transformed from a traditional way of life that has few satisfactions for any of its members to one that offers tangible rewards and hopes for all of them. The system initiates and provides the mobilizing force for many activities, as Richard Poston (1954) suggests:

> It is a process of education by which people of all ages and all interests in the community learn to share their thoughts, their ideals, their aspirations, their joys, and their sorrows, and in large measure to mold and shape their communal destiny for themselves. It is a process of self-discovery by which the people of a community learn to identify and solve their community problems. These problems may vary from the need for a new sewage disposal system to a need for becoming better informed on world affairs or on the contents of the great books [p. 194].

The strategy of community development follows Dewey's problem-solving approach and is in a sense an application of his method. The people of a locality become aware of its imperfections either gradually or as a result of some galvanizing event. They mobilize their forces to cope with their difficulties. Either by themselves or with specialist help, they define their problem, collect and analyze the data relevant to it, examine various possible solutions, choose one, put it into effect, and subsequently evaluate their progress. The habits of association or organizational structure they have developed to cope with this problem then continue in being, and the leaders choose another problem on which to work. In dealing with it, they use both the knowledge of themselves and of their community and the method of attack that they have learned in dealing with the first problem.

This strategy is also like that used in change theory and has often been powerfully reinforced by it. But the two strategies have separate histories and can be distinguished from one another in important ways. In community development, there may or may not be an independent change agent. When there is, she or he may be the central preexisting feature; thus the staff member of a university-based community development bureau may go in search of localities to help. And, perhaps most important, the central idea in community development is not to bring about planned change on some concrete specific aspect but to use the initiating episode in which such change occurs as a way of achieving sequence and continuity of a self-renewing sort.

In North America, community development has traditionally been part of the outreach service of an established educational institution. One of the most important of these is the public school, which has been suggested again and again as the proper place for mounting a unified attack on the social ills of the area it serves. This idea came to prominence in the 1930s, when a number of model programs began to appear, and has continued ever since, particularly after the activities of the Mott Foundation in Flint, Michigan, received national attention and support. Colleges and universities have also been centers for such work. The best-known program was that initiated by St. Francis Xavier University in Nova Scotia, which has served as a prototype for many other ventures. A number of universities provide expert consultants for localities that seek help, and in some cases community development bureaus have been established to carry out this function. In some places too, the work of the Cooperative Extension Service has been conceptualized as a process of community development with the farm or home adviser serving as a resident specialist.

In other countries, community development has sometimes evolved as a separate function of government. Nations with few economic resources feel the need to mobilize the energies of people in programs of self-help that are immediately rewarding in terms of such tangible accomplishments as roads, schoolhouses, or latrines and that also give the people involved a sense of progressive effort and accomplishment. Striking successes have been achieved in both respects in many communities throughout the world, and in some nations developmental programs have been institutionalized to provide widespread coverage of the country.

While the concept of community development is exciting and its broad strategy of operation is not hard to grasp, the application of its principles in specific situations is made difficult by two pervasive aspects of community life. The first is the habit pattern of the people themselves, a pattern that holds them in established ways of action reinforced by mores and folkways as well as by traditional systems of authority. An African chief is likely to regard as a threat any effort to change the nature of the community he rules, particularly when the source of that effort is a national government that he knows can grow in authority only at the expense of his own. The second difficulty arises in accomplishing the essential second phase of community development, when people who have been carefully guided through a first venture should presumably be able and eager to undertake a second task on their own using the principles they have learned. Practical people have difficulty abstracting and using theoretical principles. To build a road is one thing, to build a schoolhouse another. How can anyone learn from doing one how to do the other? Community development specialists constantly confront this question, and unless they can answer it—and put their answers into successful practice—they perpetuate the dependence of the community on them and therefore fail as educators.

Systems Analysis Systems

All of the foregoing ways of planning or analyzing educational activities can be fully understood only in terms of the contexts in which they have been developed and applied. But each could also be viewed abstractly and theoretically as a system, a set of interrelated ideas, principles, or practices that forms a collective entity. It is in such fashion that systems analysts would view each one, for their concern begins with a way of thinking and then proceeds to its application. They are interested in how a process can be conceptualized, usually in a diagram, so that its essential components are identified and put into a proper sequential order to facilitate action and decision making. They therefore work at a higher level of abstraction than do the theorists dealt with earlier in this chapter, for system building is influenced by the nature of systems themselves.

This approach has ancient antecedents but became highly visible in the 1960s. An earlier concern with such instruments of analysis as flow charts and tables of organization gradually grew into a much more sophisticated approach. Some social scientists became preoccupied with model building. Educators developed programmed learning with its linear, branching, and recycling concepts. Industrial managers developed complex ways of charting the flow of work. The concept of program budgeting was developed and spread through industry, commerce, government, and private nonprofit organizational work. The definition of systems and their analysis in terms of input, throughput, and output became common. Many methods of system building were proposed. Hartley (1969) was able to identify sixty generalized code names or acronyms, such as operations research, PERT, PPBS, cost-benefit analysis, and modular scheduling.

Systems analysis has been extensively used in education, particularly in the administration of institutions and in the structuring of learning sequences for computer-assisted or other forms of programmed instruction. While this approach might theoretically be used in any educational situation, its complexity has caused its major application to be made in large-scale and expensive enterprises. It is well suited to the direction of a national adult literacy campaign but less useful as a guide to handling a single literacy class. Meanwhile the opponents of the practice of systems analysis, as distinguished from its theory, have charged that it is too rigid, centralized, prone to a simplistic treatment of complex problems and practices, and likely to treat the individual teacher or learner as a faceless unit in a system. While defenders of systems analysis maintain that such difficulties can be overcome, no way has yet been devised for adapting its highly sophisticated approach so that it can be used as a daily guide by the learner or the educator.

Andragogy

In continental Europe, some variation of the English word *pedagogy* is often applied to the study of the education of children. When adult education appeared as a distinct field of inquiry, a parallel term (translated into English as *andragogy*) was coined in Germany as early as 1833. In the ensuing century and a half, it never became prominent but had sufficient staying power to be borrowed in several other countries, including England, Switzerland, and Venezuela. Its fullest flowering occurred in Yugoslavia where it was established as an academic discipline, at least until the dismemberment of that country in the 1990s. Few studies of the meaning of the term are available in English, and there is little evidence that it implies any consistent patterning of method.

The term was introduced into the United States by Malcolm Knowles. From the mid thirties onward, he had had a career in adult education that was unparalleled in its scope, variety, and influence.

His theoretical reflections were first presented in an early work, *Informal Adult Education*, published in 1950. In the 1960s, as the creator of an academic department of adult education at Boston University, he found that he needed a name for the new discipline he was trying to create. He discovered it in Yugoslavia, introduced the term in a journal article in 1968, and made andragogy the central theme of his influential work *The Modern Practice of Adult Education*, first published in 1970. Its original subtitle was *Andragogy versus Pedagogy*.

In the quarter-century since then, andragogy has proved to be widely popular. It has been taken up with enthusiasm in many settings, and the results of the ensuing projects have been extensively publicized. Almost immediately, critics of Knowles and his ideas were heard, and debate about the theoretical soundness and practical utility of the new term became recurrent, reaching a zenith in the late 1980s. Knowles kept evolving, enlarging, and revising his point of view and therefore became something of a moving target, particularly since he was intimately involved with many projects at every level of magnitude in both customary and unusual settings all over the world; he could bring to discussions and debates a wealth of experience that his opponents could not match. Moreover, some of his followers developed variant conceptions of andragogy, thereby enlarging the discourse.

The fluidity of Knowles's theories makes it difficult to summarize them; the following account draws primarily on *Andragogy in Action* (1984). He regarded the child as having a dependent personality, with little experience on which to draw, whose motivation is supplied by pressures from parents and teachers and is centered on advancement through the schools' system of grades. The child has only a subject-centered orientation to learning. Knowles acknowledged that such a characterization might sound like caricature, but he believed that it expressed basic reality. In contrast, the adult is self-directing, has much experience on which to draw, learns because of a felt need or aspiration, wishes to orient his or her education toward life experiences (not subject matter), and feels most deeply rewarded by such outcomes of learning as greater self-esteem and a sense of personal actualization. The andragogical program designer must (1) establish a physical and psychological climate for learning, (2) discover how to involve the learners in mutual planning with those who hope to aid them, (3) help the learners diagnose their own needs and desires, (4) assist learners to formulate and carry out both objectives and lesson plans, and (5) guide the learners' evaluation of what they accomplish.

The foregoing bare-bones summary of andragogy does not convey the richness of many of the concepts involved, the fervor with which they were expressed, or the awakening sense of mutual trust and companionship often produced in those situations in which the followers of andragogy explored a new frontier. The new ventures were also aided by the fact that in much of the world, and certainly in Europe and North America, learner-centered education (as espoused by Comenius, Rousseau, and others) had long been familiar. Dewey, the chief modern exponent of such ideas and practices, had had a great impact in the United States in the previous half-century. The quotation from him given earlier would have to be modified only slightly to win acceptance as a description of "andragogy versus pedagogy," though at that point he was actually contrasting two forms of pedagogy.

When Knowles and his colleagues realized that their ideas appeared to have as much application in childhood as in adulthood, the reason for using the term andragogy to refer only to the latter seemed to disappear along with the assumptions that had made it necessary. It also became apparent that the division of life into two stages was not in accord with what appeared to be the emerging thrust of the field, as expressed in such terms as *lifelong learning*, *recurrent education*, and *permanent education*. Both childhood and adulthood include successive major steps; in rough categorization, they are infancy, childhood, adolescence, transition to adulthood, early years of established maturity, middle age, early years of old age, and later years of old age. Developmental psychology helps educators understand each of these stages and the differences among them; program building is significantly influenced, and perhaps determined, by them. Tennant and Pogson (1995) summarize the literature dealing with the stages of what they call the life course as it has been analyzed by various investigators; they also point out the strengths and the limits of such theorizing so far as the practice of adult education is concerned.

In another respect as well, early points of view about andragogy came to seem less important. A sense of marginality had long been felt by many adult educators as they sought support in an educational world heavily dominated by institutions serving children and youth. For example, Knowles (1990) refers to the adult learner as a neglected species. Andragogists felt that they had a battle on their hands to alter prevailing systems. They advanced their position with vehemence, used strongly colored terms of discourse, and wrote in language that could be interpreted as questioning the intelligence or goodwill of any reader who did not instantly accept the new ideas. An evangelistic approach may have been required to attract attention and bring about change. Yet as one practical success in the field followed another, the rhetoric of attack and defense could be modulated into one of calm exposition. In the 1980 revision of *The Modern Practice of Adult Education*, Knowles changed his subtitle to *From Pedagogy to Andragogy*. Fifty years earlier, Dewey (1938) had followed the same pathway. In setting up his own dichotomy, his language was heavily loaded both positively and negatively, and he made it clear that he regarded his system as "education" and others as "miseducation." As he moved forward into the statement of his basic ideas, however, Dewey no longer felt it necessary to set up dichotomies of theory and practice and differentiate them in heavily emotional terms.

The presently prevailing view is that education is fundamentally the same wherever and whenever it occurs. It deals with such basic concerns as the nature of the learner, the goals sought, the social and physical milieu in which instruction occurs, and the techniques of learning or teaching used. These and other components may be combined in infinite ways as, throughout life, the individual embarks on self-directed inquiry either alone or with others, benefits from the individual guidance of a tutor, or takes part in formally structured group or institutional activity.

Andragogy remains as the most learner centered of all patterns of adult educational programming. Distinctions between childhood and adulthood are unnecessary; indeed, references to pedagogy seem irrelevant. Those who wish to do so can wholly contain their practice in the ideas expressed by Knowles and others, establishing appropriate physical and psychological climates for learning and carrying forward all of its processes collaboratively. Far more significantly, andragogy influences every other system. Even leaders who guide learning chiefly in terms of the mastery of subject matter, the acquisition of skills, the facing of a social problem, or some other goal know that they should involve learners in as many aspects of their education as possible and in the creation of a climate in which they can most fruitfully learn.

Other Systems

Many other comprehensive systems of program planning have now appeared, most of them since 1970. In a celebrated study, Sork and Buskey (1986) analyze ninety-three books and essays that described complete adult educational program models. Eighty-three of these publications presented models explicitly in narrative or graphic form, and ten implied models but did not spell them out. A complete program-planning model was defined as "a set of steps, tasks, or decisions that, when carried out, produce the design and outcome specifications for a systematic instructional activity" (p. 87). Sork and Buskey have developed a complex framework by which to describe and evaluate the models; the results of this analysis are presented for the fifty-one book-length descriptions of such models that are included in the study.

To some extent, the models build on and borrow from one another. Boone (1985, pp. 20–37), for example, presents in depth a comparative analysis of nine programming models advanced between 1958 and 1981. Throughout his book, he makes clear his own use of various elements of design drawn from a wide-ranging literature. However, Sork and Buskey believe that most models are presented in too great an isolation from one another. They report a general "lack of cross-referencing and absence of cumulative development within the literature." They also note "a low degree of theoretical explanation," too great a reliance on a few steps rather than dealing with an entire process, a tendency to focus attention on a few contexts or settings rather than on all adult education, a bias toward group instruction, and a failure to address adequately the roles played and the proficiencies required by adult educators who engage in planning processes.

Sork and Caffarella (1989) build upon the Sork and Buskey analysis but go well beyond it to include additional models. They present a brief but exceptionally well-reasoned summary of six elements or stages that the authors believe should be included in comprehensive systems of program planning. Sork and Caffarella identify as a major problem of the literature its failure to deal adequately with the relationship between theoretical systems of programming and the processes actually carried out by workers in the field. Caffarella (1994) bridges this gap by presenting a full-scale, eleven-component model supported at all points by case studies, charts, exhibits, and lists, some of which could be applied with slight adaptations in a large number of diverse settings.

The relationship between theory and practice is a central topic of Cervero and Wilson (1994), who describe how it varies from one program-planning system to another. They divide all such systems into three large groups in terms of the viewpoints of the system proposers. The *classical* viewpoint is based on the bedrock of Tyler's thought. The systems included in this category use his terms and follow his procedures, though they may devalue some elements (most commonly, objectives or evaluation) or develop some steps and processes much more fully than others. The *naturalistic* viewpoint begins not with a standard set of terms, principles, and processes but with an examination of what happens in episodes of education—particularly those bringing about changes that, either before the fact or in retrospect, are judged to be positive. Anyone who lives through or analyzes a learning episode recognizes that it has some elements (methods, materials, location, sequencing, leadership, and others) that must either be accepted as innate parts of the situation (as correspondence teaching or the use of a computer network may be in distance education) or that require decisions to be made. Out of the examination of countless cases, generalized elements can be identified; placed in the proper orientation to one another, they make up a comprehensively usable design. Cervero and Wilson classify as naturalistic the viewpoint of the system presented in this book. Programs developed according to the *critical* viewpoint are centered not in process but in a profound belief that the lot of mankind needs to be improved and that the design of education should arise from the nature of the circumstances that should be corrected. For example, if destitute peasants are to be educated so that they may exercise power in the social order that has long oppressed them, their teacher must know intimately how they express their present values and must then build bridges to knowledge and the ability and desire to change the conditions of their lives. Jane Addams and her colleagues, who went to live in the slums of Chicago so that they could identify groups who needed education, could then develop programs to help them that arose from the way they viewed their own conditions of life. The design of education must arise not from a general desire to help people but from closely observed and carefully reasoned plans for doing so.

In the 1980s, a group of scholars, primarily at Columbia University, began to develop a new approach to adult education that they called transformative learning. Works by Jack Mezirow, Stephen Brookfield, and others established theoretical and practical bases for experiment and trial in the field. Cranton (1994) has brought much of this material together and set it into the broad field of adult education. She argues that practice in that field has three perspectives: that based on acquisition of content, that based on the meeting of needs, and that based on the removal of constraints and "is a process of freeing ourselves from forces that limit our options and our control over our lives, forces that have been taken for granted or seen as beyond our control" (p. 16). This third perspective is called *transformative learning* since it changes a basic orientation of the learner toward life, sometimes very profoundly indeed.

Such learning cannot be regarded as a system of program design; it deals with many other topics that exist beyond that realm. But this new way of thinking opens up vistas in many of the components of such design as it is planned and carried out both by learners and by those who guide their education. In stimulating self-reflection, for example, methods include critical questioning, guided introspection, consciousness raising, the writing of life histories, journal writing, experiential learning, and the analysis of critical incidents. The same holds for objectives, the design of a format, the fitting of a learning pattern into larger dimensions of life, and evaluation.

The few basic treatments of modern program systems just reviewed suggest their number and variety and some of the major ways they can be analyzed and grouped. While it would be tempting to continue the comparative discussion of systems, the purpose of this book is to present a way of designing education, not to relate that design to other systems. They have all been inspirations and resources, and the design presented in the next chapter owes much to them.

Inappropriate Systems

The earlier descriptions of change theory, community development, and systems analysis have all shown that adult education is complexly related to the achievement of purposes that are different from learning or teaching. In each of those three cases, a well-developed theory of operation guides practice and helps to make clear the relationship between education and other purposes. In many situations, however, adult education is accepted as being subordinate or identical to some related function, and a way of work that is appropriate to that function is accepted as being the fundamental system to be used to guide learning or teaching.

One such function is *public relations*. Well-conducted programs of adult education can have important favorable consequences for the institutions that sponsor them, a truth not lost upon university presidents, school superintendents, industrial executives, or labor union officials. There is sometimes a temptation to design and conduct a program so that it will win support among opinion makers, achieve favorable attitudes for the parent institution, or reinforce another activity, such as the K–12 program of the public schools, the "regular" offering of the university, or the point of view of industry, commerce, or labor. When used only as a public relations endeavor, adult education can often be successful, at least in the short run. But men and women are not likely to be fooled very long by any program that, under the guise of helping them in one way, covertly seeks to win their support for something else. In the long run, the best public relations is produced by a program that is centered on the desire to achieve educational goals and is successful in doing so.

Service can be distinguished from adult education by the fact that the aim of those who offer it is not to impart skill, knowledge, or sensitiveness but to give direct assistance to their clients. In practice, the two purposes are often confused, particularly if service is elevated to the loftiness of an all-pervasive goal (as it is, for example, in a university whose officers declare that its three purposes are research, teaching, and service). In such a case, a county agricultural agent of that university may have a difficult time deciding what duties are appropriate. When should he test soils, order seeds, administer a cooperative, or grade farm produce? If he is an offerer of service, he does all these things as needed, and his method is appropriate to the task he is performing. If he is an educator, he undertakes them only for demonstration or guidance purposes and as they fit whatever system of educational design he believes appropriate. As thus stated, the difference is straightforward, but in the realities of community life, the distinction may be hard to make. For example, should the county agent give service to influential farmers so that they help support his educational program? If he does not, he may not be able to maintain it. If he does, he may discover, almost before he knows it, that his educational program is dominated by his provision of service. While such a result is not necessarily bad, it does blur the two purposes and may keep either of them from being effectively achieved.

Recreation may or may not be pursued in an educative fashion. Pleasurable activities may be undertaken simply because of the satisfaction inherent in them, but many people want to deepen their enjoyment by learning and embark upon a program of study. In many cases, recreation and education are linked together so intimately that it is hard to separate them. However, a failure to recognize that they are essentially different purposes may lead to unfortunate consequences. People who want to increase their competence may think that practice alone makes perfect and therefore fail to seek the instruction they need. Someone who wants only to enjoy herself may have the idea of improvement thrust upon her, thereby ruining her sense of satisfaction. An evening school may maintain activities and facilities (such as choruses, drama groups, arts and crafts shops, and hobby clubs) that offer little or no instruction but use public funds supposed to be devoted to education. Such practices lead to a blurring of purpose and program design that is harmful to both functions.

Closely related to recreation is *esthetic appreciation*. The enjoyment of the beautiful in any of its varied forms can be experienced directly with no thought of improvement, but satisfaction can also be deepened by education. The two purposes differ from one another as all museum directors know. They can arrange the objects on display so that each can be seen to fullest advantage by people who want to admire it, or they can put the object in some instructive order and provide helpful guides. Usually some balance is struck, but the achievement of a harmony of the two functions requires that both of them be considered.

When *fraternization* occurs naturally in life, it is usually not influenced by the desire to learn or to teach. Comradeship is its own excuse for being. If it turns into a mutually shared inquiry or a master-disciple relationship, it becomes more complex than before precisely because a new dimension has been added. This difference is sometimes not recognized when fraternization is structured, as it is in interest groups or voluntary associations. In such cases, conviviality is accepted as the equivalent of education, and a sense of enjoyment or satisfaction in being with other people is taken as the measure of accomplishment of learning. For instance, the participants in a residential conference may give it a high rating simply because they enjoyed it so much. Alternatively sociability may be lessened or ruined by the introduction of didactic elements. The members of a club attend because they want to enjoy the fellowship, but the program committee requires them to hear a lecture. In group or institutional settings, fraternization and education may be combined and may well reinforce one another, but if so, the relationship must be conceived as a complex one that combines two inherently different purposes.

The promotion of *welfare*, defined as a social effort to provide minimum standards of acceptable life for members of a society, subtly pervades much adult educational thought and practice. Many people seem to believe that learning in adulthood is essentially the effort to give a second chance for basic education to those who missed their first chance or that it is concerned solely with such goals as occupational competence for the unemployed, family-life improvement for threatened homes, or consumer skills for poor people. This conception of adult education as solely an activity of a welfare state or of private charity limits its scope and narrows its range of designs. Many programs are excluded that are educative in a broader sense and that could be improved if subjected to program analysis and planning. Among them are most liberal studies programs, management education, learned societies, literary clubs, advanced training in the performing arts, and courses that introduce new legislators to their responsibilities. Also much-needed nonwelfare learning or teaching may never be undertaken. A public school system may offer literacy and vocational courses but never try to educate those community leaders who determine the major social policies of the city. Most damaging of all is the separation of educators from learners along class or income lines and the consequent introduction of an overt or covert condescension into the very heart of the educative process.

Therapy is the hardest function to distinguish from education, in both practice and concept. Therapy implies the treatment of illness or disability in order to achieve a normal state of being, whereas education implies the realization in countless ways of an infinite human potential. But this obvious distinction is often blurred by those who relate the two functions in any one of three essentially different ways.

Some people take therapy and education to be virtually identical. Such a view is held, for example, by anyone who argues that people study only because they have needs, identified either by themselves or by others. It follows that any form of unfulfilled potential is equated with deficiency and any measure taken to remedy it is essentially therapy. A similar view is held by those who conceive certain methods of psychotherapy (such as nondirective counseling or psychoanalysis) to be ways of helping clients examine their beliefs so that they can construct a system of values to guide their lives. Thus defined, such techniques may begin by being therapeutic but are essentially educative in character and, their adherents would claim, are the profoundest methods of learning now available.

Some people subordinate education to therapy, viewing it as a methodological resource, as it is used, for example, by a physical therapist or a dietitian. In this sense, it parallels such other forms of treatment as surgery and chemotherapy.

Some people consider therapy to be merely one approach to education. While it is true that some learning and teaching endeavors arise out of and are guided by a sense of need or deprivation, others grow out of a positive zest, interest, and desire to improve. Education has at least as much to do with the achievement of outstanding excellence as it does with bringing people with deficiencies up to some kind of norm. Paralleling the therapy or needs approach should therefore be one based on interest, a feeling of curiosity, fascination, or absorption in the achievement of some goal whose accomplishment is intended to give rise to satisfaction and enjoyment.

All three approaches so clearly identify education and therapy with each other that the two functions seem virtually inseparable. Much of the literature of education is in fact influenced more or less directly by this view. But this linkage, in any of its forms, does damage to the independence of education as a distinctive process worthy of being considered on its own terms, as it has been by those who have built most of the systems previously described.

Many other functions or activities have also been misapplied as systems for educational program planning or analysis. Among them are communication, the performing arts, religion, participation, creativeness, and health. An analysis of these functions and of the seven mentioned previously reveals that they are closely related to education in three ways. Some (such as service, recreation, and religion) have purposes that are similar to education but essentially different from it. Some (such as esthetic appreciation and health) delineate broad clusters of educational goals. Some deal with one component of educational design; thus fraternization is a form of social reinforcement and public relations of interpretation. Functions can also intersect with education in more than one of these ways. For example, welfare, recreation, or esthetic appreciation may be perceived either as a parallel purpose or as a goal cluster. Therapy is both of these and, in addition, provides theories of methodology that have been influential in some programs of adult education.

Since these differences and distinctions are complex and sometimes hard to understand, the occasional domination of adult education by systems or ways of thought derived from other functions (or even by special applications of the credos mentioned earlier) is not surprising. As Cardinal Newman pointed out in distinguishing recreation from education, "All I say is call things by their right names, and do not confuse together ideas which are essentially different" (1910, p. 144). The best corrective against confusing other functions with adult education is to develop and use a system of practice based wholly on learning and of sufficient strength not to be overwhelmed by systems used in allied but essentially different fields of human activity.

A New System

All the credos and systems just described have been considered in developing the system proposed in this book. The field of adult education is old enough to make possible not merely an analysis of the theoretical bases of these credos and systems but also an assessment of their several values and limitations as they have been used in many situations. Even inappropriate systems can be useful. For instance, some of the people who have believed that the growth of fraternization is the chief end of learning have developed procedures of social reinforcement that can be widely applied.

But the system that *The Design of Education* describes is not an eclectic one. Some concepts and components of other systems have been used in constructing it but have been integrated into a pattern essentially different from earlier models, one that it is hoped is sufficiently broad to accommodate the conceptions and guide the actions of all educators of adults. The system itself is sketched in the second chapter and illustrated and described in detail in the subsequent ones.

The Fundamental System

> *Science is an allegory that asserts that the relations*
> *between the parts of reality are similar to the relations*
> *between terms of discourse.*
> —Scott Buchanan, *Poetry and Mathematics*

Adult education is the process by which men and women (alone, in groups, or in institutional settings) seek to improve themselves or their society by increasing their skill, knowledge, or sensitiveness; or it is any process by which individuals, groups, or institutions try to help men and women improve in these ways. The fundamental system of practice of the field, if it has one, must be discerned by probing beneath many different surface realities to identify a basic unity of process.

Some Assumptions

The system proposed rests on nine assumptions. The first is that *any episode of learning occurs in a specific situation and is profoundly influenced by that fact.* Every human being lives in a complex personal and social milieu that is unique to that person, that constantly changes, and that influences all of her or his experience. Any segment of that experience devoted to learning occurs in a distinctive and specific situation that can be separated out for analysis but that is inherently part of a total milieu. The purposes, pattern, and results of that learning are all profoundly affected by the situation in which it occurs. Every activity learners undertake is unlike any other; for example, every class they attend is unique. If they participate in more than one educational situation, such as independent study, tutorial instruction, group participation, or membership in a voluntary association, each kind is different from the others.

The uniqueness of situations applies equally to each person who shares in them and to the social settings in which the instruction occurs. All learners in a group and all educators who guide its members live within their own milieu and are influenced in a distinctive way by the situation in which they find themselves. If attention is shifted away from individuals toward the social entities in which they learn—groups, classes, or institutions—the same distinctiveness of milieu and situation also applies.

The analysis or planning of educational activities must be based on the realities of human experience and upon their constant change. Since every situation is unique, the effort to understand or to plan educational activities must be centered as far as possible upon realities, not upon forms or abstractions. For example, an objective is a purpose that guides a learner or an educator, not the formal statement of that purpose. Anyone who designs an educational activity may make as clear and exact a forecast as possible of what she or he hopes to achieve, but the words of that forecast do not capture all of that person's ideas, nor are those ideas the sole determinants of what will occur after the activity begins. The designer must constantly reshape all plans and procedures in order to come to terms with changes brought about by the desires and abilities of other people or the specific instructional resources available. The evolving objectives are different from the initial statement of them. The methods used are not exactly like those in the lesson plans. And no predetermined method of evaluating the results of instruction can adequately measure the achievement of goals that do not become evident until the episode is completed or that exist only in the private intentions of the teacher or the learner.

Reality is hard to grasp (as the literature of epistemology demonstrates), but that fact does not mean that the effort to discern it should be abandoned. A continuing effort to perceive the reality of an educational activity must be attempted before the learning begins, while it is occurring, and as it is appraised afterward.

Education is a practical art. As is true in such established professions as law or medicine, success in the process of education is always measured by what occurs in the specific instances of its practice. What is the verdict of the jury, how well and how speedily is the patient returned to health, to what degree does the learner master the knowledge sought? As a sophisticated practical art, education draws upon many theoretical disciplines in the humanities and the social and biological sciences. It also uses an extensive and complex body of principles that has emerged from analysis of its own previous practice, and it has a history and lore of its own. But if this abstract and applied knowledge is to prove effective, it must be used in a specific situation to bring about a desired end.

To illustrate the point further, it may be said that any learning or teaching design is similar to plans made by an architect. That person has a deep knowledge of esthetics, engineering, economics, and other arts and sciences. He or she is aware of architectural traditions; of the range of building materials available, the methods of putting them together, and their relative values in various settings; and of the ways by which harmony is achieved between a building and its environment. Yet the architect knows that each particular building must be designed in terms of its immediate terrain and surroundings, using the construction materials and labor available, and staying within the allotted budget. Educators' designs have similar imperatives. Educators may know a great deal about the theory and practice of education, but in each case they have a specific learner or group of learners to reach; limited resources of money, time, and materials to use; and a given setting in which to work. Their success is judged by themselves and others not by how much they know but by their competence in using that knowledge to deal with the situation at hand.

The entire career of educators is judged by some balancing out of the relative successes and failures of all the programs they design and conduct. These programs may be similar to one another. For example, a literacy teacher may repeat her courses over and over again for twenty years, making only changes required by different groups of students or by the appearance of new teaching aids. Usually, however, variations are complex. Just as architects build many houses, so educators deal with many different situations, in each of which they apply talents and their resources of knowledge to the task at hand. Success in each case may be judged separately, but they and others appraise their career in terms of their capacity to deal with the whole range of endeavors.

The same generalization applies to learners. They may design a program of independent study for themselves, or they may fit into an activity designed by a tutor, group leader, teacher, or institutional staff. In each case, their success is judged, by themselves and by others, in terms of their mastery of the goals they seek. Their total learning achievement, however, is not measured by the results of any one act or episode but by the fruits of all the endeavors in which they have engaged.

Education is a cooperative rather than an operative art. The distinction between these two terms is an ancient one. An *operative art* is one in which the creation of a product or performance is essentially controlled by the person using the art. The painter, sculptor, engineer, actor, shoemaker, and builder are operative artists. A *cooperative art*, though no less creative than an operative one, works in a facilitative way by guiding and directing a natural entity or process. Farmers, physicians, and educators are three classic examples of cooperative artists. Farmers do not create the crops; they help nature produce them. Physicians aid and reinforce the processes by which the patient gets well. ("God heals," said Benjamin Franklin, "but the doctor takes the fee.") Educators do not put ideas into the minds of learners nor do they give learners skills or sensitiveness. Instead they help people learn these things for themselves and, by the use of the art, facilitate the accomplishment of desired goals.

In education, the term *cooperative* is used in two major senses. In its profoundest meaning, it signifies action by both learner and educator in accordance with the dictates of nature. Learners must work in terms of their innate individualism as well as in terms of the social stimulation supplied by any learning group of which they may be a part. Also, like all other human beings, they have limitations. Some of them are generic; no hand can span two octaves on the piano. Others are specific; only a relatively few people in any generation can become master pianists. The education of learners is profoundly influenced at every point by their capacities and concerns; as these change over time, so must the goals of learners and their facility in achieving these goals. As for educators, their aims and procedures are always influenced by their abilities and interests. They must work in terms of the opportunities and limitations these abilities make possible.

In its second sense, the term *cooperative* implies voluntary interaction among individuals during learning. Even the solitary student guiding his or her own program with no fixed instructor seeks the help and encouragement that others can provide. When education occurs in any social setting, those who take part should have some sense of collaboration in both its planning and its conduct. At one extreme, this sharing is so complete that it requires a group to decide everything that it does together. At the other extreme, the sharing may be implicit in the teaching-learning situation, as when many people flock to hear a lecturer. Those who attend vote with their feet, as the saying goes, and one cannot assume from their physical passivity and silence as they sit in the auditorium that they are not cooperating fully in their instruction.

Any individual or group who designs an educational program must take both forms of cooperativeness into account. An educational program must originally be planned in terms of the estimated nature of the learner or learners and of the educator (if there is one) and then revised in the light of the constantly changing reality that appears as the program is put into effect. In some situations, it is possible to involve learners or their representatives in planning and thus foster a collaborative approach. In other situations, educators must act alone, drawing upon their experience and knowledge of people to design the program and then being alert to adjust it to meet the realities encountered when embarking upon it. Even lecturers, using what is often thought to be a highly teacher-centered method, can constantly sense their audience's response and shift their approach to deal with it.

The planning or analysis of an educational activity is usually undertaken in terms of some period that the mind abstracts for analytical purposes from complicated reality. Learning can occur in a random fashion or as the unintended byproduct of acts performed for other purposes. Even when knowledge is consciously sought, its pursuits may vary in depth and scope from the simple looking up of a word in a dictionary to the undertaking of a lifelong and intensive inquiry. But the effective planning or analysis of education requires the selection of a time dimension that sets boundaries to what is either sought or observed.

Thus an evening college instructor may design a course in introductory chemistry using an eighteen-week semester with two hours of class and four hours of laboratory work per week. He may then plan smaller segments of the course, each built on a unit of content, and may even decide in advance how he will conduct each session. He is aware that his course fits within at least three larger patterns to which thought must be given by himself or by others: the total offering of the evening college, his program of teaching, and the place of his course in the degree sequences taken by his students. All three patterns influence what he does in his own course since they help determine the answers to some important questions. What are the prerequisites for his course? How much time can he devote to it in terms of his other obligations? Is it designed as an introduction for those who plan to specialize in chemistry or as a survey course for those who want to broaden their general education? Or must it fulfill both of these functions because the evening college staff is not able or willing to separate the two groups of students?

Each student in the course also plans in terms of several temporal patterns. She selects the degree program whose successful completion requires that she take chemistry. She has some freedom of choice as to when that subject comes within the sequence of her work. During the semester in which she takes it, she determines what other courses give as balanced a program as possible. She also plans the use of her time each day in terms of her needs to work, to have time for family and recreation, to attend classes and laboratory sessions, and to make preparations for them.

As this example suggests, good program planning or analysis usually requires both educator and learner to have at least four periods in mind, each of which gains meaning by its interaction with the others and all of which are logical abstractions, patterns imposed on reality for the sake of utility. An educational *episode* is a related series of learning or teaching events making up a coherent whole. It is more than a single exposure to knowledge but less than a long-sustained series of endeavors. Examples are a course, a residential conference, a workshop, a plan of reading based on a list of books, or a series of meetings by a group studying a topic. Of the four periods, the episode is the one most frequently and most intensively chosen for planning and analysis and is therefore the central time focus used in this book. An educational *act* is a specific and relatively brief learning or teaching event. It may be part of an episode; it may stand alone (as in an isolated lecture to an audience or an educational program on television); or it may be one event in a chain of otherwise unrelated occurrences (as when a discussion group chooses a different topic each time it meets). An educational *series* is a succession of related episodes, as in a curriculum for a degree, a progression of annual conferences, or a linking of courses of graduated difficulty. An *aggregate* of simultaneous episodes is a pattern of educational activities occurring in the same span of time in the life of an individual, group, or institution. The episodes may be linked together, may include one or more courses in a series, or may be unrelated except for the common period during which they occur.

Sometimes learners or educators do not set any time limitation on educational planning. Through choice or necessity, they embark on an activity with no clear idea of how long it will sustain their interest or attention. For example, they join or accept the leadership of a group, start out to visit cultural institutions, or enter into a tutorial relationship that may be broken off at any point. In such a case, planning occurs one act at a time with only a very general idea of continuity beyond it. Later, in retrospect, the sum of their actions may be seen to have been an episode, a series, or an aggregate, but such was not their original intent.

The planning or analysis of an educational activity may be undertaken by an educator, a learner, an independent analyst, or some combination of the three. In many educational activities, two distinct roles appear: the provider of focus, direction, and content and the person or persons whose learning is shaped and led. In formal settings, the first of these is usually called a teacher and the second a student or a pupil. But the first may also be called a leader, a counselor, a coordinator, a curator, a supervisor, a mentor, or any of a number of other terms; and the second may be referred to as a participant, a member, a counselee, a patron, a client, or another similar name. The terms *educator* and *learner* are used generically here to indicate the two roles. A third role sometimes appears when somebody who stands outside the educational activity itself helps to plan or analyze it. An administrator, a curriculum specialist, a consultant, an external examiner, or other people may plan, study, or appraise a program either independently or in collaboration with the educator, the learner, or both. This third role is here designated as that of *analyst*.

While the usual patterns of collaboration among these three are well understood, it is not always realized that each can operate independently of the others. An educator may do the whole job of planning, conducting, and appraising an educative program by himself, as when a public health specialist devises and provides a series of posters to teach the basic principles of nutrition. A learner may work completely on her own, as when she plans, carries out, and appraises a series of visits to Civil War battlefields because she is interested in American history. An analyst can design an activity that never comes to fruition, or he can study the operation of a program for which he has no responsibility and with which he may never come in direct contact.

Any design of education can best be understood as a complex of interacting elements, not as a sequence of events. In theory, the process of education usually goes through the stages of identification and refinement of objectives, selection of means of accomplishing them, conduct of the planned activity, and retrospective evaluation of it. If these various elements are to be identified and understood, they must be recorded in some fashion, and the temporal order is as good as any other for the purpose. It provides a structure that helps beginners to learn the system and more accomplished users to be sure that they take account of all relevant elements. But practice usually does not follow this logical pattern. An activity may be initiated because some resource is available or intriguing. For example, the director of an educational television station may begin his planning when a time slot opens up on his schedule, or an experimenter with computerized instruction may develop a course that tests that method. In such cases, the objective is chosen to fit the means, not the reverse.

Even more important, the mind seldom works in a completely logical fashion. The procedure of planning or analyzing an educational program is often very like the process of research. A distinguished group of scientists representing the American Psychological Association once observed:

> [Research] is a rather informal, often illogical, and sometimes messy-looking affair. It includes a great deal of

floundering around in the empirical world. . . . Somewhere and somehow in the process of floundering, the research worker will get an idea. In fact, he will get many ideas. On largely intuitive grounds he will reject most of his ideas and will accept others as the basis for extended work. . . . If the idea happens to be a good one, he may make a significant positive contribution to his science—"may" because between the idea and the contribution lies a lot of persistence, originality, intuition, and hard work [1959, p. 169].

From beginning to end, the design of an educational activity is usually in a constant state of reformulation. It emerges first in at least an embryo form when the possibility of the activity first appears, and it is reconsidered frequently during the time of planning, the time of action, and the time of retrospection. All the component parts of the design mesh together at every point at which it is considered. Only when they are separated for formal analysis do they appear to be logical and linear.

A *generalized educational design should be used to strengthen (not replace) the values that arise from profound belief, dedication, or creativeness.* Pioneering educational programs often spring from powerful desires to aid humankind: to bring people into a profounder relationship to God; to help them achieve a rewarding economic life; to give them power over the political decisions that affect them; to enable them to share in the arts and humanities; or to foster a greater awareness of and support for innovation in the various sectors of their lives. Success in such endeavors has often resulted from procedures and activities, often improvisational, which helped people understand the need to achieve the goals desired; such goal-driven programs often gained added strength when sponsored or carried out by a powerful and energetic leader or group.

The educational designer should try to reinforce the strength and effect of such programs, not to replace them with a generalized way of work. For example, an innovator who goes into either urban or rural slums with the passionate desire to help people learn how to live more healthy lives is likely to develop a program that bears fruit almost no matter what she does. To argue that a system should be fastened down upon her activities would be to suggest that conformity of process is more important than the purpose that illuminates her whole enterprise. But if she is not gaining all she hopes to gain, it might be wise for her to examine what she is doing by comparing it with ideas and standards found to be useful in other adult educational ventures. The effort to provide such helpful systematization has been the motivating force for the literature on program development whose growth was described in the last chapter. Most of the authors of that literature have themselves engaged in highly purposeful programs, and sometimes when those authors had achieved less success than they wished, they turned to the analysis or creation of generalized patterns that might be of help to themselves and others.

A *program design should be based on decision points, not prescriptions.* It is often easy to believe that adult educational programs must follow didactic rules, often laid down in other settings. It was once believed, for instance, that a baccalaureate degree could only be achieved by following a pattern originally developed for late adolescents and young adults that required full-time residence on a college campus for thirty-six months; completion of a prescribed number of required and elective bundles of content called courses, all of them strikingly uniform in length and design; and sometimes the completion of examinations or set tasks, usually highly cognitive in nature. Some adults find it possible to follow this pattern and may gain unexpected benefits from observing their young classmates, thus adding a new dimension to their education. It is now generally recognized, however, that most adults who want to earn the baccalaureate require a system of learning created in terms of the challenges and rewards of living a mature life. Such programs now flourish throughout the land.

It must be added that some programs designed especially for adults can be prescriptive in nature; this approach almost suggests that if specified rules are not followed, learning cannot result. Sork and Caffarella (1989, p. 235) pay their respects to one frequently advocated dogma by saying, "We believe that direct participation of client or learner in planning is desirable but not essential." The advocates of some systems (Verner was mentioned in the last chapter) suggest, directly or by implication, that if a program developer does not follow their rules, he or she is not really engaging in adult education.

A generalized program design can escape from such dogmatism if it is proposed as a network of decision points. The proponent of such a system asserts that an educational episode has influential elements that require its planner to make decisions or to accept the consequences of not doing so. Let us suppose that a resident of a retirement home wants to start a self-help computer group. At a minimum, all she really needs to decide in advance is the time, place, and means of announcement of a first session. But she may feel it wise to narrow the focus of the group in some ways, such as to limit it to users of DOS systems or to people who want to concentrate on word processing. She may want to involve a specialist consultant; she may want to suggest an initial series of topics so that the group can feel immediate rewards and learn how to work together; she may want to make available copies of a simple guidebook to computers; and so on. Most importantly perhaps, she must decide how much structure it is wise for the meetings of the group to have. Shall the group from the beginning decide everything? Shall it have an initial control by herself that will be replaced by control by the group? Or shall it continue indefinitely under her own caring guidance? From the time that the idea for the group first strikes her, on through its establishment and continuing existence to its end, affairs will be conducted either by deliberate decisions on key elements or by the way ongoing practice influences action, thereby making decisions by default.

Since the beginning of philosophic discourse, much has been said about the distinction between ends and means and their proper relationship to one another. In educational programming based on decision points, the goals to be sought and the ways of achieving them are inherently interactive. The aspirations of program design-ers and their accommodation to practical necessities are constantly interwoven both in initial planning and in the revisions required by experience. Cervero and Wilson (1994) offer three fully devel-oped case studies to show how this process occurs; they also develop the principles that should govern responsible decision making.

When stated baldly as propositions, some of these nine assump-tions may sound platitudinous since they underlie so much excel-lent practice. They are presented here, however, chiefly because they are so often violated. All too often, abstract systems of teach-ing, such as textbooks, lesson plans, or course outlines, are worked out on the basis of a generalized conception of content, method, evaluation, and the nature of the "typical" student and are then imposed virtually intact upon many different situations. An insti-tution builds up a generic pattern of service, such as a ten-session course meeting one night a week for ten successive weeks, and then seems unable to vary it, implying that all knowledge relevant to its purpose should be conveyed in this fashion. These and similar rigidities deny in practice the situational approach to education expressed in the foregoing assumptions.

Practically speaking, learners or educators may use this approach in either of two ways. They may work wholly within the situation in which they find themselves, building up designs of activity deter-mined entirely by its dictates. Or they may begin with a generalized system but adapt it, profoundly if necessary, to fit the requirements of the situation. The failure to use this second approach creatively leads to excessive formality of education.

A Two-Part System

The foregoing nine assumptions might undergird many different systems of program planning or analysis. The one proposed here requires two complementary actions: (1) the examination of the situation in which the learning activity occurs to determine the basic category to which it belongs and (2) the application (in ways profoundly influenced by its category) of a basic framework or model to that situation in order to produce a design or program. These two actions must be described separately here, but in practice they are closely interrelated.

Categories of Educational Programs. The most familiar category of educational programs is instruction in a classroom, where a group of students learns from a teacher, usually under institutional sponsorship. Classroom instruction is in fact so commonly used in the schooling of young people from kindergarten through graduate instruction that many people carry over into their adulthood the belief that it is virtually the only possible learning situation. This view is shared by many educators of adults. An extension dean may believe the only university-level instruction that is intellectually respectable is one in which an acknowledged master of a field of content teaches it to a group of well-prepared students. The dominance of classroom instruction is further reinforced by both professional and lay discussions of education, many of which imply that it is the only form of learning and teaching worth consideration.

But as earlier parts of this chapter suggest, both processes also occur in countless situations that do not fit the classroom form. Among the most popular of these are the small self-directed group, the residential conference or institute, the voluntary association, and the tutorial relationship. Each of these has sufficient clarity of form to be widely understood, and each has its own protagonists. To some people, for example, the small self-directed group is the only valid form of adult learning; to others, the residential conference is supreme. An advocate of a "new" category often helps make a case for it by disparaging the classroom, thus unintentionally accentuating the dominance of that form.

If overall harmony of process is to be achieved in adult education, it is apparently necessary to have some typology of the categories into which learning and teaching situations can be fitted. Five such categories have already been roughly identified. When they are arrayed side by side, they can be looked at dispassionately as being alternative ways to undertake the educative process. Some people may still like one form better than others, may wish to work wholly within it, and may try to establish their personal preference as a panacea. However, those who seek to make sense of the field as a whole (as it is and not merely as they wish it to be), or who hope to broaden their range of personal competence to include a mastery of various categories of process, will find it useful to look speculatively at each of them, understanding its form and assessing its relative utility. The central question is not "Is Category A better than Category B?" but "In what circumstances is Category A better than Category B?"

Anyone who tries to answer this question must look beneath the surface of the formal settings in which learning and teaching occur. The essential distinction among categories is not to be found in their outward form. On that basis, it is often hard to distinguish a class from a group or either of them from a conference. The inner reality lies in the chief source of authority and direction so far as planning and control are concerned. In the class, it is the teacher; in the group, its own members; and in the conference, a committee. Each of these forms can use a great variety of methods and resources. For example, a teacher can lecture, hold recitations, lead discussions, provide demonstrations, use role playing, arrange field trips and work experiences, require readings, invite visiting speakers, show films, or ask that the students write themes. Yet in every case, the teacher, though using all the arts of cooperation, is the chief designer of the program; thus it is distinguished from either the group or the conference.

Eleven educational planning categories are suggested here as those most common in current practice. Each is somewhat broader in scope and more exact in definition than the five popularly designated categories to which reference has just been made; thus "classroom instruction" becomes "a teacher or group of teachers designs an activity for, and often with, a group of students." These eleven are classified into four sets relating to their central foci and are usually referred to subsequently by their numerical designations as C-1, C-2, and so on. While the reader may find this method of reference to be initially awkward, it has the advantage of brevity as contrasted with the relatively lengthy description in words that would otherwise be repeatedly required. Each category will be described in detail in Chapter Four but is identified and illustrated here (in Table 2.1 and the following paragraphs) in order to establish the nature of the first of the two essentials in the system.

One set of situational categories is centered on individual learning.

C-1. An individual designs an activity for herself. Examples: a woman decides to broaden her knowledge of music by reading about it, systematically listening to it, and attending courses in it. The educational director of a prison undertakes to improve his performance by reading the literature on the rehabilitation of criminals and by visiting other prisons and detention centers.

C-2. An individual or a group designs an activity for another individual. Examples: a supervisor in a department store tries systematically to help one of his staff to become a better salesman. A librarian in the natural sciences collection of a large public library works out a bibliography of readings to suit the special needs of a patron. A group of specialists in the State Department in Washington briefs a newly appointed ambassador on various aspects of life in the country to which she is being sent.

A second set of situational categories is centered on the learning that occurs in a group activity.

C-3. A group (with or without a continuing leader) designs an activity for itself. Examples: a club of faculty members drawn from the various departments of a university meets regularly to keep its members abreast of new scholarly developments. The pastor of a

Table 2.1 Major Categories of Educational Design Situations.

Individual	
C-1	An individual designs an activity for herself
C-2	An individual or a group designs an activity for another individual

Group	
C-3	A group (with or without a continuing leader) designs an activity for itself
C-4	A teacher or group of teachers designs an activity for, and often with, a group of students
C-5	A committee designs an activity for a larger group
C-6	Two or more groups design an activity that enhances their combined programs of service

Institution	
C-7	A new institution is designed
C-8	An institution designs an activity in a new format
C-9	An institution designs a new activity in an established format
C-10	Two or more institutions design an activity that enhances their combined programs of service

Mass	
C-11	An individual, group, or institution designs an activity for a mass audience

liberal church organizes a group of its members to read and discuss the writings of Paul Tillich.

C-4. A teacher or group of teachers designs an activity for, and often with, a group of students. Examples: a home economist teaches a group of low-income mothers how to select and prepare inexpensive foods that provide a balanced diet for the family. A team of heart specialists conducts a course for the nurses in a hospital, teaching them new techniques of caring for cardiac patients.

C-5. A committee designs an activity for a larger group. Examples: a committee works out the program for the annual conference of a professional society. The officers of a study club plan its activities for the next year.

C-6. Two or more groups design an activity that enhances their combined program of service. Examples: the presidents of a number of voluntary groups in a city neighborhood form a council to identify common problems and study ways to deal with them. Delegates from all the clubs in a settlement house meet together to develop a combined program for it.

A third set of situational categories centers on the learning that occurs under the auspices of an institution.

C-7. A new institution is designed. Examples: a businessman starts a private correspondence school. Congress establishes and funds a program to provide basic vocational education for the persistently unemployed. A national association is formed to educate its members on foreign affairs.

C-8. An institution designs an activity in a new format. Examples: a university extension division creates a new curriculum that prepares adults for a master of liberal arts degree. A museum staff designs a new exhibit. A local YMCA sets up a program to help its members learn new recreational skills.

C-9. An institution designs a new activity in an established format. Examples: the staff of an educational television station selects and develops the broadcasts that will highlight its programming for the coming season. The director of a community college adult educational program chooses the new courses it will offer. A conservation association plans its program emphasis for the year.

C-10. Two or more institutions design an activity that enhances their combined program of service. Examples: the heads of the major agencies of adult education in a city develop a program of collaborative action to deal with the common needs on which their institutions should be working. A county extension director and a regional public librarian develop a number of systematic ways by which each can foster the other's program.

A final situational category is centered on the provision of education to a mass audience. The learners can be identified only in terms of very general characteristics and not as specific groups or individuals.

C-11. An individual, group, or institution designs an activity for a mass audience. Examples: a professor presents a course by television. A publisher issues a set of books intended to educate readers on various subjects. A voters' league holds a series of mass meetings to inform the public on current political issues. A state department of agriculture issues a number of farmers' bulletins, each written to tell readers how to cope with some practical problem.

Central and subordinate categories. The process of education is strongly influenced by the nature of the category in which it is conducted. This fact is considered at length in Chapter Four, but it may be useful to illustrate it at this point. If the pastor of the liberal church referred to as an illustration of C-3 leads a discussion on the writings of Tillich, using the books themselves as the fundamental sources of content and accepting any interpretation of them that seems reasonable to the group involved, he or she is acting in C-3. If the pastor treats the writings as a text as a base for expressing a personal knowledge of the matters with which they deal and presents an individual interpretation of Tillich's ideas, he or she is acting in C-4. Neither category is inherently superior to the other, but the two are different in establishing both the ends and the means of the learning process. That difference is particularly sharply felt when a group believes itself to be in one situation and its leader believes himself to be in the other. The church members may feel frustrated if they seek instruction from their pastor (C-4) but find that he or she constantly throws them back on their own resources (C-3). Learning is hampered until the difference in viewpoint has been resolved.

Once planners or analysts have identified the basic category or categories with which they are concerned, they may want to shift focus from time to time. Thus the pastor may view the course on Tillich as being essentially a C-4 situation but want to have some sessions in C-3. In such a case he or she may need to make the shift in category dramatically clear, perhaps by having a member of the group lead the C-3 sessions and remaining apart in order to symbolize a temporary abdication of authority as a C-4 teacher. The use of central and subordinate categories may become very complex. For example, an evening college professor of introductory chemistry knows that the central focus of his course is on C-4, but he also knows that when one of his students is considering his total program of educational activities, he is working in C-1. Within his course, the teacher may need to design subcomponents in C-2 (if he finds it necessary to work with individual students), C-3 (if he makes provision for group-directed discussions), and C-5 (if he encourages a group of students to prepare and present a demonstration on some special topic). He also knows that his course is but one episode in a series of courses, most of which are also C-4 but which may include a number of other categories as well.

Framework and components. Even as central and subordinate categories are being identified, the planner or analyst is performing the complementary task of fitting together a framework of interrelated components that compose the design of the activity. These components and the process of harmonizing them are detailed in Chapters Five and Six. At this point, the overall framework is merely sketched to make the outline of the model clear. Two parallel presentations of the same material are given, one in Figure 2.1 and one in the textual analysis.

In conformity with an assumption identified earlier, these components are to be understood as a complex of interacting elements, not as a logical sequence of steps. In applying the model to a situation, one may begin with any component and proceed to the others in any order, and in many cases the program needs to be

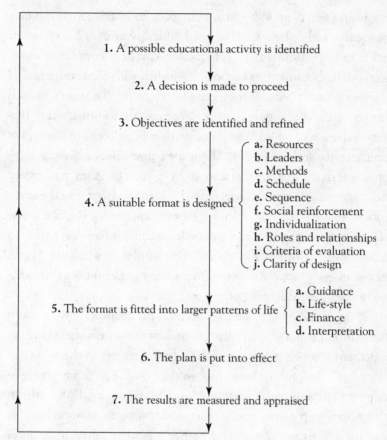

Figure 2.1. Decision Points and Components of an Adult Educational Framework.

reviewed many times during the course of the activity. But the general framework must be introduced to the reader by presenting the components one after the other in some rational fashion, and long experience with various overall designs has shown that the series of decision points used in Figure 2.1 and in the text is the one that brings about the most rapid understanding and the firmest eventual grasp of essentials.

1.   A possible educational activity is identified. The impulse to learn or to teach may arise from almost any source within or without

the life pattern of an individual, a group, or an institution; and it may
be created either by a sense of need or deprivation or by a sense of
desire or opportunity. In C-1, individuals may contemplate a learning activity because they become dissatisfied with the routineness of
their existence, because they get a different job, because a branch
library opens in the neighborhood, because they must learn to live
with a disease or a handicap, because they have come to the end of
one activity and are casting about for a new one, or because they
grow interested in a new avocation. In C-10, a program may appear
desirable because a major social need is identified, because the institutions involved are not achieving maximum results, because a new
source of financing becomes available, because influential figures in
a community think it wise to imitate a similar program elsewhere,
or because the appearance of a major new organization threatens
the work of existing institutions.

2.   A decision is made to proceed. This decision may be taken
for granted, it may be rapidly reached, or it may emerge slowly as
judgment is brought to bear on the relevant factors in the situation.
It is usually helpful to think through the possible program, trying to
conceptualize how the various components will be dealt with. In
this way, a preparatory design of a possible future activity is built. It
can then be examined to see whether it is worthwhile in terms of
available resources and probable accomplishments. Sometimes (as
is often the case in C-9) some choice must be made among various
possible alternative programs. If the decision to go ahead with an
activity is negative, the process of program building ends. If it is
positive, the next steps are taken.

3.   Objectives are identified and refined. Every educational
activity is based on some conception of the ends it should achieve.
Out of the complex array of complementary or conflicting possibilities present in the situation, dominant and guiding purposes emerge
to give shape to the educational program. A class in art (C-4) may
be based on the desire to improve its students' painting skills or on
the attempt to increase their understanding and appreciation of

mankind's great art treasures. Every aspect of the course is influenced by the decision as to which of these two purposes is dominant. Often several objectives must be sought simultaneously, as when a cluster of groups (C-6) seeks by collaborative effort to improve existing separate programs, to find and remedy gaps in service, and to discover new activities that its members can jointly sponsor. These three goals may be pursued separately, but in the total setting they are intimately interrelated. That fact influences every component of the design.

Usually some hierarchy of objectives, in which broad purposes comprehend limited ones, must be developed. Sometimes this ordering is based on a logical analysis of content; a tutor teaching introductory Spanish to a student (C-2) knows that to convey a basic capacity in the language, she must teach vocabulary, pronunciation, and grammar. Sometimes the hierarchy is based on a balancing out of complementary goals; a course designed to train secretarial workers must provide occupational skills, a knowledge of office procedures, and an awareness of the need for good personal grooming. Hierarchical analysis is particularly significant when several educational periods are considered simultaneously. If the staff of a public school adult education program decides to introduce a complete curriculum leading to the high school diploma (C-8), a broad objective is required for the series and more specific ones for the episodes. Meanwhile the educator in charge of each episode must identify its general purpose but also define specific goals for each of its acts.

4. A suitable format is designed. Any educational activity, however brief or extended, has a distinctive shape or pattern that gives unity to its various elements. Each of them may be considered or planned separately and in any order, but a successful program requires a fusion of all such elements in terms of the situation in which the education occurs.

4a. Learning resources are selected. Such resources include any persons, facilities, or materials that can be used to achieve the purposes identified. In some situations, a program planner must try to provide resources where they do not currently exist. Most of the people of the world have no access to books; where this situation is true, a first step in an educational program may be to create a library or other materials center (C-7). In other cases, the task is one of selection. A group wishing to study modern art (C-3) in an American city can choose from many possibilities, among which are a packaged course provided by a publisher, a self-selected list of books or pamphlets, films, slides, and collections of works of art.

4b.   A leader or group of leaders is chosen. In one sense, this leader is a learning resource since she or he often possesses some knowledge or competence that the learner must master. And as is often true in C-4, this knowledge or competence may go far in determining the whole course of the learning activity. But the leader also plays a dynamic role. She or he takes the initiative to guide, direct, instruct, question, demand, or interact in other ways and by taking any of these actions becomes more than a resource.

4c.   Methods are selected and used. They are often automatically established as soon as learning resources or leadership are determined. If a computerized game is to be played, the group involved must use the method required by the game it chooses. If the leader is viewed as the chief source of content, the lecture method may be required. Methods set limits to both resources and leadership. In mass programs (C-11), the very nature of the medium (publishing, television, radio, CD-ROM) helps to define both the content and the human resources that present it. But despite the close relationship of method to other elements, it should usually be considered independently since in most situations several methods could be used, and it is important to choose the best one for the immediate setting. Also variety is often important; the planners of a weekend residential conference (C-5) may decide to use several methods so that none of them becomes dull or fatiguing.

4d.   A time schedule is made. Often the schedule is inherent in the situation, for many educational institutions operate in terms of fixed allocations of time. An educational television station may offer one-hour programs on a subject once a week for thirteen weeks, and an evening school may have classes on Monday and Thursday evenings for ten weeks. Such established patterns as these define the boundaries of time available, and the overall schedule is accepted as it stands. However, if a program is being newly planned by an independent learner (C-1), a group (C-3), an institution (C-8), or in any other category, it is necessary to decide how long the activity should last and when it should occur.

4e. A sequence of events is devised. Even within a single learning act, progression occurs; for example, a lecturer develops a theme according to some ordering of ideas. The arrangement of events so they will be maximally educative grows in importance as activities increase in complexity and length. Sequence may occur in terms of a logical principle, such as early to late, simple to complex, easy to difficult, specific to general, or general to specific. Sometimes several such approaches must be designed, as when a course in history proceeds in terms of successive chronological periods. But in each one certain basic themes are considered. The sequence of events may also be wholly psychological, growing out of the developing interests and interactions of learners and educators, as happens in T-groups or other forms of sensitivity training.

4f. Social reinforcement of learning is provided. Whenever two or more people are involved in an educational activity, they have feelings about one another, and these feelings can either aid or limit the learning that occurs. In a tutorial situation (C-2), for example, a nondirective counselor may play a wholly supportive and reinforcing role, while an athletic coach may develop a pattern of challenge, demand, and reward. The emotional aspects of interpersonal relationships are always keenly felt by groups of learners; in most cases when they are asked to appraise an educational activity, they begin by expressing their feelings toward its leader or their fellow students.

4g. The nature of each individual learner is taken into account. Each person is unique and learns in a distinctive way, a fact that should never be forgotten by the planner or the analyst. The task of taking this element into account grows more difficult as groups or institutions increase in size; but even in mass learning programs (C-11), efforts may be made to reach a few individuals. Thus a poster in a public health campaign may urge its viewers to consult a physician or dentist; an educational radio station may give close consideration to letters of inquiry; and a lecturer may focus attention on several individuals in the audience to observe their reactions to what has been said.

4h.   Roles and relationships are made clear. When people are related to one another in an educational activity, as in any other, each person develops both expectations toward the others and beliefs about what they expect. When a supervisor is instructing a staff member (C-2), for example, their superior-subordinate position is important to the learning relationship. Ambiguities are always present in social interaction, but it is usually helpful to the learning process to have duties and responsibilities as clearly understood as the situation allows. When the voluntary groups in an underprivileged neighborhood work together to inform their members and the whole community of the need for urban reform (C-6), attention must be paid to the allocation of functions, the definition of authority of the officers and members of each group, and the manner in which existing power structures and emerging leaders can be duly recognized.

4i.   Criteria for evaluating progress are identified. An educational activity should bring about those changes in the learners that are indicated by its objectives. If goals are stated in behavioral terms ("to be able to demonstrate the proof of any Euclidean theorem"), they suggest both a form of measurement and a criterion for the judgment of success. If goals do not establish such criteria, the planner or analyst must identify them if he or she is to make an appraisal. Thus a conference on industrial management offered to executives may set three standards for itself: satisfactory completion by all members of a multiple-choice test on the content, expression of a personal sense of heightened competence by all members on a form provided for the purpose, and active participation by all members from beginning to end as observed by the staff. At least some of the criteria of appraisal and methods of measurement should be clear from the very beginning of an activity, though they may be altered and others added as time goes on.

4j.   The design is made clear to all concerned. A perennial complaint in every kind of educational activity is "I didn't know what I was supposed to do" or "nobody told us what was expected of us." Many a beautifully planned convention (C-5) has failed because its organizers understood it so well that they forgot that the other people involved (speakers, panel members, discussion leaders, chairmen, and participants) did not know how they were to carry out the plans made for them. At the start of an activity, its design should therefore be made clear to all concerned, and any changes in it should be fully communicated as they occur.

5.   The format is fitted into larger patterns of life. The learning activities of men and women must ordinarily be introduced with some care into a complex milieu that includes work, home, civic, and other responsibilities. At least four kinds of adjustments must usually be considered.

5a.   Learners are guided into or out of the activity both at the beginning and subsequently. Since any given program is appropriate for some people but not for others, some means must often be found for including the first and excluding the second. Much of this differentiation occurs by self-selection; courses in calculus or in gourmet cooking have such clear purposes that student choice may provide adequate guidance. But special planning and procedures may also be required; the staff of a university extension center considering its courses for the following year (C-9) may devote a good deal of attention to identifying present and potential clienteles and to finding ways by which individuals and groups can discover which of the varied activities are most rewarding for them.

5b.   Life-styles are modified to allow time and resources for the new activity. In most cases, educational activities cannot simply be added to whatever the learner or educator is doing. Something else—work, home, or leisure—must be changed. An individual (C-1) or group (C-3) planning a program of study must give up some other existing or potential pursuit, and that relinquishment requires alteration of a total plan of life. If several evening colleges in the same city develop a coordinated program of offerings (C-10), each institution may have to drop some courses and add others, thus changing the shape of its previous independent offering.

5c.   Financing is arranged. The cost of adult education includes not only the outlay for instruction and such allied expenses as travel, meals, and child care but also, in at least some cases, the loss of income that might be derived from an alternative use of the time. Other goods and services that might be bought with the money spent on education are denied. In the long run, expenditures for education build human resources and thereby often produce increased income. Yet for many people, the funds required to make the initial expenditures are either lacking or are so limited that their use requires a sacrifice or the choice of a low-cost pattern of learning rather than an expensive one. The problem of finance is also often crucial to the educator, particularly when new institutions (C-7) or major new formats (C-8) are created. The high death rate among them is chiefly due to the fact that they have inadequate funds to stay alive.

5d.   The activity is interpreted to related publics. This step usually requires that those who belong to any such public both understand it and assent to it. Since participation in adult education usually depends heavily on voluntary choice by the learners, interpretation plays an important part in most situations. A man needs to make it clear to his wife and family why he wants to be away from home one evening a week. The relationship between tutor and student needs to be understood by those who observe it. Participants need to be recruited for groups, courses, conferences, and institutions. Collaborative arrangements among associations or organizations need to be explained to their memberships or constituencies.

Sometimes proper interpretation is crucial to the success of learning activities. Sometimes it is merely facilitative or tension reducing. But it must always be actively considered as part of a design.

6.   The plan is put into effect. In this process, what was abstract is made concrete; education becomes in the fullest sense a cooperative art. Much of the direction and content of the activity may be determined only after it begins, particularly in learning that is centrally concerned with problem solving or human interaction. In other cases, constant adaptation is needed to adjust to problems or opportunities. Often it is wise to have a periodic reinspection of purpose and format to see whether they need to be adjusted to changing situations. Thus a conference or convention may retain its original planners (C-5) or choose a new steering committee to make decisions about such developments as an unexpectedly large attendance, a missing lecturer, or a demand from a group of participants that the program be revised to meet its needs.

7.   The results are measured and appraised. Measurement is based on quantitative data, and appraisal is an estimate of success based in part upon the results of measurement. Taken together they make up evaluation. Both processes go on simultaneously during an educational activity but are culminated at its conclusion. While the two are intimately related, they need to be considered separately. It is important to gather all of the evidence that can be economically collected both by the means originally devised in the program and by any other means that may appear subsequently. To use a very simple example, a teacher of word processing may plan to measure the speed and accuracy of her students by giving them timed tests. During the term, she may also note an unusually high repair bill and frequently jammed machines. When she appraises her own accomplishments and those of the members of her class, she takes into account both the factual data and her subjective observation. Was the students' progress as good as expected? If not, why not? Was it better? If so, why? Were the students careless with their machines, or did the electronic difficulties arise from other causes? The answers

to such questions as these provide the bases for the judgment of success. In educational activities, it is never possible to measure every outcome—a fact particularly true when goals are less tangible than are inputting speed and accuracy. The learner or educator must always supply some appraisal that goes beyond the data if she or he is to arrive at a final judgment concerning the degree of success of the activity and to probe into the causes of that success.

8.   The situation is examined in terms of the possibility of a new educational activity. Here the cycle of program planning recommences, and if the decision to proceed is made, a new design must be created. In some cases, that decision is virtually automatic regardless of either measurement or appraisal and may even be made before they can occur. Thus teachers often take it for granted that they will repeat their courses again the next year—an assumption that leads at least a few of them to forget the continuing need to be creative, cooperative artists. Similarly a group or an institution may cling to a continuing existence long after it retains only a shadow of its original substance. Rejection can be as automatic as acceptance; many students end a course or a program with the belief that it completes their education or the judgment that learning has been so distasteful or profitless that they will never undertake it again. But the completion of an activity also often leads, either immediately or subsequently, to a reexamination of the situation to see whether a new act, episode, or series would be desirable. The consideration of this question requires as critical an examination as does the decision to undertake an initial activity.

Using the System

This two-part system is proposed in a spirit of pragmatic utilitarianism. If it works effectively and economically in either explaining or improving educational practice, it can be used. If it does not work, some other system should be tried. In every case, the learners or the educators should be the masters since only they can comprehend the situation that they choose or in which they are placed by circumstance. Anyone who becomes inflexibly attached to the following of a process rather than to the achievement of ends is by definition doctrinaire.

The system suggested is a natural one, using familiar terms and components that have a common-sense foundation, requiring neither special terminology nor elaborately intricate exposition. It can be used with some success even by those who have little knowledge of educational theory and practice. Figure 2.1 and Table 2.1 can in fact be readily grasped by volunteer lay leaders in a single training session. The great body of educational research of the past seventy-five years has been focused on the several components of design, so that no matter how sophisticated educators may become, they can still fit their knowledge about these components within these categories and frameworks. Unless they do use some such systematic plan to provide order to their approach to the designing of educational activities, they cannot work effectively as practical artists. The more knowledge they have, the less efficient they are.

All the components of the system must be kept in balance. Each depends upon all the others; the change of one influences the rest. For example, effective social reinforcement should be considered separately, but it is also a product of decisions made about leadership, resources, individualization, clarity of design, and other elements. If any is given undue stress, it negatively influences all the others. When any component, such as finance, schedule, or measurement, is fixed, all the others must be considered in terms of it. Otherwise the system loses its equilibrium and therefore its fullest effectiveness.

The scarcity or misuse of time often limits or destroys the balance essential to an effective design. A planner may have too short a notice or too many programs to allow her to pay attention to separate components or to their blending. In other cases, so much time is devoted to particular aspects of the system that other aspects suffer. A group may spend so many hours on refining objectives that it has no time left to fulfill them, or a teacher may become so obsessed with evaluative procedures that finally he teaches only what he knows he can measure. In the practical world, overplanning is as bad a habit as underplanning.

As the copious earlier illustrations suggest, the framework is fundamentally the same in all categories of situations, though its applications vary from one to another. Individuals who wish to think through these applications systematically might find it useful to guide their thought by a two-way grid in which the eleven situational categories are listed on one coordinate and the components of program design are listed on the other. Such an examination shows a few places where format elements are inapplicable or have only limited relevance. Self-guided learners (C-1) do not need to think about creating social reinforcement within the activity itself, though they may need to find ways to maintain positive attitudes of their own. In a mass educational activity (C-11), instruction cannot be individualized, though as noted earlier, an effort may be made to personalize it in some fashion. In most cases, however, the components apply in all categories, even if in different ways.

The mastery of this system of planning and analysis, like that of any other complex process, is initially tedious since it requires close attention and application. One must examine many cases, looking beneath the specifics of each activity to discover the basic structure that gives a common design to all of them. Chapter Three presents and interprets a few cases in order to introduce the practical use of the system, and sources of additional cases for study and discussion are suggested in the list of references. But the major way by which anyone can learn the system is by the analysis of his or her own practice. In time, the ability to identify categories and construct designs is greatly facilitated. Experience provides not only skill but speed, particularly in the delicate art of balancing components.

Chapters Four and Five return to the categories and the components respectively to give a somewhat fuller account of each of them than was possible in this overview chapter. The primary effort in both cases is to convey an understanding of how the system works in the creation of an activity or in the process of revision that occurs as the cycle of planning is repeated.

The final brief chapter returns to the topic of how the system can be incorporated into the thought and practice of both learners and leaders and serve as the skeletal base on which either a lifetime learning program or a career in adult education can be enriched.

3

Five Cases

*Studies themselves do give forth directions too much
at large, except they be bounded in by experience.*
—Francis Bacon, *Of Studies*

A system of program planning can win acceptance only to the
extent that it credibly describes the myriad activities of adult
education and is useful in designing new ones. In this chapter, the
system described in the previous chapter is used to analyze five very
different learning situations. None of the activities described was
designed or conducted by people who had knowledge of the model;
in one case, they were not even aware that theirs could be called a
venture in adult education. Following each case is my analysis of
how it relates to the model, but the reader may wish in each instance
to make an independent interpretation before reading mine.

Learning Among the Destitute

Background. The leaders who first established an American adult
education movement in the 1920s and 1930s were primarily concerned with formal instructional settings and broad political, economic, and social issues. Their horizons were abruptly enlarged by
a paper written by Walter Dan Griffith, first published in the *Journal
of Adult Education* and later reprinted widely elsewhere. It was clear,

forceful, original, and distinctively American. This condensed version is taken from Ely (1936).

"*A Hobo School*." In the matter of barging about the world, I've had a bit of experience. During the World War I was in France and Mesopotamia with the British, and after that I followed the sea, until the depression put me high and dry on the beach.

Shanghai, Hong Kong, and Rio are spots that I can look at with sated eyes. In my time I've been shipwrecked off the Great Barrier reef and, all in all, I've lived what the lady reporters call "an eventful life."

Nevertheless, looking backward, I can think of no episode that can hold a candle to my recent adventure in pedagogy.

But to start at the beginning, when I was a youngster in school I would study nothing but geography. The pictures in the big geography book seemed to hypnotize me and, using the pictures as a starting point, I would dream of far-off places—green seas, dense jungles, and snow-capped mountains. So zealously did I concentrate on geography, to the detriment of all other studies, that in the fourth grade the teacher set me down as the class dunce and told my parents that it was no use to send me to school. After the war, I endeavored to recapture the romance of my childhood days, only to find myself approaching the two-score mark, with a fringe of graying hair, a past resplendent with bizarre episodes, and a future black as a wailing wall in the Holy Land.

In fact, last year I found myself shuffling along day after day in a Seattle breadline and wondering if, after all, the big adventure did not lie under the turbulent waves over which I'd sailed so many years.

However, I found a haven in the reference room of the public library. At first the place was just four walls and a ceiling to protect me from the rains that usually prevail in the Pacific Northwest. But with every passing day the association grew dearer, life took on a purpose, and I looked forward to the hours of study.

I was staying in a shelter for homeless men down on Second Avenue when purpose began to shape my life. There were over a hundred and fifty of us derelicts—eager-faced youngsters, tottering lumberjacks, rheumatic sailormen, and frost-bitten prospectors. Most of them had played a part in building the Pacific Empire, and the same reckless vagabond spirit that had urged these fellows to the Orient, to Alaska, and into the tall timber had also landed them in that municipal flop-house.

Every night at nine o'clock, after the public library closed, I would rush to these quarters with a book and a pad of paper under my arm. This accouterment of erudition earned for me the title of a knowledge tramp, or library bum, and on the strength of these credentials I was able to horn into any bunkhouse arguments in progress.

One night when I came in, Milsudski, a Slav who slept in the deck above me, eyed the textbook under my arm, I thought, somewhat enviously. "You read 'em book?" he asked.

"Sure," I answered, "I read 'em all but the big words."

"I like t' read 'em," he said, "not big book, but fonny paper."

"There's nothing to stop you." I waxed into quite an enthusiastic oration on what a man could do with his spare time. "You're on the bum, walk' the pavement twelve hours a day. If you would use an hour of that time every day for three months, you'd be able to read Moon Mullins and Boob McNutt."

"You t'ink so?" he asked.

"I don't think so. I know so. A guy can do anything with his spare time. Look what Lincoln did!"

"Dat's good car: I ride one time; go like hell!"

"Not a Lincoln car—Abe Lincoln, the President of the United States."

"Roosevelt, him President."

Finally the talk veered back to adult education, and Milsudski pinned me down as to what book he should read in order to get the full import of the comic section. I was quite vague, I admit, but in a generous moment I promised to help Milsudski in his quest for knowledge, and with that promise I inadvertently founded Dumbbell

University, a school that weeks later was to become a joke along the "Skid Road," the waterfront district of Seattle.

The next day I went to the children's department of the Seattle Public Library and asked the lady in charge for some material on a method of teaching a "Bohunk" to read the funny papers. And did she supply me with material! That woman stacked books and magazines in front of me in huge piles. I muddled through this maze of knowledge but for the life of me I couldn't see where any of it would help me in teaching a dense Slav.

I was discouraged and regretted that I had been so enthusiastic about Milsudski's chances of learning to read. Yet, the next day I took him down to a tie pile along the railroad track and produced a paper and pencil. "Now," I said, drawing a large A, "that's A."

"Yes, I know, that's A."

"And this is B," I said, drawing a generous B.

Then I pointed to the A. "What's that?"

"That's B."

"Nobody but a thick Hunky would say that; at least, not after it was pointed out as an A. See, A. Catch 'em A."

"Sure, I catch 'em A."

Day after day the lessons proceeded, with me goading Milsudski during every lesson.

A Swede lumberjack, Ole, who wished to learn to figure lumber, joined the class. He could add a little, subtract a little, but could neither multiply nor divide. Ole would not respond to goading in the manner of Milsudski; instead of digging into his lessons harder than ever, he would sulk a bit and tell me to jump in the lake. However, when I praised the Scandinavian people, asserting that they were the pure Nordic stock that supplied the world with the explorers who discovered America long before Columbus, the lumberjack would swell his chest and strive his utmost to solve the intricacies of the decimal system.

In contrast to this pair of students, the next fellow to enroll, an Irishman, would work well when his efforts were challenged. I found that by being dubious I could spur him on to greater endeavors. He wanted to learn how to do crossword puzzles, and I shook my head. "You'd better give up the idea; a Laplander might learn to do puzzles, but it's all beyond the ken of an Irishman."

"Is that so?" O'Malley retorted. "I'll show ye that an Irishman can learn to do anything an Eskimo can!"

Excepting a sing-song school I saw in Constantinople—where all the students were reciting the Koran aloud—I think that Dumbbell University was the queerest fountain of knowledge the sun ever shone upon. We had no schoolroom, but in fair weather we congregated on a pile of ties in the Northern Pacific Railroad yards. During rainy days we sought shelter in a convenient box car.

Later, along with the three students I had to goad, to praise, and to challenge, were two Filipinos, a man who had put in years in South America, and a Negro who wished to learn some "big dictionary words."

I think the remarkable thing about this class was that each man achieved his goal: Milsudski learned to read the comic section; the Swede learned to scale lumber, after a fashion; O'Malley solved the mysteries of the easier crossword puzzles; the man from South America brushed up on his Spanish; and the Filipinos learned a patter they fondly believed to be English. As for the colored member of the class, yesterday I met Booker T. Jackson on Pike Street, and he hailed me with a wide, white-toothed grin: "Perfesser, let's me an' you git t'gether on a high-brow confab. I'se got t'talk colloqualisms t'mah customers."

It's strange, but only I, the teacher, am left on the breadline. However, the goal that I've set for myself is higher and the road leading to it more rocky than the pathway to the palms of the other students.

Analysis. This memoir of the Great Depression contains evidences of both independent study (C-1) and tutorial teaching (C-2). The first, the effort of Mr. Griffith to use the reference room of the Seattle Public Library as the center of his own self-education, is so briefly mentioned that the program design cannot be analyzed, though he makes it clear at the end of his account that his unstated goal had not been achieved. The six episodes of tutorial teaching are sketched out fairly clearly and suggest—as in the contrasting approaches used with Milsudski, Ole, and O'Malley—how the tutor must adapt his approach to the desires and nature of each student. Milsudski wanted to read the comics, Ole wanted to figure lumber, and O'Malley wanted to do crossword puzzles. Milsudski had to be goaded, Ole's national origin praised, and O'Malley's national origin challenged.

The steps in the progress of the Hobo School are fairly clear. The possibility of the group of related episodes was raised by Milsudski's interest and Griffith's sense of evangelism; the situation was not tested at all; and "in a generous moment" the decision was made to proceed. The specific objective was unique to each student, but the broad goal of learning to read and write was common to all. In all episodes, the elements in the format were probably similar, though each episode had unique features. In Milsudski's case, for example, the *resources* were the paper and pencil, the open-air classroom, and eventually perhaps the library books. The *leader* was Griffith, the *method* was teaching by rote, the *schedule* was a daily session, and the *sequence* was that imposed by the acquisition of literacy. The *social reinforcement* was established by a man-to-man goading; the *individualization* was inherent in the situation; the *relationship* was that of two equals, one of whom was guiding the other; the proposed *criterion of evaluation* was the ability to read the comics; and the *clarity of design* was established by the facts in the situation itself.

This tutorial teaching was fitted into the overall situation imposed by the shelter for homeless men and the lumberyard where the teaching occurred. Each of the men taught was *guided* into the relationship by his own goals and changed his otherwise rather aimless *life-style* to accommodate it. *Finances* were covered by the resources provided by society—library, breadline, shelter, and Griffith's contribution of his time. The *interpretation* required that the activity violate all the folkways of the situation; Dumbbell University became a joke on "Skid Road," and only 6 men out of 150 took part. After the plan had been *put into effect* and run its course for an unstated length of time, Griffith *measured* the capacity of each of his students to perform the task he sought to master and *appraised* the program as being a success. The memoir does not say whether there was any further educational sequence in the lives of either Griffith or his students.

Rural Educational Program

Background. For almost three-quarters of a century, Americans who live in rural areas and small towns have been intimately familiar with what they usually called extension. In its total service, this program has been massive in size and pervasive in spread, reaching virtually all of the nation's 3,000 rural counties; but it is intensely local in both governance and service. As American life has changed, so has extension. Even those who know well the activities of yesteryear may be unfamiliar with what is occurring today. Therefore, at my request, Dr. Terry Gibson has prepared the following account of a modern extension leader and the program he chairs in a Wisconsin county. Dr. Gibson is director of program support of the University of Wisconsin–Extension in Madison.

Extension in Endurance County. Both Wayne R. Griggs and Endurance County, which he serves, are fictional, but they are based on reality. Wayne is a composite of contemporary extension educators, each of whom is highly individualistic but all of whom relate to extension in common ways. The program described resembles the work of an actual county in Wisconsin but some of its attributes and activities have been changed to provide a more rounded view of a countywide extension service.

The Cooperative Extension Service (CES) began over seventy-five years ago in response to a congressionally expressed need to help farmers and farm families make better use of the knowledge gained from research on agricultural and homemaking practices. Extension is jointly funded by the local county government, the state government through the land-grant university, and the federal government through the United States Department of Agriculture. The program is operated as a true partnership with control and responsibility at each level of government but with the focus of attention being the local community.

Endurance County had a population of 115,400 in 1990, about equally divided between rural and urban people. Extension's priorities are established in consultation with a communitywide advisory committee and with the Extension Education Committee, a subcommittee of the elected county board of supervisors. The operational budget of the county office is provided by the county, and the personnel costs come from county, state, and federal funds. The functions carried out by the staff and volunteers in Endurance County are similar to those conducted by extension offices in other counties and other states. The participants are both rural and urban, but this case study focuses on educational programs for rural residents, especially those engaged in agriculture.

Wayne Griggs and his colleagues spend most of their time on locally designed and delivered educational programs for various family members; such programs are the hallmark of extension. The local extension educators also work closely with campus-based faculty members to design and conduct educational programs based on current research. Endurance County is in a major milk-producing region, and Wayne is in frequent contact with extension specialists in the Dairy Science Department at the University of Wisconsin–Madison. Together they design educational programs that will meet local needs, adapting general content to meet specific and individualized concerns; in some cases, campus-based faculty members travel to Endurance County to make special presentations.

While lifelong learning did not fully emerge as a concept in the field of adult education until the 1960s, it has been the practice in extension from its very beginning. The central focus of the educational program is on the total family, and the CES has meaning for people of all ages. It is a part of life for many children as they grow in consciousness; they see their mothers and fathers, their aunts and uncles and grandparents, their older siblings and cousins, and their parents' friends taking part in a clearly identified stream of educational activities.

But the members of a family are not merely the recipients of service; they also help plan it. This point may be illustrated by mentioning the participation of the members of one dairy farm family during two recent years. The father served as a member of the education committee of the regional cooperative and with extension's assistance helped plan an educational program on the international marketing of dairy products. The mother and teenage son served together on a 4-H study group called Youth Futures that planned a series of educational programs for urban and rural youth in Endurance County. The grandfather was a founder of an association concerned with community problem solving related to land use, urban sprawl, and its impact on agricultural property taxes. The high school–aged sister served as a representative on a team to design an educational program on nutrition and health cosponsored by the University of Wisconsin–Extension and the local medical clinic.

Wayne Griggs currently serves as chair of the Endurance County Extension Office. He was born in 1950 in Lyon County, Kansas, where his father was an agricultural agent. (Multigenerational families are not uncommon in extension work.) He graduated from Kansas State University with a B.S. in animal science. He then completed an M.S. in extension education with a minor in dairy science from the University of Wisconsin. He and his wife, Lisa, have two children. They were in another Wisconsin county extension office for almost ten years before Wayne accepted a position in Endurance County.

His colleagues there work in the areas of family living, 4-H youth, and community development. The newly arrived family-living educator uses her expertise in consumer affairs to recruit and train volunteers who provide counseling on family financial planning. She also recently held a series of workshops called "Raising Responsible Teens" for parents in the community. The longtime youth development educator works with the adult leaders of many active 4-H clubs in the county that serve children and adolescents interested in agriculture, natural resources, biotechnology, and community development. He also helps supervise the county fair. The community development educator works with county and town government officials and local citizen groups on community issues such as land-use planning, waste management, and community revitalization.

Wayne and his colleagues play diversified roles. They are educators, counselors, advisers, evaluators, researchers, and representatives of not only the local office but also the state university and the national government. Most have master's degrees in fields related to their areas of expertise. In recent years, the interdisciplinary nature of many problems has required a good deal of teamwork both within their own group and with other community resources. Wayne and others in extension provide leadership for educational programs on many topics such as managing growth, creating positive environments for youth and families, and maintaining quality water for drinking and recreational purposes. They try to help solve community problems and, in doing so, to build the capacity of individuals and the community to solve future problems.

The number of staff members in county offices varies widely. In some sparsely populated sections of the United States, one educator may serve several counties. Large metropolitan counties, like Milwaukee County, may have over a hundred staff members, including those who conduct special activities. For example, the Expanded Food and Nutrition Education Program has nutritional aides who visit low-income families every few weeks to discuss food buying and preparation, nutrition, and ways to cut costs.

In recent years, travel by the staff has become less frequent because extension is able to use technology to bridge the distance between university-based resources and community needs. Outside the Extension Office is a satellite dish twelve feet in diameter that receives video programming available from the University of Wisconsin and forty-nine other institutions that are a part of A*DEC, A Distance Education Consortium of land-grant universities. The office also receives programs via compressed video and audioteleconferencing. Publications are printed on demand from a CD-ROM or downloaded from computer data bases located throughout the world. Electronic mail has largely replaced surface mail as the preferred way to communicate with colleagues and with many of the clientele served by the Extension Office. Many of the top dairy producers have computers, and they frequently send E-mail messages from their farms to Wayne at the County Extension Office, to the campus-based faculty specialists, or to authorities in another state. However, the more traditional methods of weekly newspaper columns, monthly newsletter, call-in radio and television programs, and the plain old telephone are still important vehicles for supporting extension's educational activities.

Wayne and his colleagues are action oriented and find it difficult to take time to do a good job of documentation and reporting. As best they can, however, they keep records on their programs and report their results to their stakeholders at the county, state, and federal level. The program is primarily supported by tax dollars; the elected officials and the general public need to feel that they are getting a good return on their investment. Being "politically savvy" is part of the job, and the extension staff members know they must be accountable for program impacts. It is no longer enough to have satisfied clientele speak on extension's behalf at the monthly meeting of the subcommittee of the county board of supervisors. Elected officials and other stakeholders want to know the inputs and the outputs of the educational program. Did the dairy program increase the profitability of dairy farms in the county? Did the land-use planning committee develop a plan acceptable to the community? What was unique about extension's program, and how did it differ from those of other organizations serving the county?

The grand sweep of extension's success during the years of its existence must be seen in terms of the changing social scene in which it has operated. In 1910, at the time when the early beginnings of extension were being shaped, the great majority (55 percent) of the American people lived in rural areas. All too often, those who farmed the land were ill educated, superstition ridden, and full of contempt for "book learning." They feared that any change in their practices might cost them their livelihood, and many of them felt that the preservation of their way of work had strong moral overtones. According to extension lore, an agent sent into a community by "the government" might well find himself being escorted to the county line by a posse of hostile farmers. Today scientific agriculture has triumphed, as has the use of knowledge in dealing with the problems of personal, family, group, and community life. This change has been brought about by the operation of many forces and the work of many institutions, but few would doubt that extension has played an important part in this vital transformation of American life. Its history should give hope to those who confront the massive problems of today.

Analysis. As its name implies, the Cooperative Extension Service is an example of a C-10 situation in which three centers of power (the United States Department of Agriculture, the land-grant university, and the county government) have designed an institution that enhances their combined program of service. In its programming, the CES often works within this same situation; many collaborative programs are mentioned in the case study.

Wayne and his colleagues also work in all of the other ten situations. Staff members are both subject-matter specialists and adult educators, and must constantly update and advance their knowledge by independent study (C-1) and group learning (C-3). They have many tutorial contacts with clients (C-2) in their offices and elsewhere and design many activities in this situation, such as the training of counselors for family financial planning. The staff also makes many presentations and schedules other people who do so

(C-4). In the course of a year, many committees plan activities for larger audiences (C-5), and others create programs in the C-7, C-8, and C-9 situations. Mass media (C-11) are constantly in use.

While there is no indication that a single programming model is used in Endurance County, much thought is clearly given to the design of educational activities. For example, five members of one family were contributing to design decisions: the mother and son who helped plan the Youth Futures program (C-3 or C-5), the father who served on the education committee of the cooperative (C-5), the sister who helped plan the nutrition education program cosponsored by the local clinic (C-6), and the grandfather who helped found an association for community problem solving (C-7). The extension staff has long-established patterns for its work, but much thought has been given to the use of new learning materials and methods.

Prevocational Academic Instruction in the Army

Background. This case was written by R. H. Heylin in April 1964 and with his permission was published in an abbreviated form in the first edition of this book. I intended to replace it here with a more modern case, but diligent search failed to turn up another account that, with equal economy and charm, described fully one of the most frequently found situations in adult education. It occurs when an activity such as a course, workshop, or conference is repeated periodically with such modifications as seem wise or necessary. In military, industrial, or professional education, these repetitions are sometimes called "iterations."

High School–Level Education for Servicemen. In early June, 1956, I was reassigned duty with the US Army Support Detachment, Chicago, as an Education Advisor (Administrative). The reason for this reassignment was to organize an educational development program for Army Antiaircraft Artillery units in the Chicago-Gary Complex. I was to be the first Education Advisor to be assigned full-time duty with non-Post Units in the history of the Army's General Educational Development Program for Military Personnel. Up to that time Education Advisors were rather stationary at a military post. Units not physically located at that Post received educational development services only by personally visiting the Army Educational Center proper. In short, this opportunity (?) promised to be a real challenge and I wasn't convinced in my own thinking that the concept was practical. I was only too willing to give my all, sensing the possibility of rapid promotion for myself and the opportunity to lend more than lip service educational development services to deserving Army personnel who through no choice of their own happened to be assigned to Units from five to fifty miles away from our Education Center. To further complicate the implementation of any program, these AAA Units were all in the process of converting from the World War II antiaircraft guns to the new NIKE Surface-to-Air missile. I was to work with three Battalions of these people, totaling approximately 3,000 officers and men located at fifteen separate sites and scattered over the West, Southwest, and South Suburban areas of Greater Chicago plus Northwest Indiana. I had the full-time use of one enlisted man from the Education Center who would accompany me daily to one of these fifteen installations on a prepublished schedule. All funds for the conduct of educational development services within these three Battalions were to come from the operating budget of the Army Education Center. There was adequate financial support available to cope with any success I might enjoy.

My two-and-one-half years' prior experience in the Army's GED Program—part as an Enlisted Man on Okinawa and part as an Education Advisor in Korea—prompted me to take careful stock of the situation before attempting to promote any program(s). I spent the first full month in just (a) evaluating education level surveys from March, 1956, (b) obtaining such information as was available from my immediate superior, the Post Education Officer, and (c) introducing myself to AAA Unit Commanders, Personnel Officers, and Training Officers, and discussing general Department of the Army educational goals with them.

By mid-July, 1956, it appeared to my thinking that priority consideration should be given to promoting formal classroom instruction for a great number of Enlisted Men who possessed less than high school completion or its equivalency. These men were not of the illiterate category, just below the academic level generally considered necessary to absorb Army technical training and/or meet civilian institutions' admission requirements for further academic study. I felt that classroom instruction should encompass English, arithmetic, geography, history, and basic physical science. The previously mentioned educational level survey of March, 1956, disclosed that approximately 50 per cent of all Enlisted Men had achieved less than high school completion. While this rate was considerably above the United States' average for adults, it was unsatisfactory for potential career soldiers who were soon to face training for handling highly technical equipment as a team. I just couldn't see how this group could possibly absorb any technical training without first acquiring a proper academic base! To further document my position before approaching each of the three Battalion Commanders on the problem, I directed a letter of inquiry to the Antiaircraft and Guided Missile School at Ft. Bliss, Texas, to establish minimum academic requirements for the Electronics Sub-Course which preceded each of their missile service school courses. Reply was received before the end of July, 1956, affirming my hypothesis that a minimum of current 8th grade capability in arithmetic and English were necessary to handle the Electronics Sub-Course. The Electronics Sub-Course presented algebra and those areas of high school physics, for example, heat, electricity, levers, light, which were considered basic to the study of radar operations, missile launchers, and missiles themselves. I reiterate at this juncture that we were concerned not with a once-recorded academic level, rather a current proficiency therein. I must also include the item that the officers and senior Non-Commissioned Officers in the three Battalions appeared to be well-qualified for any retraining required in this missile conversion operation ahead.

Armed with the data on the number of Enlisted Men below apparent training potential and with the correspondence from the AA and GMS, I approached each Battalion Commander individually before the end of July, 1956, with a request for a discussion of the possibility of conducting formal classroom instruction at each Battalion Headquarters as a means of reducing the number of untrainable Enlisted Men in their respective battalions. Each Battalion Commander agreed to the proposal. It was agreed that I would serve as moderator. At each Battalion discussion, the following key individuals would participate: Battalion Commander, Battalion Training and Operations Officer, Battalion Personnel Officer, and the five Battery Commanders. Discussions were scheduled for mid-August, 1956.

Although I had enjoyed some nominal success in Korea with advanced elementary/junior high school level pretechnical instruction, I had felt that the predominant Army-wide concept of half-day instruction for two or three days each week left much to be desired. Consequently, at each of these three Battalion discussions on the subject, I pushed for a schedule of half-day instruction each afternoon, Monday thru Friday, once we could administer appropriate diagnostic testing and individually counsel each untrainable Enlisted Man. I also decided to push for formal instruction for only voluntary students, based on undesirable consequences from earlier experience. In summary the following ramifications were agreed upon by majority opinion during each Battalion discussion:

(1) It would be my responsibility to administer the California Achievement Test (Advanced Elementary Form) to all Enlisted Men below high school completion or equivalency prior to October, 1956, but only after preliminary group counseling.

(2) I or I and another Education Advisor as supplied by my Supervisor at the Education Center would individually counsel only Regular Army examinees between October 1 and December 1, ascertaining in writing as to whether or not such instruction before AA and GMS training or High School Equivalency Testing should be considered. I regretted each Committee's decision not to give Drafted Enlisted Men the same opportunity, but felt this group could be reached later on if the program were to be successful.

(3) Between December 1 and January 1, 1957, each of the five Battery Commanders would nominate five students from his Battery for the initial class to start at the Battalion Headquarters the first week of February, 1957. These nominations would come from the list of those who indicated a voluntary interest after counseling. The Battalion Headquarters were situated at Orland Park, Illinois, Skokie, Illinois, and Gary, Indiana.

(4) The curriculum would consist solely of English and arithmetic. This majority decision also disappointed me but I felt I could possibly mediate this prevalent attitude in subsequent classes after the first one.

(5) Class would meet each Monday, Wednesday, and Friday (Federal holidays excluded) for four hours per day in the afternoon. Those students requiring less instruction would be permitted to terminate instruction sooner than those requiring more instruction. A range of eight to fourteen weeks of classroom activity would be anticipated. This decision also disappointed me but once again I felt I could temper this attitude in the subsequent classes.

(6) Students would be exempt from military duties during the scheduled hours of instruction and each Battery Commander would be responsible for providing transportation to and from each session.

(7) Standardized elementary final examinations would be administered by the instructors upon the completion of each student's time with the group. In addition, the Battalion Personnel Officer would readminister the GT (General Technical) Aptitude Area tests

(average of reading and arithmetic) and I or my accompanying Enlisted Education Specialist would administer the High School Equivalency Test upon the completion of each student's time in class.

(8) I would interview, select, and contract part-time teachers from the nearby community(ies). This appeared to present no obstacle since a number of fully qualified mature ladies were registered with local elementary schools for substitute teaching at this level.

As indicated already, several facets of the initial class organization were less than satisfactory to my thinking. I had confronted this difference in opinion in Korea and so I wasn't exactly unprepared for this turn of events. I felt that a half loaf was better than no loaf at all! Certainly, I thought, I could present a better and more convincing position if the initial class in each Battalion proved successful. In short, I felt all future possibility of curriculum expansion, all possibility of consolidating the class hours, and the inclusion of drafted EM into the program rested squarely on the results of our maiden attempt in each Battalion.

During September, 1956, while I was heavily involved with both administering the CAT diagnostic instrument, and group counseling expectant examinees, one of the three Battalions received Reassignment Orders from the Department of the Army. Obviously this sudden announcement forced cancellation of preliminary arrangements for classroom instruction in the Battalion concerned. I have often wondered since what prevocational instruction was afforded the needy EM at their new designation(s). All that I could do was to insure that a resume of testing and counseling activity—on individuals already tested and counseled—was made a portion of their Personnel Records for release to an Education Advisor at the next Duty Station.

Also during September, 1956, I established contact with—and interviewed—a number of prospective part-time lady instructors residing in communities near the remaining two Battalion Headquarters. Local school principals and superintendents were very cooperative in this respect. I was seeking particularly married ladies

within each Battalion! Commanders and first Sergeants found the every-other-day schedule quite perplexing to any training schedule and duty roster. Students were confusing "class afternoons" with "nonclass afternoons." Teachers tactfully mentioned to me that excessive class time was required at the start of each presentation in recapping the previous session's accomplishments. In mid-March, 1957, I requested each Battalion Commander to call an urgent meeting of the planning officers. Each Battalion Conference was held prior to April 1! By unanimous agreement, the conferees decided that Class 2 would meet every afternoon (holidays excluded), Monday thru Friday. Also, since the first class would probably be concluded by May 1, Battery Commanders were requested to forward nominations for Class 2 by April 15. I needed adequate time to continue my project of furnishing each instructor with a class roster and biographical sketch of each new student. Also, time must be allowed for negotiating new teacher contracts and procuring additional text materials.

Class 1 concluded the last week of April, 1957, after twelve weeks. Some students had completed in but seven weeks. The eighth grade standardized tests in English and arithmetic had been successfully administered to all 25 graduates. The Battalion Personnel Officer readministered the General Technical Aptitude Test and my Enlisted Education Specialist administered the High School Equivalency Test. Department of the Army Certificates of Training were provided each student and placed in each student's Military Personnel Folder. In brief, no student required more than 144 hours of combined instruction and terminal testing, though some had started at as low as the fifth grade level!

Class 2 started the second week of May, 1957, within each Battalion. The teachers and I projected an eight week term as adequate for the extreme student. Classes were now meeting every weekday afternoon for four hours each day. Students were scheduled for Battery Duty only in the mornings and initially everyone seemed pleased. During the 4th week of Class 2, one of the two arithmetic teachers suggested that she could eliminate the "grade" concept of placement with slight modification of the material, thus permitting all students to start arithmetic together and to finish together. Consultation by me with the other arithmetic teacher revealed that she, too, thought this innovation workable. Thinking perhaps that the English teachers might be "open" to some suggestion for improvement, I posed the problem of eliminating "grade level" distinction for English. After several days' deliberation, each English teacher expressed a desire to experiment and promised to jointly prepare a modified English curriculum for Class 3 to come. The noble experiment, if successful, could open the door to several very beneficial changes. The more needy students could conceivably enter more freely into classroom recitation and discussion, additional subjects might be introduced into the program with no appreciable—if any—lengthening of the term, and, last but not least, the teachers would have incentive to further upgrade the quality of the instruction by continued curriculum improvement. I was convinced by now that I was blessed with four fine teachers who were going to keep me on the go to keep up with them!

No student in Class 2 required more than seven sustained weeks of instruction and terminal testing to satisfy requirements. Three students completed after four weeks. All in all, it seemed as though the more compact schedule was as beneficial as the planning officers, teachers, and I had hoped it might be. Everyone was swelling with success; I felt it was just a matter of time now until I could "sell" the planning officers on full-day instruction with a curriculum of five subjects. One little misfortune occurred during Class 2 per the Courts Martial Procedure, causing us to have not twenty-five graduates, but only twenty-four!

Class 3 started during the 1st week of August, 1957. During the four-week interval between Classes 2 and 3, I thought it advisable to individually follow-up on a minimum of 50 per cent of the graduates of Classes 1 and 2. My primary purpose was to attempt to establish some further area(s) for suggested improvement in classes beyond upcoming Class 3. Student opinion of the teachers was extremely high (I passed this on to the teachers!) but this was normal for this type of activity. Many students were awaiting action on applications for an AA and GMS course. One suggestion that arose from these graduates—but was expressed in varying degrees of forcefulness—was that a student in this type of class was the target of unkind slurs from other soldiers of his Battery during the time he was in the Battery. Study facilities within an individual Battery were limited and interviewed graduates thought this could be improved somehow. A minority of graduates reported that they seemed to catch more than their fair share of routine housekeeping jobs during the mornings when attending school. I decided to cross-reference these comments during the conduct of Class 3 with the ten Battery 1st Sergeants. Possibly this course of action would be my big opening for full-day resident instruction.

Class 3 was concluded in mid-September in but six weeks' time! This signified a reduction of twenty full class hours of instruction and terminal teaching over Class 2's 140 hours, that is, a 14 per cent time savings. Complete course outlines were introduced by both English and arithmetic teachers and distributed to each student prior to "start of business" on the opening day. I secured a copy of each outline for each planning officer in the two Battalions. Teachers reported appreciable increase of participation by the more needy students throughout the initial days of the course. By sheer coincidence during the conduct of Class 3, a Department of the Army directive placed greater emphasis on broadening this "preparatory" instruction to include study in the social sciences. This provided all the ammunition I felt necessary to press for expansion of the curriculum to include world geography, world history, and basic physical science. Due to the fast-approaching close of Class 3, I decided to broach the matter with the Battalion Commanders *only* after the added benefit of interviewing graduates of Class 3 and upcoming Class 4. I laid plans to interview 50 per cent of the graduates of Classes 3 and 4, after completion of Class 4 in late November, 1957.

Class 4 was very successfully conducted during the six week period of early October to mid-November, 1957. No change in curriculum or materials was introduced during this Class. Had not the misfortune of that Court Martial in Class 2 occurred, this Class 4 would have signified the graduation of exactly 100 students in each Battalion in only slightly over nine months of part-time activity. Ninety-four of the 100 graduates in one Battalion, and ninety-two of the ninety-nine graduates in the other Battalion, produced not only successful High School Equivalency Test results but also considerably above average results on the English and arithmetic portions thereof. All 199 students improved their GT Aptitude Area Score appreciably.

In view of the approaching Christmas-New Year Holiday, both Battalion planning committees decided against offering Class 5 until after the holiday period. This met with my personal approval since I did not particularly relish the prospect of interrupting a class of this nature for a full two-week period. During the last week of November and first week of December, 1957, I interviewed 50 per cent of the graduates of Classes 3 and 4, per my previously discussed plan. I limited my interview with each graduate to two questions, namely (a) his opinion on the relative merits of half-day, nonresident instruction or full-day resident instruction, and (b) his sentiments on adding geography, history, and physical science to the curriculum. I must admit I was pleasantly flattered by the results of the interviews, since twenty of the twenty-five strongly favored adding the three subjects, and seventeen of the twenty-five favored full-day resident instruction. One graduate was noncommittal on the matter of curriculum expansion, and three were noncommittal on the matter of full-day residential instruction.

Encouraged by this favorable response of my interviews, I once again requested each Battalion Commander to convene his Planning Committee. (Note: Some replacements in each Committee had occurred due to Transfers.) I requested this conference in each Battalion be held not later than mid-December to permit any approved changes to be reflected in Class 5. I forthwith proposed that Class #5 be a full-day, resident program and expanded to include world geography, world history, and basic physical science. I supported this dual proposal with interview summaries from graduates of Classes 1 thru 4, comparative statistical summaries of the results achieved by graduates on the English and arithmetic parts of the High School Equivalency Test as contrasted to results attained on the social studies, natural science, and literature parts, and naturally the early September, 1957, change in concept at DA level on the extent of curriculum. I stated that additional teachers, if necessary, could be procured. I also offered to have the 5th Army Printing Plant reproduce the expanded curriculum in booklet form. Visual aids, I explained, were available through local business firms to enhance the presentation of geography, history, and physical science. I assured the Planning Committees that not more than nine weeks would be necessary. I mentioned that each Battalion Headquarters' Battery Commander had stated that living facilities were available at each Battalion Headquarters' site to accommodate the switch from nonresident to resident instruction. The meeting in one Battalion consumed five hours, the same meeting in the other Battalion consumed six hours, on different days in mid-December, 1957. In each meeting, there was much variation in opinion represented. (Note: I had hoped that the bringing up of a wide range of issues would force each Battalion Commander to make the decisions because there was enough in the package to partially please all members of the Planning Committee and make them willing to accept the total platform because of personal interest in a segment of the platform.) Each Battalion Commander decided about the matters at hand. I'm certain, to this very day, that the good Lord and not my approach, turned each Battalion Commander in favor of accepting the program expansion and concept of resident instruction. The first week of February, 1958, was set as the starting date of Class 5.

A personal conversation with each of the tried and true four teachers disclosed that in each Battalion there was sufficient professional training and experience for the present teachers to split the now five subjects among them. By the first week in January,

1958, each teacher was provided materials to handle the expanded curriculum. Each morning and each afternoon was so organized as to provide a suitable blend (we hoped!) of subject matter presentation, study, individual attention, variety of instructional media, and breaktime. The credit for development of the new curriculum was entirely attributable to the joint planning of the four teachers. I merely served to have the end product neatly printed and bound by the 5th Army Headquarters' Printing Plant, and to secure copyright releases from publishers and photographers for certain extracted items. While the majority of course materials were still USAFI stock, approximately 75 per cent of Class 5's materials were USAFI as compared to 100 per cent in the previous four classes. I should note that all teachers were now being compensated at the hourly rate of $7.50 per early agreement.

The first class under the new approach was conducted as scheduled, February to April, 1958. The fondest expectations of myself and the four teachers were realized in this undertaking. The most significant improvement noted was in respect to the significantly positive deviation in the social studies, natural science, and literature parts of the High School Equivalency Test results. As pertains to the personal satisfaction of the students, their egos did not suffer in the resident setting as had happened in the nonresident setting of the ten Batteries. The classroom used during the day was available each evening, Sunday through Thursday, for study purposes. The teachers noticed a greater degree of mutual problem-solving and a closer group relationship. I was so thankful that our projections went as planned that I was breathing a series of sighs of relief! The teachers, the two Battalion Commanders, and I had gambled heavily on a combination of unproven variables. I believe to this very day that it just was Providence that made things happen in our favor.

This same curriculum and full-day resident concept was continued with equal success through Classes 6 and 7, both concluded by mid-November, 1958. It is significant to note that Class 7 in each Battalion was comprised of individuals assigned to the Battalion since February, 1957. All in all, a total of 329 students were graduated by this program within the two Battalions in twenty months' time. The Classes 6 and 7 did not accommodate the capacity of twenty-five students each. The need for sustained, or even additional classes, had been met at a local level.

What happened to the curriculum? I turned this prized product over to the Education Director, Ft. Sheridan, Illinois, for implementation in both On-Post and Off-Post military organizations to which he furnished educational development services. Since early 1959, he has conducted resident instruction at Ft. Sheridan, Illinois, for Enlisted Men from Chicago, Gary, Minneapolis, and Milwaukee on a consolidated basis since there have not existed—nor do exist today—a sufficient number of Army personnel at any one of these metropolitan centers to warrant separate classes nor to attract and hold qualified instructors. One such class is conducted quarterly at Ft. Sheridan but diagnostic testing, individual counseling and advisement to Unit Commanders is still furnished at the local situation. Draftee Enlisted Men are now accepted and Commanders have been quite cooperative in this regard.

As it turned out, this full-day resident preparatory instruction program was the first such attempt recorded to date in the Army's General Educational Development Program for Military Personnel. The proof of the pudding, so to speak, was the individual and collective success of its graduates in AA and GMS courses (now renamed the US Army Air Defense School), the planting of the seed for further academic and technical self-development, and the broadened perspective gained by the Commanding Officers involved as to the role of continuing education in the modern Army. This undertaking remains yet in my memory as the outstanding example—of which I have direct or relayed knowledge—of how patience, cooperation, and pooling of ideas can ultimately develop a new program of adult education.

Analysis. This case might be analyzed from several points of view: that of the academic instruction program as a whole (C-8), that of each teacher in it (a series of C-4 episodes), that of a particular group taught by a teacher (a single C-4 episode), or even that of a hypothetical student (a single C-4 episode). The first of these alternatives is chosen here since the central point of view of the paper is Mr. Heylin's and since it offers the richest interpretation. It might be argued that the program should be ascribed to C-7 because in a sense Mr. Heylin created a new institution, but his need to fit everything carefully into the dictates of Army procedures and command structures suggests that C-8 is the more relevant ascription.

This account describes a series of seven episodes. In the first, the program design was clearly established, and in each of the following four it was rethought and significantly altered. In the final two episodes, the design had become so well established that it was merely repeated, and the novelty of the approach was no longer present. At the conclusion of the series, the failure to recruit the desired number of students needed for another episode led to the appraisal that "the need for sustained, or even additional classes, had been met at a local level."

The program was initiated with Mr. Heylin's appointment, which was presumably brought about because someone in the army hierarchy thought that more education was required at the anti-aircraft artillery units. Mr. Heylin presumably identified a number of possible educational activities and finally made a decision based on available facts and his own judgment to proceed with an eighth-grade school completion program to prepare students for further vocational instruction. This broad objective was thought by Mr. Heylin to require instruction in English, arithmetic, geography, history, and basic physical science, but the army officers who controlled the program allowed only the first two subjects to be taught, thereby limiting specific objectives while retaining the broad one.

The format was designed by Mr. Heylin in collaboration with the officers, and in several cases he was required to accept decisions he regarded as undesirable. The resources were provided by several army units; for example, the classroom furniture came from battalion headquarters and the textbooks and other materials from the

United States Armed Forces Institute. The leaders were carefully recruited, as demonstrated by their retention in the later episodes of the series. Methods were those customarily used in courses of this sort, and the teachers were not only provided with preservice training materials but also supervised by Mr. Heylin. The schedule, worked out to fit army customs, was less than satisfactory to Mr. Heylin. The sequence of presentation of learning units was probably dictated largely by the arrangement of the content of the materials available. The provision of social reinforcement, essentially the responsibility of each teacher, was aided by support secured from military authorities and by initial counseling. To some extent, students were permitted to move at their own rates; some finished the program much earlier than did others. The roles and relationships among the students, their teachers, and their army supervisors were worked out as carefully as possible. Success in the program was to be measured by standardized achievement tests. The program design was explained by an opening session addressed by the battalion commander, Mr. Heylin, and the teachers.

A great deal of attention was devoted to fitting the program into the established and all-embracing life-style of the army. Mr. Heylin is explicit at many points about his efforts to involve the collaboration of the various officers whose support was essential to the success of his endeavors. In this process, he did much shared decision making and interpretation. He describes in detail the testing and guidance procedures he used in selecting the students and his efforts to fit instructional time into the army's on-duty schedule. In this last respect, he was not wholly successful at first since the commanders and first sergeants found the every-other-day scheduling confusing. The direct and indirect costs of the program were borne by the army.

When the plan was put into effect, various alterations of procedure were required. Presumably some of them were made at once, but others were noted as desirable changes to be incorporated in later episodes. At the end of instruction, which required individuals from seven to twelve weeks to complete, all students had achieved the desired eighth-grade standard, though some had started as low as the fifth-grade level. The program was judged a success.

The subsequent episodes incorporated many changes in format, both at the start and as instruction proceeded. The program was generally tightened up with the result that completion of required standards consumed less time than before. A follow-up sampling of the graduates of classes 1 and 2 indicated that the interpretation of the program to fellow soldiers and to first sergeants still left something to be desired. Mr. Heylin noted this need and tried to do something about it during the third episode. Other changes of format were made both in it and in the fourth episode.

It was not until the fifth episode, however, that Mr. Heylin was able to broaden the objectives to include the content areas he had always hoped would be in the program. He describes graphically how the change was brought about by a general army directive, the wishes of graduates whose opinions he sought, the discussion of planning committees, the decision of battalion commanders, his own persuasion, and the intervention of "the good Lord." This change in objective made it necessary to revise several elements of the format, most significantly the instructional resources, the schedule, the methods, the sequence, and the criteria of evaluation. The perennial problem of program interpretation was also removed because the program became full time and residential, so that the students no longer had to confront nonstudent fellow soldiers and duty-time first sergeants. The social reinforcement within the group was also significantly improved by various other elements in the format.

As Mr. Heylin took leave of his program, he had many evidences of its success. The reader may well share with him some of the enthusiasm expressed in his final sentence.

Community Improvement Programs

Background. Some cities have associations of outstanding local leaders apparently created for convivial or fraternal reasons but also exercising a powerful influence over the life of the community. As a student of governing boards, I have long been interested in the nature and activities of such associations and, despite their passion for privacy, have been able to learn something about them, all of it with promises of confidentiality. Fortunate acquaintanceship has enabled me to participate as a guest in two such clubs, half a continent away from one another but astonishingly similar in structure and methods of operation. To serve the present purpose of providing a case study—and to keep my promises—I have merged these two into an imaginary 528 Club and assigned to it actions similar to those carried out by both of its prototypes as well as by other elitist associations elsewhere. The following account is therefore wholly fictitious, but I hope it provides a valid picture of how adult education works in a kind of setting not often described, one at the opposite end of the social scale from the hobo school.

The 528 Club. At the close of World War II, the 528 Club was the most elite group of men in a city of about 500,000 people. The membership was highly selective and included the chief wielders of the city's financial, industrial and commercial power, a few patricians, and two or three men whose charisma did much to establish the jovial good fellowship characteristic of the group. It was a luncheon club whose members attended every working day if they could. It met in a private suite of rooms on a secluded floor of what the general public believed to be the best club in town. The group was in fact a club within a club and was known solely by the number on the door of its suite. It sought no publicity, and its name was almost never mentioned by the mass media, whose owners were members.

Amid the badinage of the lunch table and during the poker and bridge games that sometimes followed it, many purposes were accomplished, most of them private but some of them aimed at the improvement of the community. For example, a few of the men were on the board of the city's largest private hospital. When it needed a new wing, they asked for the financial backing of other members. Or if in the general conversation it became evident that several men thought the quality of a public service—health, welfare, education, transit, or any other—was falling seriously below acceptable standards, the word went out through the channels of power that the controlling board and its staff had better strengthen the system or face serious consequences.

One day in the early 1950s, the conversation took an unusually serious turn. Several community problems were discussed in turn by individuals particularly concerned with them, and the conviction gradually grew in the group that the people of the city should stop their piecemeal approach to community improvement and consider what a unified city plan might be like. Some members argued that any total plan would stifle the individual initiative of various campaigns for civic betterment, but gradually these opposing voices were either won over or fell silent. No decision was reached, but the members thought about the matter and perhaps talked it over with some of their associates. The next day the discussion was resumed almost as soon as lunch began. Before long, the members present seemed to have reached a consensus that the club itself should undertake to guide and direct the growth of a master plan, though some men still argued that the club's purpose should continue to be good fellowship or that if a total city plan was contemplated, it should be undertaken from the start not by the club itself but with much wider community involvement.

Perhaps it was this sense of a continuing division within the group that led one of its wiser members to suggest that the club itself had better know more than he thought it did about the subject of municipal planning. Taking up this idea, the group undertook several informal sessions, at each of which a local or imported expert on urbanism talked and answered questions about the essentials of a city plan, its possible value in the current situation, and the processes by which one should be evolved. Some sharp questions at every session indicated that some of the members still had grave doubts about the feasibility of comprehensive planning. But after the series had run its course, the group reaffirmed its prevailing belief that the city did need some kind of overall blueprint. The president of a large corporation said that his company foundation would make a grant to the local university to guide the development of such a plan; and the chairman of the board of that university, after making the proper telephone inquiries, promptly accepted the grant.

During the next year, the club retained a proprietary interest in the development of the plan. The university staff members involved needed some help and advice from specialists employed by the banks and by industry, and it was quickly provided. A few centers of resistance to the whole idea were encountered in various units of the local government, and members of the club undertook to "reach" the opponents with generally satisfactory results. Various tentative formulations and ideas were brought before the club and discussed and criticized by its members. Finally the task was completed, and a model was developed of the ideal city as it might appear after fifty years' evolution.

Long before this model was prepared, the members of the club realized that a task of public enlightenment lay before it if it hoped to win acceptance of the plan. Therefore, under the leadership of a member who was head of an advertising firm, a public group representing many segments of the community was formed. Most of its members had no idea that they had been handpicked by the club; many of them in fact did not even know of its existence. For its part, this City Planning Association (CPA) sought publicity. A fanfare greeted its formation, and its meetings were covered by the mass media. In a series of well-timed releases, the association told the citizens about the various stages of the model as it progressed.

When the final design was prepared, the CPA launched a careful campaign of widespread study and discussion among other voluntary associations and neighborhood groups. In this process, it became apparent that some of the aspects of the plan had to be revised, some compromises had to be worked out, and some interest groups and individuals had been permanently alienated. Despite the sharp objections and the necessary modifications, the basic integrity of the overall plan was maintained. When it was finally presented to the city council for adoption, all but two members voted in favor of it. The CPA went out of existence with as great a burst of publicity as that which had heralded its inauguration.

There then ensued a series of special discussions. By direction of the mayor and the council, the health, educational, welfare, transit, police, and other public agencies of the city undertook their own approaches, each built around its distinctive requirements. The private institutions in the same fields responded by reexamining their own projections for the future. As this phase evolved, the planners were realistic. While they knew that the overall plan had won city-wide acceptance and had the support of the central local power bloc, they also knew that the design would never be fully achieved in its totality, since changes would be required by unforeseen happenings, new conceptions, social pressures and resistances, changing political alliances, and other events. But what should be done during the year following the adoption of the plan to make it appear that at least one-fiftieth of the way toward the ultimate ideal had been reached while still holding fast to institutional values? The staff and citizen board of each substantive agency studied this question so that it could formulate the results in its program and budget. Since the 528 Club felt a proprietary interest in the plan, various members made sure that it was kept alive by their active participation on the boards to which they belonged and by their influence on other community agencies.

A quarter-century after the adoption of the formal plan, anybody who compares its provisions and the ensuing accomplishments would discover that some proposals have been carried out, some forgotten, some discarded as a result of unexpected difficulties or opportunities, and some adopted for a time but later outgrown. Perhaps the major change in the city, resulting in part from the plan itself and the discussions preceding it, has been the unforeseen

growth in both government and private life of monitoring regulations and organizations: planning boards, zoning ordinances, his-
toric preservation trusts, tenants associations, block groups, the
requirement of open hearings and meetings by public boards, and
many other ways of assuring that overall balance is maintained
among the ventures and missions designed to meet the city's special
needs. The uncoordinated growth first deplored in the 1950s is now
being resisted by checks built into the social systems of the city.

The 528 Club has also changed but not in profound ways. For
example, its parent club began to accept women and—a bit later
and with many expressions of dire foreboding—so did the 528 Club.
As a result, the language has become somewhat less coarse than
before, and a painting of a voluptuous nude has disappeared from
its former place of prominence. The women members have little
desire to change the essential nature of the club; it was the old order
of things that had attracted them. A native son who had gone on
to world fame has come back home in his retirement, has been
elected to the club, comes there for lunch every day, brings a fresh
viewpoint to its discussions, and has opened up many channels of
exploration outside the city.

The club has continued to avoid publicity and remained a place
where, under the cloak of conviviality, its members can advance
their personal and public interests. The club has never taken votes,
has seldom reached complete consensus on any topic, and has never
taken a public stance on any issue. Its function has been to provide
a networking mechanism by which its members can achieve their
private and public goals by informally working out agreements with
one another. The experience of creating a city plan had established
the idea of initiating and guiding projects aimed at improving the
quality of the city's life.

The sequence of development of most such projects follows a
common pattern: the suggestion of an idea at the lunch table; the
subsequent discussion of what might be done and how to do it; agreement on how to secure and disseminate the relevant data, usually by

some community organization; development of a concrete plan of action; decision by key members of the club to go ahead; the winning of support by other members who could be of help; and then the initiation of the project. Many ideas are dropped at various points along the way, but a few survive. One of them occurred after several youth-related crimes occurred in the city and aroused great publicity. A discussion of the situation at the club revealed a general desire "to keep the kids off the streets." A board member of the city's Parks Department said he would ask its bureaucracy what could be done. The professionals who operated the parks prepared a report that identified the chief need as being the provision of both paid workers and corps of volunteers at the park field houses. This report was discussed by the club. Several of its members offered to help raise funds for a pilot program at several parks, and in due time it was begun. Its progress was reported to the club, and a few members retained a continuing interest in helping the Parks Department to enlarge its budget so as to broaden the pilot project to other parks. Interest in this project gradually moved into the background of attention of the club, but some of its members have kept a sense of identity with it.

Most new ventures have not required the attention of very many people or the expenditure of much time; for example, if a natural history museum needs help in strengthening its educational outreach, a member of its board can talk with members of the board of education and the university board of trustees. The whole club does not need to be involved. If a topic is of broad concern, however, it can be brought to the center of attention at the luncheon table and may in time arouse frequent and deep discussion, particularly when the proponents of an idea or project have to counter sophisticated challenges with informed statements. Once an idea seems to have won general support in the club, it is likely to succeed in the larger community, and money can be found for its implementation. Most of the changes thus brought about have had to do with the needs of the city for specific areas of service: economic growth, health, welfare, the schools, public safety, and the arts.

The members of the club have also had the feeling that they should pay attention to the city as a whole. They have compared its social statistics with those of other cities. They have looked at the ratings of the country's "best" or "most livable" cities, paying special attention to the elements on which their city scored lowest. They have encouraged studies of the status and trends of the local economy, allocating funds to do so from their family and company foundations.

When the city grew to a population of 800,000, the club members believed that it still did not have the resources to support a world-class symphony, opera house, art museum, or university, but some people thought that less expensive ventures could be found to give distinction and individuality to their city. Among them were a children's museum, a regional theater, a ballet company, and a community chorus. Perhaps too, something might be done to enhance the general quality of life. What could be done, for example, about the excessive noise of certain highways or the airport? The municipal government of Paris was said by one club member to have put into effect a new theory of street lighting, and a fortunate group of local government engineers was delegated to go there and find out about it. Some of the other members talked about how the "winter cities"—such as Minneapolis, Buffalo, Toronto, Stockholm, and St. Petersburg—had collectively found ways to alleviate the rigors of their climate. Among them were the use of bright colors to contrast with the whiteness of the snow, the sheltering of walkways, the use of ornamental plantings in both winter and summer, and the sponsoring of ice festivals. Though their own city was at a more moderate latitude, perhaps they could find ideas for local use.

Over the years, the members of the 528 Club have never doubted that it is a wholly admirable enterprise that has achieved many worthy goals, including the increase of their personal economic stability. They are also well aware that many of their fellow citizens would not understand or agree with that assessment. These citizens might hold that the club is a self-chosen instrument of the city's economic elite that lacks any representation from many of its most important and vital segments. Debate on this subject must surely have occurred at some places and times, but it has not been publicly reported in any prominent fashion. It could be argued as well that its community-based projects are merely a screen to hide personal deal making among its members. These individuals might concede that both contentions are correct, but they would want to add that the club has survived because of its ability to maintain confidentiality, its delegation of the sponsorship of programs to other agencies, its ability to identify and respond to deeply felt themes, its sensitivity to troublesome topics ("we'd better not touch that one"), its capacity to provide support and reinforcement in many ways to many institutions, the intimate knowledge of its members about many aspects of community life, and its insistence upon getting the facts about a situation before moving ahead. Whatever the causes of its success, the club thrives and so do most of the projects it originates or supports.

Analysis. This case illustrates adult education as it is often found: learning is intermingled with action and serves to support and reinforce it. The unique element here lies in the relationship of the 528 Club to the programs that it has caused to be initiated. Its own central purpose has been fraternal and its members also see it as an instrument of power brokering; they would scoff at the idea that they belong because they want to learn. But in each episode of their community programming, the members concerned wanted to be informed about what they did or proposed to do. Recurrently at least some of the members entered into a C-3 situation. Except for such cases, the club stimulated, planned, and supported various educational ventures and evaluated their results. It did not sponsor or administer them.

Looking only at the data here provided, an analyst could speculate that several program-planning categories were involved in the establishment of the master plan. The club planned its own activities (C-3) in two episodes: the use of a series of experts to inform the group about the essentials of city planning, and the study of successive phases of activity while the plan was being evolved. The subsequent support of the plan was essentially action, not education. The CPA program was an example of the creation of a new educational institution (C-7). Most of its successive campaigns were based on C-11, the provision of a program by the mass media. As for the separate substantive agencies that took up the task of studying their programs after the city plan was improved, their program development situations might take any of a number of forms depending on the distinctive nature and operation of each. C-6, C-8, C-9, and C-10 would be prominently represented, though perhaps the latter two would be most common.

The other educational episodes generated by the club could be analyzed in terms of categories and processes if there were sufficient data to do so. An experienced adult educator could speculate about their probable nature, but any such effort would be incomplete. For example, in the case of the Parks Department, the senior staff probably carried on a process of inquiry, and later a training program was almost certainly required for the new personnel. If such activities did exist, each could be analyzed as an example of a basic program design. Any such analyst, however, would be likely to miss the influence of the 528 Club at several points: the pressure of the club on the board member of the Parks Department; the way by which financing was arranged for the pilot program; and the assistance club members were able to give to the expansion of the program to other parks.

Education for Health

Background. Disease- and health-related education is now to be found everywhere in our society. Much of it is carried by the mass media or transmitted by voluntary associations to their members or to the public at large. Of all the institutions that offer direct instruction on disease and health, the most comprehensive and directly personal is the hospital. A case study of one such program is presented here. The information comes from the staff of the hospital (particularly its director of educational planning), its publications, and both extended and intensive personal experience.

Sarasota Memorial Hospital. Sarasota is a beautifully situated city sixty miles south of Tampa on the west coast of Florida. It is estimated to have about 300,000 residents. (All figures in this study unless otherwise noted are for the mid 1990s.) It is a center for recreation (particularly for beaches, boating, golf, and tennis) and for the arts. It has an extensively used, large performance hall, a symphony orchestra, an opera house, a magnificent art museum, several theatrical companies, a ballet troupe, a liberal arts college, a university extension center, a municipal auditorium, many parks, and other amenities. A solid core of longtime residents has been greatly augmented by people who work in a number of substantial businesses and by many retirees (most of them middle class) who spend part or all of the year in the city. About 39 percent of the citizens are over the age of sixty. The tourist industry is very important, bringing just over a million visitors every year.

Looming large on the skyline are the white pavilions of the Sarasota Memorial Hospital, the most prestigious and wide-reaching institution in the community. It is prepared to serve the health needs of everyone in the city and, if need be, to face with each of them many of the starkest realities of their lives. In addition to its 2,800 employees, the hospital is served by eight hundred volunteers, many of them highly educated. Both paid and unpaid workers come from all parts of the city and permeate its many life patterns; they bring constant word to their daily associates of happenings at the hospital. Everything it does is news, often on the front page or mentioned prominently by the electronic media. The meetings of its board are televised. What the cathedral was to the medieval city and the mill to the nineteenth-century New England town, the hospital is to Sarasota.

Its basic service statistics can be quickly given. It has 952 beds and admits about 28,500 patients each year. In the same period, it has about 50,000 visits to its emergency section and about 106,000 visits to its outpatient clinics. Its structured outreach activities for the community (such as lectures, classes, short courses, publications, and support groups) serve an uncountable number of people, but one indication of size is that eighteen thousand individuals are registered to take part in the senior care program.

The purpose of Sarasota Memorial, as of any other hospital, is the achievement and maintenance of health. To carry out these purposes, many patterns of learning and teaching, chiefly of adults, are required; this section describes some of them and how they fit within the structure and operation of the institution.

Everybody aided by the hospital is to some degree acculturated by it, learning its rules and procedures and ways to derive the greatest value from what it has to offer. In addition, many of its clients, both inpatient and out, must learn how to redirect their lives: what to eat and when; how to breathe or swallow or talk; and how to use prosthetic devices, change dressings, follow strict medication schedules, and pursue other therapies. In many cases, family members or other care givers must learn how to provide continuing or emergency assistance.

An example will illustrate how much learning is sometimes necessary. A newly diagnosed diabetic patient must confront complex life-style changes. He or she must master facts and skills dealing with insulin administration, medication, diabetic diet, foot care, signs and treatment of hypoglycemia and hyperglycemia, sick day management, exercise, and coping strategies, as well as gain an understanding of the disease and its complications. Inpatient and outpatient diabetics and their families are given a four-day course in personal diabetics management that is offered every week. Teaching the program are diabetic educators, nurses, physical therapists, dietitians, and social workers. It is given high ratings by its students.

The staff of the hospital is the second major audience for learning endeavors. The 2,800 people involved represent all levels of occupational skill, but every employee is expected to engage in some form of personal advancement. Most such education is offered by the hospital itself, but it is increasing the number of educational institutions with which it has collaborative relationships. It also has a liberal policy of tuition reimbursement for people who want to study elsewhere. Many of those who work in the hospital belong to professional or professionalizing associations that have adopted continuing education requirements for their members. Similar mandates have also been set in some states for relicensure; for example, the Florida State Board of Nursing requires twenty-four hours of continuing education every two years. It is the hospital's policy to require all individuals in its employ to carry out the continuing education requirements established for their occupations. In addition, there are countless groups (such as those based on the various specializations of medicine) that have regular seminars or presentations centered on the theory or practice of their work.

The patterns of education offered by the hospital are many and varied. Careful attention is given to the induction of workers. All new employees are required to take an orientation course that includes a one-day overview of the vision, mission, and operations of the hospital; also included is a review of the skills and equipment needed to work in specific jobs. All newly employed nurses are given a special orientation to the hospital. These initial learning experiences are followed up for each employee. Each person's personnel record contains among other items a statement of expected personal development and a list of concrete goals to be achieved during the current year; educational desires or needs are included as they seem appropriate. All of the items in the personnel record are taken into account in the annual evaluation of every worker by his or her supervisor. The training of volunteers follows the same general pattern as staff training: an orientation to the hospital, instruction concerning special assignments, and refresher education as needed.

The focal point for education in the hospital is the appropriately named Educational Development Department (EDD), a unit within the Human Resources Division. It administers a number of all-hospital or specially assigned services, such as a program to train hospital managers, a literacy program, continuing nursing education, career counseling centers, and a resource unit for audiovisual equipment. In addition, the department provides liaison to non-clinical units, assigns educational specialists to help anywhere in the hospital, and works with other divisions to develop teaching programs for patients. It also serves as liaison to educational institutions and services outside the hospital; for example, the Tampa-based University of South Florida offers two external bachelor's degree programs at the hospital, one in interdisciplinary science and one in business administration. Three master's level programs are also offered, two in nursing by Andrews University and one in adult education by the University of South Florida.

The EDD has twelve full-time members and is headed by Mary Lou Proch, known throughout the hospital by her first name only (a fact in which she takes some satisfaction). Eleven of the educational specialists are nurses, and the entry requirement is a bachelor's degree. Two of the staff members have master's degrees, and the rest are in graduate programs. All of the positions require competence in adult learning principles, consultation expertness, interpersonal skills and teamwork.

Mary Lou is of Polish descent, and her parents came to Florida from West Virginia when she was very young. She was raised in Sarasota, went though its parochial school system, holds a bachelor of science in nursing from Duquesne University and a master of arts in adult education from the University of South Florida. She is currently working at the latter institution on her doctorate in adult education. Her husband, Dave, also works at Sarasota Memorial. As of 1995, they had children aged fifteen, thirteen, eleven, nine, and seven. She has had a varied career in nursing in Colorado, Montana, and Florida. Since 1984, she has been on the staff of EDD and was appointed its head in 1991.

Mary Lou's workday begins at 6:00 A.M. and goes to 2:30 P.M. Her responsibilities are so complex that she has no such thing as a "typical" day, as evidenced by her schedule on one day in mid 1995.

She arrived at her office at 6:00 A.M. In the next hour and a half, she answered her E-mail, dealt with her voice mail, completed her monthly departmental report summarizing past activities and setting priorities for new ones, scanned her mail, and reviewed her schedule with her secretary.

At 7:30 A.M., the EDD staff met for an informational and decision-making meeting. It began with a reporting of individual successes and mistakes and went on to a review by Mary Lou of new hospital concerns and policies. Attention then turned to several matters having to do with computer instruction: the effectiveness of current classes, the implementation of a mobile computer laboratory, and the desirability of using two instructors in basic computer classes. Several other minor concerns were also dealt with briefly.

From 9:00 to 10:00 A.M., Mary Lou discussed various matters with her immediate superior, the vice president for human resources. The major theme of the meeting had to do with possible liaison arrangements for education with several public institutions; Mary Lou got a sense of how to proceed in each case. She also brought up several matters that concerned her, one of them having to do with the staffing needs of the literacy program.

During the next two hours, Mary Lou worked with staff members from the Operating Room on a project to promote teamwork in the OR. The staff had developed a list of the values they hoped to establish; specialists from EDD helped to design a curriculum of classes to establish these values. The classes will be taught by both EDD and OR staff.

At noon, the available EDD staff members had an informal lunch together at which the discussion concerned mainly personal and family matters. But the session also had some bonding effect as the group members discussed the highlights of their day and shared observations, fears, and successes.

Immediately after lunch, Mary Lou had a supervisory meeting with one EDD specialist who reviewed her report on her activities for the past two weeks, summarized her plans for the next two weeks, and described some classes she had taught. Other topics at the session were the computer education schedule, the record-keeping system Abratrain, the plans for AIDS and HIV therapy education, and the progress of the Discharge Planning Committee.

During the day, Mary Lou found brief intervals of time in which she dealt with many immediate matters: making decisions, smoothing out misunderstandings, passing along information, heading off difficulties, answering questions, writing notes and letters, and doing all of the other things required of busy administrators. In the last half-hour of her work day, she made telephone calls, signed letters, jotted down notes, and the like.

While she was thus engaged, her EDD colleagues were busy with their own responsibilities. One taught a course in how to use the computer software Excel and later met separately with two hospital employees in career-counseling sessions. Another specialist helped plan a seminar for physicians and nurses on cardiac and pulmonary topics. Still another conducted the hospitalwide orientation course. A fourth, who is an expert on organizational development, consulted with the manager and staff of a department undergoing massive change. A fifth, who coordinates community health education, worked with other departments in the hospital to plan the programs needed for the next year, using current health data as indicators of need. And so it went, each person taking assigned parts in an intricate web of activity.

The hospital library, a part of EDD, is a highly regarded learning resource. Its collection of books, monographs, and journals is current, authoritative, and relevant to the needs of the hospital employees and other users. On request, it does literary searches through a data-based system on CD-ROM that contains MEDLINE and HEALTH. Thus a physician confronted with an unusual case can get immediate help in knowing how to handle it, or a therapist seeking a deeper understanding of some aspect of her work can consult relevant texts.

As with most hospitals today, Sarasota Memorial is generally considered to be chiefly a center for the care of seriously ill or handicapped persons. This mission must continue, but virtually every publication that the institution issues stresses the desire of its board, administration, and staff to be health preservers as well as care givers. It seeks to reach this goal primarily through educational programs offered both in the hospital and elsewhere in the community. These include large and small meetings on various health themes, seminars, short courses and reinforcement groups for people with various ailments and their family care givers. Periodically a one- or two-page advertisement in the local newspaper will list some of the currently available activities. A brief sample of these are counseling for senior adults to help them locate and initiate contact with needed health services; nurse-supervised walking programs in a local mall; courses in low-fat cooking; and lectures, courses, and seminars on such topics as foot care, female stress incontinence, coping with the impact of a divorce, learning to deal with loss and grief, and making end-of-life decisions. Obstetrical tours are held for expectant parents to help them understand what they will encounter when babies come to term.

The ideas for such activities flow in part from the experience gained by the hospital staff in direct service to the community. Two examples may be cited. First, two evenings a week, significant numbers of the people who work in the hospital volunteer their time to conduct free clinics for people who would not otherwise be able to afford health care; thus some of the special needs of the poor are emphasized. In 1993–94, almost 4,800 people were served. They are, a hospital report says, "young and old, many . . . marked by desperation." Second, hospital employees are encouraged to serve as volunteers in community enterprises so that they will personalize the hospital in many places and will bring back to it new or deeper insights into social needs. In 1993–94, about 500 people worked almost four thousand hours on twenty-two community projects.

Mary Lou and many of her colleagues hope to help the hospital evolve into a wellness center for the whole community and are designing learning and other programs to bring about that result. An observer senses that they take seriously the quotation highlighted in the hospital's 1994–95 annual report. It was written by Henri Frederic Amiel, a nineteenth-century Swiss essayist, and reads, "Happiness, grief, gaiety, and sadness are contagious. Bring your health and strength to the weak and sickly, and you will be of use to them. Give them not your weakness but your energy, so you will revive them and lift them up. Life alone can rekindle life."

Analysis. Memorial, as the hospital is often called, has gone a long way toward institutionalizing the idea of lifelong learning and creating an educative society in the workplace. The continuing educational requirements required by the professions of many of the staff are supplemented by an annual performance review for every employee. This is guided by the expectation that he or she will set and achieve new levels of personal accomplishment brought about by educative or other means. The ideal of the continual upgrading of performance is strongly expressed from the beginning of employment by orientation programs for everyone and reinforced by instruction aimed at personal and collective needs. For example, the improvement of teamwork in the operating room is treated as an educational as well as a supervisory goal. Patients accept the fact that training is an integral part of their therapies, and the efforts to preserve wellness are almost entirely educational in character. Total institutional involvement is perhaps most fully indicated by the fact that the EDD does not merely operate its own programs; it puts its expertise to work as a collaborator with all other parts of the hospital.

Every one of the eleven educational design situations can be identified somewhere in the hospital's program. Library and computerized resources for independent study are available. Much of the therapy provided to patients is dyadic. Learning groups and courses abound. Various occupational groups carry out programs planned by committees of their members. The EDD works with other departments to enhance their combined services. The hospital helps create new institutions to carry out functions best performed independently. It is constantly at work enlarging the number of learning activities in familiar formats and seeking new patterns of service. It works collaboratively with other community institutions and is seeking new affiliations. It uses mass media in many ways, particularly in its outreach and community service activities.

Those who design new forms of instruction or analyze existing ones do not follow any formal model of program planning; they rely pragmatically on collective judgment based on experience. The hospital now has in place a number of courses created after much thought and refined after many repetitions. Examples are the orientations given to new employees and volunteers, the course for diabetics, and the systematic rehabilitation procedures designed for the handicapped. At any given time, a number of new learning programs are under development, often on an interdisciplinary basis. In such ventures, the staff members of the EDD are accepted as educational specialists bringing their expertise to bear on the shaping of the program.

Unanswered Questions

The analyses of these cases suggest that the program-design framework proposed in this book can be applied to a wide variety of educational situations. In making any such application, variant interpretations are quite possible, particularly since the accounts do not give exhaustive details about what actually occurred during the educational process. Thus the reader may prefer to assign any of the programs described to different situational categories than the ones here suggested and may consider certain procedures to illustrate other components than the ones to which they have been ascribed.

In addition to this possible variance in interpretation, at least three other questions remain. First, would some other theoretical program design be more accurate and helpful in analyzing these and other cases than the one proposed in this book? Anybody who seeks to grow in understanding and ability should come to some kind of answer on this point since a basic design establishes the structure for later learning. Second, if the design proposed here is accepted, does it need to be revised to be more accurate or useful? If readers add or subtract any component or category or prefer a different ordering of the present ones, they will have increased the utility of the framework for themselves and may have helped in its evolution toward a more precise and meaningful instrument of analysis and operation. Finally, in analyzing any case, are there hidden or obscure elements that are significant in determining its relative success? The example of the 528 Club suggests that adult education can be powerfully influenced by factors not readily apparent. The successful designer of adult educational programs must be alert to the possible existence of such factors and try to replicate them if she or he can.

4

Categories of Educational Situations

'Tis to create, and in creating live
A being more intense, that we endow
With form our fancy, gaining as we give
The life we image.
                    —Lord Byron, *Childe Harold's Pilgrimage*

Much has been said, and rightly so, about the unity of human experience and the impossibility of separating and defining all the attributes and actions of the seamless web of life. The eleven categories of educational situations suggested here do not come from an attempt to sort out all existing learning or teaching activities in terms of their form or sponsorship. Instead, the categories are dynamic. Educational planners or analysts examine the milieu in which they work, define or choose what appears to be the most logical or productive situation, identify the category in which it falls, and shape or guide their work according to the distinctive nature of that category.

At first sight, the eleven appear to reflect a shifting point of view. In C-1, there is at best only a fancied semblance of a leader, and in C-11 the leader has no clear awareness of the nature of all the learners. C-1 through C-5 and C-11 are based on the act of education itself while C-6 through C-10 deal more broadly with the creation or operation of an administrative pattern. But beneath these surface differences lies a central unity—the categories define the basic configurations of action used by an educator, a learner, or an analyst in pursuing a creative process, either alone or with other people. Each of them has also been described by Elias (1982).

C-1:Independent Study

Since independent study is by definition a wholly self-guided way of designing and controlling an educational activity, it can be examined in depth only by those who analyze their own experience or that described to them. As a result, knowledge about this category of situations is based largely on anecdotal accounts, some of them drawn from the biographies or autobiographies of distinguished men and women and others from self-reported case studies. Episodes in which learning plays a primary or significant part may occur in a life that is essentially private and contemplative (as was that of Montaigne or Spinoza), or in one fully rounded with activity but in which all actions aim at the fullest possible enlargement of the individual's potentialities (like that of the idealized "Renaissance man"). It has been taken for granted that any scholar at the forefront of a field must direct his or her own study, either alone or with the advice of colleagues. Such general patterns of independent study as these have long been celebrated as providing one of the wellsprings of major human achievement and as setting ideals for less supremely gifted people.

Little is known about the nature or frequency of independent study in the lives of the undistinguished individuals who make up the great majority of mankind. Johnstone and Rivera (1965), in an investigation based on a national sample, estimated that in one year in the early 1960s 8,960,000 American adults were engaged in episodes of this sort. It was discovered that "some subjects are almost always self-taught"; among them are technical arts and hobbies, gardening, and home improvement skills (pp. 38, 57–59). The incidence of independent study is probably highest among those who have had an extensive formal education. In a Canadian study, Tough (1965) found that all but two of forty-four college graduates he interviewed had recently engaged in self-directed study. But, as the examples of Walter Dan Griffith in Chapter Three and many another workingman suggest, this kind of learning can exist at any social level. Even in economically disadvantaged societies, such as those of Africa, some individuals find ways to study, often in situations in which their objectives are dictated by the fact that they have access to only a single book or other learning resource.

The available evidence suggests that self-directed learning takes place in a number of different ways. For some people, it is an inherent part of the pattern of life itself. A scientist, for example, may systematically keep up with the literature of her specialty, attend conferences, and take part in continuous discussion with her colleagues. When she engages in research, she informs herself about relevant theoretical work and previous studies and by collecting and interpreting data acquires new understanding and insight. The expression of the urge to know may be sufficiently paramount in the life-style of such a person that learning and life merge together. She has so completely mastered her own educational design that she scarcely realizes that it exists.

Other equally self-reliant independent students are well aware of the need to plan their learning. Their typical pattern is to accept some component of a learning design as central to what they wish to do and let everything else fall into place around it. One young librarian decided that she wanted to broaden her knowledge of the world and of her profession by spending about two years in each of five libraries in various parts of the United States. She carried out this plan, centered on her chosen method, altering it in one case to go outside the country to gain foreign experience. At the end, she felt that she had fully achieved her purposes, though she had never been certain precisely what they were.

Another example can be found in a prison experience of Malcolm X (1964):

I saw that the best thing I could do was get hold of a dictionary—to study, to learn some words. I was lucky enough to reason also that I should try to improve my penmanship. It was sad. I couldn't even write in a straight line. . . . I spent two days just riffling uncertainly through the dictionary's pages. I'd never realized so many words existed! I didn't know *which* words I needed to learn. Finally, just to start some kind of action, I began copying. In my slow, painstaking, ragged handwriting, I copied into my tablet everything printed on that first page, down to the punctuation marks. I believe it took me a day. Then, aloud, I read back, to myself, everything I'd written on the tablet. Over and over, aloud, to myself, I read my own handwriting.

He woke up the next morning, thinking about the words and proud of what he had done. So he went on, day after day, until finally he had copied the whole dictionary (pp. 172–173).

Most learners who start such a program soon realize that their original plan lacks one or more important elements. Malcolm X found that he could read books with increasing understanding. "Anyone who has read a great deal can imagine the new world that opened," he said and embarked upon a broad venture in learning. But many people find resources denied to them. Even so resolute a man as Winston Churchill had his difficulties. As a graduate of Harrow and Sandhurst, he had had an excellent early formal education. But when he undertook a program of independent reading of history and philosophy while stationed as a young officer in India, he soon felt the need for guidance. "It was a curious education," he later wrote,

First because I approached it with an empty, hungry mind, and with fairly strong jaws; and what I got I bit; secondly because I had no one to tell me: 'This is dis-

credited'. 'You should read the answer to that by so and
so; the two together will give you the gist of the argument'. 'There is a much better book on that subject', and
so forth. I now began for the first time to envy those
young cubs at the university who had fine scholars to tell
them what was what; professors who had devoted their
lives to mastering and focussing ideas in every branch of
learning; who were eager to distribute the treasures they
had gathered before they were overtaken by the night
[Churchill, 1930, p. 127].

Most people do not know of any systematic way to design their
own learning activities. They choose independent study because
they want the flexibility of approach it allows, because they are
attracted by some new resource or method, or because they are
unaware of any other way to learn what they want to know. Almost
at once, most of them begin to feel inadequate. Tough's detailed
record of forty learning episodes undertaken by college graduates in
a metropolitan area shows that some learners felt they required assistance in every aspect of their programs and that the average learner
turned to about ten other individuals for some kind of aid or support. In general, those who conducted the episodes felt inadequate
about what they were doing, underestimated their accomplishments,
and believed that their style of learning differed from that of everyone else (Tough, 1965). Like Churchill, such people approach
learning with an empty, hungry mind, and what they get, they bite.
But when they encounter the confusion and difficulty usually posed
by the reality of independent study, they grow insecure, stop far
short of attainable goals, abandon their efforts, or try to find some
other way of learning.

Why is this sense of stress and uncertainty so common? The
answer may be that young people are seldom taught how to design
and conduct their own education. A zest for knowledge may be fostered by a series of absorbing learning experiences in childhood and

youth, but that zest does not automatically bring with it either awareness of the intricacies of a complex program or competence in designing one. What children and youth may learn from incessant practice is that education is a process guided by a teacher and conducted in a classroom. They may not be taught to separate the process from its embodiments, to understand its components, or to master their use.

It is interesting to speculate what would happen if such instruction were to become an established part of the schooling of the young, being taught by precept, demonstration, and practice, so that young people left school fully prepared to undertake independent study. The net result might be a vast increase in the number of people who initiate and carry out their own projects. It is less certain that such efforts would be more calmly and purposefully managed than is now the case. As a quotation in Chapter Two suggested, even researchers with extensive training and experience still proceeded in a floundering and messy-looking way. Anyone who confronts the unknown with no sure guide is likely to be uneasy. But the researcher knows and accepts the canons of science that can be used for guidance at times of doubt or stress. The independent student has a similar need to be aware of the fundamental design of learning.

In the system proposed here, the model used in self-directed study is the same as that in any other category, though a few of the elements or adjustments may be omitted or applied in special ways. An independent learner who works wholly alone may not need to think about leaders, social reinforcement, individualization, roles or relationships, or guidance. Alternatively the learner may want to test a plan with each such component in mind, particularly since he or she might wish occasionally to move into another situation, treating it as subordinate to the central endeavor. Thus a man who wants to learn statistics may seek guidance from someone about the best way to do so. If he decides to work his way through a textbook, he may find it useful to ask a friend to tutor him on the hard parts; in this way both leadership and roles and relationships would be involved. He may also find it pleasant to work in a library surrounded by other people, many of whom are studying independently but giving silent social reinforcement to one another. Heim and Wallace (1990) have described very fully how public libraries provide adult services.

As foregoing comments suggest, independent study is an idea whose essence is easy to grasp but that can in practice have many ramifications. Since the 1960s, a very large literature has grown up on self-directed learning, a related but much broader idea than independent study. The effort to distinguish between these two concepts and others related to them has grown ever more difficult. This entire realm of discourse has been described and analyzed in masterful fashion by Candy (1991).

C-2: Tutorial Teaching

Tutorial teaching exists in many forms and in some fashion or other it is universal to human experience. Most frequently it arises spontaneously as one person shows another how to do something, but it may be consciously fostered in institutions by the process that the English colloquially call "sitting next to Nellie." Such learning is an established aspect of some continuing relationships, such as that between a supervisor and a subordinate, and an occasional part of others, such as that between a physician and a patient. Tutorial instruction is also offered by private teachers who are usually paid for their work. The study by Johnstone and Rivera (1965) has estimated that in a single year 1,670,000 American adults studied with such teachers.

Patterns of tutorial teaching may also be institutionalized. In vocational rehabilitation and other ways of helping people reshape their lives, the counselor focuses directly on the specific needs of each client. The reader's adviser in a public library helps patrons choose the learning resources they need. In many occupations, such as medicine, teaching, or industrial management, a master performer sometimes accepts an intern and gives her close and personalized instruction. In other situations, it may appear that instruction is occurring in a larger group (and in some sense it is), but the heart of the teaching lies in the relationship between the instructor and each student. The master painter or sculptor moves about the atelier helping students one by one, and the same technique is used in teaching most of the other fine or practical arts and crafts.

The collaborative aspect of education as a cooperative art has its fullest expression in tutorial teaching, for the educator and the learner face one another directly. The starkness of this confrontation has led to deep analyses of the proper roles of the two members of the dyad. As Georg Simmel has pointed out, it "contains the scheme, germ and material of innumerable more complex forms," but is itself completely unlike any other: "Each of the two feels himself confronted only by the other, not by a collectivity above him." If either party withdraws, the relationship ends, whereas if there are three or more people, the withdrawal of one person still leaves a collective social unit. The failure to have external social reinforcement gives the dyad its strength since it creates a "feeling of exclusive dependence upon one another and of hopelessness that cohesion might come from anywhere but immediate interaction." This bond is so great that larger groups often dissolve back again into smaller units. Thus the bonds and disunities, even in a triad, may "result in three parties of two persons each" (Wolff, 1950, pp. 119–137).

In tutorial teaching, the dyadic relationship has been worked out in many different ways, some of which have taken established form. The Platonic dialogue was a method of eliciting truth by the process of directed questioning. Disputation by scholars in the Middle Ages demonstrated how subtly a line of investigation could be carried forward by the making of theoretical distinctions. In modern times, educational practice has relied heavily on work done in such allied fields as counseling, psychiatry, psychoanalysis, and industrial psychology, but many different ways of identifying the teacher-learner relationship have also arisen from practice or have been evolved from pedagogic theory. The following four patterns are among the most widely espoused.

The most common is straightforward exposition in which both parties expect the teacher to demonstrate or instruct and the learner to be a ready and willing recipient of knowledge or skill. This pattern may be worked out in many ways, but all of them assume that the two roles will be clear-cut and well established and that the members of the dyad will move through a series of formal steps. In a manual on industrial training, for example, the following procedure, paraphrased here and stripped of its reinforcing discussion, is recommended under the title *How to Instruct:*

> *Part I.* Prepare the Worker (Put him at ease. State the job. Find out what he knows about the job. Get him interested. Place the learner where he can see the operation clearly.)
>
> *Part II.* Present the Operation (Tell, show, and illustrate. Present one important step at a time. Stress key points. Instruct clearly, completely, and patiently. Teach no more than the learner can master. Summarize the operation in a second run-through.)
>
> *Part III.* Tryout Performance (Have learner do the job. Have learner explain key points as he does the job again. Make sure he understands. Continue until you know he knows.)
>
> *Part IV.* Follow up (Put him on his own. Designate the person to whom he can turn for help on the job. Encourage questions. Taper off by returning to the learner at longer or longer intervals. Continue with normal supervision) [Magill and Monaghan, 1967, pp. 117–120].

A second pattern (actually a special adaptation of the first but one now being heavily stressed as an independent system) is programmed instruction in which an educational task, usually the learning of a body of content or an established skill, is analyzed into a series of logical units, each of which is mastered by the student before going on to the next one. Cooley and Glaser (1969) suggest that this instruction follows a general sequence of operations:

(1) The goals of learning are specified in terms of observable student behavior and the conditions under which this behavior is to be manifested. (2) When learners begin a particular course of instruction, their initial capabilities—those relevant to the forthcoming instruction—are assessed. (3) Educational alternatives suited to the students' initial capabilities are presented to them. The students select or are assigned one of these alternatives. (4) The students' performances are monitored and continuously assessed as they learn. (5) Instruction proceeds as a function of the relationship among measures of student performance, available instructional alternatives, and criteria of competence. (6) As instruction proceeds, data are generated for monitoring and improving the instructional system. A special feature of programmed tutorial instruction is that the human teacher may be supplemented or sometimes replaced by an inanimate one, such as a specially developed book or sequence of videotapes.

The fullest expression of nonhuman programmed instruction so far has been computer software where units of content are presented to learners either sequentially or as a "menu" from which they choose topics. Their rate of learning is determined by their ability to select the sequences they need and react appropriately to these sequences. But the computer's ability to provide tutorial instruction seems to extend without limits as new kinds of software are developed and new possibilities of contact are made on the internet. Currently it is conventional wisdom that teenagers find computers more "friendly" than do adults, but nobody seems to know why. Perhaps experience leads men and women to perceive ambiguities and tolerate subtleties that computer programmers (in their need for exactness) now find it hard to plan for. But if the difference between the generations does exist, it seems likely to disappear as computer pioneers become more sophisticated and teenagers grow up.

A third pattern is coaching, most commonly understood in its application to athletic and artistic accomplishment but also widely adopted in the teaching of other complex skills, including those of management. Anselm Strauss defines this relationship as existing "if someone seeks to move someone else along a series of steps, when those steps are not entirely institutionalized and invariant, and when the learner is not entirely clear about their sequences." In each case, the learner "has yielded himself (whether he knows it or not) to a teacher who guides him along at least partly obscure channels." The coach dominates the instruction by thrusting the student into unfamiliar situations, imposing demands, functioning "like a playwright, arranging episodes, setting scenes, getting supporting characters to act in a certain way," setting the timing, and devising such tactics in a delicately balanced process as "the prescription, the schedule, the challenge, the trial, and the accusation." From the beginning, however, students impose resistances and controls; eventually they achieve independence, and usually they decide when the relationship will end. Strauss concludes, "The best pupils, like the best children, get out from under the control and the vision of the best teachers, and the best teachers are pleased that this is so. At the outer limits of learning, the stages can no longer be as standardized as at the beginning; and the pupil discovers his own style, whether we are talking of religious conversion, musical composition, or anything else. For the coach, too, the process may be open-ended; he may develop a different identity" (1959, pp. 109–118).

A fourth pattern is nondirective instruction, often cast in the form of counseling or therapy. Learners ask for help, but the person who guides them (counselor, therapist, pastor, teacher, or any other) knows that the seekers must find answers within themselves. They may do so by putting together previously unrelated elements of knowledge, by searching beneath the surface level of consciousness, or by discovering the purpose and motivation that will lead them to seek out independently the information, the skill, and the understanding they need. In this permissive approach, the guide is far from being a vacuum but is so strong and independent that he or she can focus wholly on the needs of the person who wants help. Various specific methods have been proposed as appropriate to differing situations, but Carl Rogers has suggested that in all cases the greatest help results from the ability of therapists to communicate their own trustworthiness in an unambiguous fashion, recognize their essential separateness as persons from the individual they are trying to help, "experience positive attitudes toward this other person," respect his freedom "to develop a personality quite different from that of his therapist," "enter fully into the world of his feelings and personal meanings and see these as he does," act so sensitively in the dyadic relationship that the client "can begin to experience and to deal with the internal feelings and conflicts which he finds threatening within himself," free the client from any "threat of external evaluation," and accept him as a person who is in the process of becoming, of confirming or making real his own potentialities (1961, pp. 39–58).

As these four patterns suggest, tutorial instruction can be dominated from beginning to end by an established theory of the proper roles of the two members of the dyad, this theory being imposed on the relationship by the person who is cast as the educator. If such a theory is followed, its dictates influence all choices and actions taken during the designing and carrying out of the program. A coach and a nondirective leader will differ greatly from one another in how they behave and how they require their learners to behave. However, some leaders are eclectic, choosing whatever pattern seems best to fit the situation or evolving a fresh approach out of the dictates of the moment. When such is the case, the relative importance of the definition of roles may diminish somewhat, but the very directness of confrontation of the two members of the dyad always causes such a definition to be an important element, even though it may be expressed in action, not words. Vella (1994) has explored deeply the variable relationships between leaders and learners.

Leadership is sometimes provided by a group, not an individual. For example, a new public administrator may go through a formal indoctrination program provided by future associates. If each person sees her separately with no collective planning in advance, she is subjected to a series of tutorial experiences. If the leaders work in terms of an overall plan, each experience will be limited and directed by that fact since each leader operates in terms of his assigned function. Occasionally the leaders provide instruction simultaneously, so that the tutorial teaching ceases to be dyadic. In such cases, conflict sometimes arises among the leaders, particularly if they differ on their theory of approach; one person may feel he or she should be a coach and another that he or she should be nondirective. If this conflict cannot be resolved, the education of the learner will be impaired.

In the later stages of an episode, the nature of the C-2 situation often changes. The interaction gradually broadens, and the role distinction between educator and learner disappears. In such a case, tutorial teaching is replaced by another situation, that in which a group of two or more people share in the learning.

C-3: Learning Group

A group is any collection of human beings that has a common purpose and among whom interaction occurs. Thus runs the austere sociological definition; but since some of the most crucial, creative, and inspiring elements of the human spirit result from the relationship of one person with another or others, there is great emotional power in the idea of the group, however small or large it may be. The goal to be collectively sought furnishes one source of inspiration, but the very sense of interaction provides another. Thus Martin Buber, who applied Simmel's thought to his own career as an adult educator, identified the central importance of the group by distinguishing between collectivity and community:

> Collectivity is not a binding but a bundling together: individuals packed together, armed and equipped in common,

with only as much life from man to man as will inflame
the marching step. But community . . . is the being no
longer side by side but *with* one another of a multitude of
persons. And this multitude, though it also moves toward
one goal, yet experiences everywhere a turning to, a dynamic facing of, the other, a flowing from *I* to *Thou*. . . .
Collectivity is based on an organized atrophy of personal
existence, community on its increase and confirmation in
life lived towards one another [1947, p. 31].

All groups are learning groups in the sense that their members
are constantly influenced by interaction with one another, but some
groups have education as a primary or facilitative goal. Most of them
are probably autonomous, arising from some spontaneously discovered sense of interest or need and continuing as long as they find
their experience rewarding. Others are fostered and developed by
an institution, such as a public library, a senior citizens' center, a
sensitivity training program, or a health or welfare service.

Learning groups are so numerous and so variable in form that
they can be neither counted nor cataloged. Some are brought into
being by the common desire of several people to study a specific
body of content. Others are created as literary clubs, scientific societies, or other associations designed to provide a generalized opportunity for learning; many clubs of this sort outlive their founders,
occasionally by several generations. Others focus on the group
process itself as a way to provide increased sensitivity to individual
personality and human interaction. Others are designed to be vehicles of advanced study; most professions and scholarly disciplines
have self-selected groups of leaders (known collectively as invisible
colleges) who inform one another of outstanding new developments
and research contributions.

Such learning groups as these are often highly significant both
to the individuals who compose them and to the society of which
they are a part. Few men in human history have had as thorough a

formal education in childhood as did John Stuart Mill; yet he said of a discussion group to which he belonged as a young man:

> I have always dated from these conversations my own real inauguration as an original and independent thinker. It was also through them that I acquired, or very much strengthened, a mental habit to which I attribute all that I have ever done, or ever shall do, in speculation; that of never accepting half-solutions of difficulties as complete; never abandoning a puzzle, but again and again return-ing to it until it was cleared up; never allowing obscure corners of a subject to remain unexplored, because they did not appear important; never thinking that I perfectly understood any part of a subject until I understood the whole [1944, p. 187].

Illustrious learning groups may have a powerful impact on their socie-ties, sometimes (like the Royal Society) continuing to influence it for centuries. Also the cumulative influence of many humble groups can sometimes be very great. In the twentieth century, Swedish study circles have done much to lay the foundation for the social advance of their country, and voluntary groups have had a powerful influence on the development of responsible electorates in Africa.

When a learning group is formed, its program may be created afresh, borrowed, or dictated by some aspect of the situation. In the first case, the members themselves decide how to deal with all com-ponents of the design. The success or failure of the group's endeav-ors reflects the extent to which an effective program was devised and followed. In the second case, the group that follows the example of another may find that the design it adopts fits its own need exactly, or it may wish to consider how differences in the two situations require the original pattern to be altered. In the third case, the group accepts the fact that it cannot have full freedom to do as it wishes. Such a decision is necessary, for example, when a local chapter of a national association is formed, when a group decides to undertake a packaged instructional program, or when process is controlled by purpose, as in some forms of sensitivity training.

Even when the situation requires that some of the components of the design be borrowed or accepted, a great deal of decision making must usually be left to the group if it is to flourish or even survive. The quality of its life and experience depends on its capacity to be creative and to have the right to choose as freely as possible among alternatives. Thus a national association ordinarily allows its local chapters as great a freedom as is consistent with established overall policies.

The leadership of a learning group may take many different forms. The group may have no formal leader but may let itself be guided only by the push and pull of the personalities in its membership; the individuals who exert more influence than others have a fluid kind of power that may shift at any time to other hands. In such cases, the role is not consciously accepted or ascribed by others, but it exists and upon scrutiny can be identified and defined. There may be both a titular and a real leader, and the two may or may not be in conflict. The group may have an amalgam of factions, each with its own leader. It may have a rotating leadership from among its members. It may recruit a leader from outside or accept a leader at the time of its formation. This person may or may not be trained for the job and may be completely pragmatic in her or his approach to the task, or the leader may try to use some formal process. But essentially she or he is first among equals, and, though that role sometimes may come very close to that of a teacher, some distinction is ordinarily preserved so that the group retains the power of decision and action in collectively achieving its aims.

Of all the design components in a C-3 situation, social reinforcement tends to be most important, being at once a beginning point, a major determinant of continuity, and a basis of appraisal. It often transcends objectives in importance; the group remains in existence though its purposes change. As Hodgkin points out in his

and courses is professedly broader, purporting to deal with educational psychology, curriculum, administration, or the history of education, the customary central reference of the author is to the young person in the classroom in the school. Many of the findings and conceptions of this literature, if generalized sufficiently to remove it from the immediate situations from which it was derived, can have significance for the improvement of adult education. The principles used to state objectives, demonstrate a skill, determine readability, or construct achievement tests are as relevant to the learning of men and women as of boys and girls, particularly when the adults are engaged in teacher-directed group instruction.

Yet there are important characteristics of both the maturity and the life-style of adults that make the application of the C-4 category to them different from its use with young people, and this difference is worth exploring at some length. Adults have had more experiences than children, including some that boys and girls cannot have, such as getting married, acquiring and holding a job, and sensing the body's full maturity and subsequent decline. They may therefore bring to learning a background of knowledge, skill, and judgment that can enrich their knowledge and that of classmates. Adults may also grow rigid, opinionated, or forgetful, particularly if they do not keep their minds and bodies active with use, and thereby present special problems to anyone who tries to teach them. The instructor of adults does not have the same generalized power over the students as does the teacher in a school or college. She or he has a specialized authority unique to the situation based on mastery of subject matter and teaching skill. When the class is ended, so is the teacher's power. But she or he can be challenged by the very maturity of the students to go far beyond the exposition of the familiar. The teacher of children almost never conveys a message of profound original truth to them. The teacher of adults at least occasionally does.

In the education of children, the teacher-directed group is a customary, familiar, and continuing experience that students take for granted. A high school girl, for example, spends most of the day attending classes that often have much overlapping of membership among them. More than that, she has moved through the previous school years with the same age cohort and expects to continue to do so. In adult education, the group is usually formed especially for each situation. The students may not know each other. For many of them, the experience is a unique and unusual one, and they are of varied ages and backgrounds. As a result, each class is a venture and often a challenge in building a new network of interpersonal associations.

In the life-style of the learner, there are significant differences between children and adults. Children conform to some degree to the expectation of society that their main occupation should be learning, much of their time is spent within the environment provided by the school or university and under its administrative controls, and they expect to have a number of simultaneous classes. Adults usually accept noneducational tasks as primary to their way of life; learning must be secondary to other major occupations. They may have little contact with an educational institution except as it provides the environment that they enter periodically for class, and their schedules may contain only that one experience of formal learning. This limited effort may mean that education becomes so peripheral to experience that it has little impact. At the other extreme, it can mean that adults continuously use the knowledge gained in class to look with new insight at their own affairs and those of society, thus enriching not only their learning but also their understanding of the whole pattern of life.

Children usually proceed through the steps of an orderly and successive educational progression. Society carries them along for ten to sixteen years of schooling, sometimes longer. Ordained completion points exist, and while they may not achieve them, the system is set up to encourage them to do so. But when children end their formal instruction, age-grading ceases. In the adult years, any learning activity must usually be initiated by individuals themselves or by someone else, such as an employer. The impetus to study comes not from the established expectations of society but from interaction with the conditions of life. Adults may elect to undertake a long-range series of episodes, perhaps one leading to a certificate or a degree. But the choice is made by the adults, not by society. If by decision or default they do not continue to study, they will gradually lose their learning skills, a fact that adults may not recognize until they undertake a new educational program after a hiatus.

Such distinctions as the foregoing make clear the fact that adult C-4 situations, while similar in form to those encountered in childhood, must be handled by both teacher and students with a special awareness of the distinctive nature and life-styles of the latter. This necessity falls on both parties, but its burden lies heaviest on teachers since the designing of the activity is centrally in their hands. They usually begin by accepting their own role as a leader but then take account of all the other components, either by themselves or with the collaboration of the students. Heimlich and Norland (1994) show how each teacher may develop a distinctive teaching style.

A C-4 situation is more likely to be repetitive than is one in any of the other categories, since the teacher's usual pattern of employment requires recurring activity of the same sort. This repetitiveness can lead to staleness or rigidity. Early episodes may be planned creatively. Yet with the passage of time, routines are established and in increasingly rigid fashion applied to succeeding groups of students. This process can also occur in C-2 situations, but there the directness of confrontation with a single student tends to reduce the danger. In a C-4 situation, the very generality of the group may blur the differences between individuals and lead teachers to the comfortable belief that each succeeding class is made up of pretty much the same kinds of people. Teachers begin to treat education as though it were an operative rather than a cooperative art. This danger can be resisted only if they set themselves the task of rethinking each act and episode in terms of its unique components.

C-5: Committee-Guided Group Learning

A C-5 situation is one in which the educational activity of a group is guided by a committee, usually composed of the group's own members. This guidance may be required because the group is too large to plan for itself, does not wish to do so, or does not have adequate time. Alternatively committee planning may be required because the learning group has not yet been created, as when a council is appointed by a mayor to plan and undertake a conference on an important social problem. A C-5 situation is essentially a collective decision-making process that aims to make a proposed educational experience more truly cooperative than it would be if planned by a single person. But the committee must not allow itself to consider only its own concerns and thereby act as though it were in a C-3 situation. Throughout its deliberation, it must think about what will be most educative for the learners for whom it is planning.

Program committees have highly variable tenures of existence. One may be called into being for only a single session. Another may have a life that begins with its first meeting and ends with the completion of the activity it has planned. Still another may have permanent status, though with rotation of membership; such might be the case in a continuing voluntary association. It sometimes happens during the course of an activity that one committee succeeds another. Thus a teacher-education workshop may be planned by one small group but, when the program begins, be replaced by another elected to represent the wishes of the participants in attendance.

The composition of a program committee also varies greatly among situations. It may be wholly derived from among the potential learners, as is the case with the education committee of a local union. Alternatively its membership may be drawn from many sources and be destined to play various roles in the activity itself. For example, the planners of a conference at a university center for continuing education may include faculty members from several disciplines, programming specialists from the center, delegates from institutional cosponsors, experts in the topic to be considered, and representatives from funding agencies.

A C-5 situation may arise naturally and spontaneously. Often a learning group, perhaps because of growth in its size or a sense of frustration, designates a few of its members to assume the planning function. Program committees have also become established parts of the work of many highly formalized institutions. Thus the Cooperative Extension Service has made great use of such committees in all its work; they provide an important experience in the continuing education of lay leaders. Some institutions or program formats are chiefly or entirely concerned with C-5 situations; such is the case, for instance, with university conference and institute offices.

Planning groups ordinarily have a limited time in which to work and must often use much of that time to resolve individual or role differences in points of view. In order to compensate for the brevity of the planning period, specialists in program design have developed standard check sheets of decision points and components designed for use in industrial training centers and other settings where C-5 situations are common. Such a list presented to a committee makes it aware of the decisions that it must either make or delegate, and helps fix its attention on the total situation in which it finds itself. Even when such a check sheet does not exist, many institutionally based program planners have evolved a pattern of standardized decision making. As a result, systematic design may be more characteristic of institutionalized C-5 situations than of any others.

C-6: Collaborative Group Education

Every voluntary group is held together by the bonds of interest created by its purposes, activities, structure, and interpersonal associations. When a number of groups work together to enhance their combined programs, they are essentially trying to fuse these separate loyalties into some larger pattern of interconnected interest. Suppose, for example, that in a small city, the various voluntary associations (such as Rotary, Kiwanis, PTA, and the League of Women Voters) decide to sponsor an educational activity that none of them can undertake separately, such as a lecture-forum series of distinguished speakers. Every decision made in such a program-planning situation reflects not merely the capacity of the separate groups to accommodate one another but also their ability to transcend their separateness and join in a common effort.

While retaining this essential quality of supragroup cooperation, C-6 situations vary in many other ways. The planned educational activity may be designed for members of the constituent groups, for some other special audience (such as the functionally illiterate, the "downtowners," or the elderly) or the entire community. The collaboration may be undertaken solely for one activity or it may be continuing, as is the case with the countywide councils maintained in some Cooperative Extension Service programs. It may occur on a completely independent basis, or it may be sponsored by an institution, as when the clubs in a settlement house plan for some general activity. The planning group may do all of its own work, or it may have a full- or part-time secretariat.

The formal structure for planning in a C-6 situation often looks very much like that in a C-5 situation, since both center on small groups working out the design for large group learning activities. There is an essential difference, however, since the C-6 planners are delegates assigned by groups to speak for them. Usually these delegates have only limited powers; they act under direct instruction or with clearly defined authority. Even when they are given unlimited freedom, they feel informal constraints and are careful not to go beyond the wishes of their constituents or even of factions within them. These delegates must move collectively through the stages of program planning, making the decisions and acting upon them. All the delegates are obliged to express the will of their own groups as they understand it or alternatively be prepared to urge their groups to adopt a new position. In the latter case, the delegates know that they have no power other than their personal stature or persuasive ability to win the support of their groups for the educational programs in question.

Knox (1993) refers to a cooperative venture (including those in both C-6 and C-10 categories) as a *synergism*, a program carried out jointly by two or more entities whose effect is greater than would be the sum of actions taken separately. He argues that such problem areas as continuing professional education, rural development, and community problem solving are so complex that they require the concerted efforts of the multiple institutions concerned with their solutions. In a monumental undertaking, he has collected and edited 175 case descriptions of such collaborative activities in thirty-two countries and has grouped these accounts into twelve clusters, each dealing with a problem area. After analyzing all of this experience, he identifies ten guidelines that should be used by adult educational leaders to strengthen their collaborative efforts.

Institutions, Associations, and Organizations

Since the next four categories all deal with institutions, it is useful to begin by making several distinctions concerning their basic nature and their typical pattern of growth. The term *institution* itself is used as an overall designation to mean any comparatively stable, formally—and often intricately—structured body of persons that carries out common purposes or advances common causes and whose members share a standardized and complex system of habits, attitudes, and material facilities. Institutions of adult education have countless structural patterns but usually can be classified as either associations or organizations in terms of their allocation of function, the flow of power within them, and the intended beneficiaries of their services.

An association is a complexly structured body of members who join together, more or less freely, because of a shared interest, activity, or purpose and who, by the act of joining, assume the same basic powers and responsibilities held by other members. This collective membership elects its officers, thereby giving them some degree of temporary authority. Sometimes this upward delegation is carried out at several political levels. Thus a large association may have local, county, district, state, regional, and national decision-making bodies. An association usually has its own members as its beneficiaries. It is distinguished from a group largely by its size and complexity and may in fact be a constellation of groups. It cannot maintain direct interaction among all its members. Instead it must create an interlocking system of roles and relationships, often of a complex sort.

An organization is a body of people who work together to achieve a common purpose and whose internal structure is characterized by a hierarchical flow of authority and responsibility from the top downward. There are relatively permanent (rather than periodically rotating) occupants of the seats of power who, when replaced, are ordinarily designated from above rather than from below. The basic authority of the organization may be derived from the general public, from stockholders or other owners, or from a self-perpetuating board, but its visible exercise is in the hands of a layered succession of policy makers and administrators. Organizations ordinarily exist to benefit their owners, a defined clientele outside their own membership, or the public at large.

An association or an organization is seldom found in a pure form, for each type tends to evolve toward the other. As an association grows in size, it creates a bureaucracy that may in time achieve dominance in both policy and its execution, though paying lip service to the all-encompassing power of the membership. An organization is often greatly influenced by the associations that enter intimately into the exercise of its power. A university has its academic senate and its student and alumni associations. Industry and government must deal directly with unions, professional societies, and employee groups. But though there are few pure examples of either an association or an organization, both are essentially different models for the exercise of power. In analyzing or dealing with any particular institution, it is thus important to know how the two different forms are mixed in its composition, which is dominant, and how each is tempered by the other.

Since many institutions, particularly public ones, are organized in a complex and interlocking fashion, it is often hard to define their boundaries. The term *institution* could be applied, for example, to any of the following entities of what is essentially an interwoven system: the government of a state, its legislative branch, the state university system, the land-grant university, the college of agriculture, the agricultural extension service, the statewide group of field agents, or the staff of a county extension program. In practice, those who design a program, operate it, or analyze it usually concentrate on whatever level of structure they believe to be most relevant to their actions, meanwhile taking account of the influence of the larger systems of which it is a part and the subsystems that make up its internal structure.

The founders and supporters of an association or organization usually believe it to be wholly unique. They are concerned chiefly with the immediate social and physical environments in which they work and with their own personalities, interactions, and processes. But while every institution is in some respect like no other, students of organizational theory and practice have found a number of patterns and classifications that are useful in analyzing particular instances of institutional creation and growth.

In testing this point, William S. Griffith studied five dissimilar adult educational institutions: the Great Books Foundation, a suburban evening school, the educational activities of a central-city YMCA, the educational department of an international trade union, and the correspondence division of a university. Using a general growth model proposed by Herbert Thelen, Griffith established the fact that these five institutions all passed through the same stages, though sometimes going back and forth among them and sometimes, with a new surge of life, repeating the sequence of steps.

This growth model has six stages, which can only be sketched here. (1) "A 'sense of issue' develops in a potential leader or leaders who feel that a strain in an existing system is not being reduced satisfactorily in the conventional, routine operating procedures." (2) The leaders are supplemented by the addition of other people and become a larger group that refines its objectives and develops a means of reducing the strain: "Decisions, both firm and tentative, are made concerning the structure, functions, and methods of the new institution." (3) The institution comes into being and has its "first working interactions with the clientele and the environment. . . . As a result of the decisions made at this stage the institution may be said to acquire the beginnings of a 'personality' which includes . . . the generalized images held by those who work within it." (4) The institution expands at an accelerating rate, and its program "is focused upon the successfully proven combination which produces a channeling of interest and resources and the productive utilization of resources that had been engaged in testing previously." (5) For any one of a number of internal or external reasons, a strain sets in. Compensatory adjustments are made, and some growth continues; "but when structural adjustments are no longer made and growth effectively ceases, the institution is mature." (6) The institution "comes into a fairly steady state in which a constant level of input and output is maintained. . . . The functioning is at that level which is adapted to the established structure, functions and methods of the institution in a particular environment. The personnel direct their efforts toward increasing the efficiency of each of the operating segments and may lose sight of the cosmic *raison d'etre*" (1965, pp. 139–142).

At every stage of its development, those responsible for an institution must pay attention not merely to its program but also to its pattern of administration. The two constantly overlap, since the objectives, format, external relationships, and measurement of results of an educational activity are never separable from the staffing, budgeting, and reporting processes required to undertake it. Yet in practice a distinction is often made between a program staff and an administrative staff. In some cases, a whole institution becomes bureaucratized into many interlocking units. Those who deal with various components, such as the provision of resources, the selection of leaders, interpretation, or finance, develop a sufficient tradition, size, or complexity of interacting operation so that each administrative unit develops a purpose and structure of its own distinct from that of the organization or association itself. The maintenance of one part of the system becomes the chief end of the people concerned with it, however much they may cloak that goal by using the rhetoric of service. As a result, the institution achieves a steady state that may be difficult to change.

The same result can be brought about when the program becomes unalterable. Even inspired administration can then do little to change the situation. One national association with adult education as a central purpose has maintained for years a membership of between 39,000 and 40,000, though its program invites the participation of all adult males. It is richly financed and has a large and skillful staff that has worked out refined administrative procedures and is innovative in trying new promotional practices. Yet unceasing effort can do no more than to keep the size of the membership stable, replacing those who drop out each year with an equal number of recruits. The reason for this failure to grow is clearly that the basic design of the program was "perfected" long ago and a conservative board refuses either to alter any element of it or to add new activities that might increase the membership.

The growth cycle of associations and organizations gives rise to many situations, but only the most common categories will be dealt with here.

C-7: Creating an Educational Institution

Adult educational institutions are constantly being created—by the government, by industrial and business corporations, by profit-minded proprietors, by people with a cause or those enamored of a solution to a social problem, and by countless others who seek to learn or to teach. Sometimes these institutions are wholly new in form; more often they are imitations or adaptations of existing structures. Their sponsors usually hope they will become enduring parts of the social fabric, and occasionally this hope is realized. For the most part, however, their life is relatively brief; they come into existence, survive as long as they are sustained by hope or need, and then disappear. The creation of institutions also occurs in elementary, secondary, and higher education but with nothing like the frequency that it does in adult education.

Perhaps the most dramatic and consequential adult educational institution created in the last half of the twentieth century was the Open University of the United Kingdom, proposed in 1963 and opened in 1968. While it used many forms of instruction, linked together with increasing skill, its activities were most conspicuously carried out by the electronic media. A description of its origins and early growth was provided by Perry (1977), its first chief administrator, who was later elevated to the peerage as a recognition of his efforts. Many other countries around the world almost immediately created institutions based on the same general principles and practices as those used in the British prototype. A summary account of this movement is provided by Rumble and Harry (1982).

In a relatively few cases of which the original Open University was one, the creators of an adult educational institution have substantial freedom to design it in any way they choose. A sponsoring group may decide that its community needs a new cultural resource and make whatever plans for it they like, or a foundation may be created by an endowment of funds that imposes no limitations on those who administer them. Most states have laws and regulations governing the nature and operation of various kinds of institutions; but once these broad requirements are met, the founders need only consult their own sense of what is appropriate and design whatever mix of components seems best to them.

Usually, however, the planning for a new institution is anchored by the acceptance of one or more components as being unalterable.

The scarcity of money may impose limitations. The desire of the founders to remedy the wrongs or inadequacies of an existing social system may restrict them to the selection of certain goals. Personal capacities or resources may set limits to the format, as happens when the founders want to be the leaders themselves, to employ a method they favor, or to spend funds for already-defined purposes. When the controlling desire is to replicate or adapt an existing institution, a fairly complete model of the proposed activity is already in existence. Thus a community group that decides to establish a museum has by defining that goal identified the major components of its program.

Freedom to choose may be further limited when new recruits to the cause are found, since they will have their own ideas about what is to be accomplished and by what means. The sponsors of a new public library may win support from the Chamber of Commerce by agreeing to stress industrial and technological books and from a local film society by promising to have an audiovisual service. While such alliances as these help make an institution possible, they influence the distinctive pattern that it evolves and that it may never subsequently be able to change.

Despite initial limitations, the range of choices open to the founders of an organization or association is usually greater than that available to their successors, who will always have to deal with both the tangible and the intangible legacies of its past. Therefore those founders should think through their program very carefully, considering each of its components and making choices that reflect the best available judgment as to what is required for initial success. The elements that must be accepted as unalterable can then be combined as effectively as possible with those in which freedom of choice is present.

It is also useful for the founders to retain an experimental approach, for the program will seldom work out exactly as planned. Early calculations, however expertly made, will be faulty in some respects. New staff members will want changes to be made, as will the people served. The social system that the institution enters will have aspects not taken adequately into account in advance calculations. Unexpected opportunities and resistances must both be coped with, and counterinfluences created by the program's presence must be met. One sector of the program may flourish and another wither, requiring a rebalancing of the total service. As time goes on, the social and physical environment will change, sometimes as a result of the program's success. These and other internal and external factors require that constant change in the design be contemplated. However steadfast of purpose the founders may be, they need to be as pragmatic as possible concerning the format of the services they provide and the way by which those services are fitted into the larger patterns of life of the society.

A growing modern sophistication about institutional growth models has led many founders of organizations and associations to be concerned with the rigidity of form and function that they often display. Occasionally programs are planned to have only a limited life because self-destruction is thought to be preferable to inevitable staleness; thus a legislative act creating a new service may limit its funding to a short period of years. Alternatively mechanisms or procedures are devised to aid creativity. Among them are the deliberate seeking out of innovative staff members, the provision for a periodical review of the program, the creation of a special staff freed of operational responsibility so that it can constantly plan for the future, and the engaging of consultants to provide independent critiques. These and other devices can be helpful, but only if they are consciously and continuously used by institutional managers. Innovativeness is the product of human thought and can never become automatic.

C-8: Designing a New Institutional Format

An institution's total program usually becomes established as a relatively limited number of accepted formats. For instance, a university extension division may maintain off-campus centers, a conference and institute staff, a correspondence division, and a lecture bureau; and its customary planning is entirely devoted to these four kinds of activity. Then the prospect may arise of a new kind of service, perhaps the creation of television programs, the development of a special baccalaureate degree sequence, or the local sponsorship of a national project. In any such case, the policymakers and administrators of the institution must ponder the new format, not merely thinking about it as a different kind of activity but also considering how it might be fitted into the aggregate of the present patterns of service.

An institution may add a new format for any of a number of reasons, among which the most common are to respond to an expressed desire or demand, to meet a need perceived by the staff, to capitalize on past experience by using a new approach to a continuing goal, to provide itself with a broader base of service than before in order to spread opportunity or risk, or to take advantage of resources made available to it. Sometimes the decision to go into the new activity is swiftly made and executed. Sometimes it is reached only after long and agonizing consultation, which may involve a debate between those who want to remain true to the traditions of the past and those who insist that the demands of society or the needs of the institution require a broadening of scope. The strain is usually felt most keenly when an institution that has always specialized on one format adds a second one. A broadly generalized institution has less of a problem; if it already uses ten formats, it can fairly readily add an eleventh.

While a new pattern of service should always be examined on its own terms, it will be influenced at every point by the nature of the sponsoring institution and of the other educational activities it maintains. Sometimes the institution is not centrally concerned with education, as was the case with the Fifth Army training activities described in Chapter Three, in which an academic program was strongly conditioned by the system of military control in which it was operated. In predominantly educational institutions, the staff draws on its past experience in designing the new format and usually tries to make it complement or supplement the existing pattern of services. In a sense, the distinctive difference between C-8 situations and those in other categories is the influence of the history of the sponsoring association or organization on the design of a new format.

The creation of a pattern of service can also cause profound changes within the institution itself. When it adds the new kind of activity, its administrators usually hope not merely to meet individual and social needs but also to reap such advantages as may come from greater financial and material resources, a larger staff, a better balance of programs, and more adequate ways to take advantage of equipment, public relations, and other methods of facilitation and control. These gains may actually be achieved, but it is equally possible for losses to occur. Resources may not grow as expected so that the costs of the new format must be borne by the well-established programs. Long-time clients may be alienated, or alternatively their shift to the new activity may hurt the old ones, thereby providing no net gain in service. New staff members may be incompatible with existing ones. For these and other reasons, the institution may be weakened, not strengthened, by its larger responsibility.

A new format also alters the overall image of the institution held by those outside it, and that change may have either positive or negative consequences. When a community college that has offered only degree sequences begins to sponsor noncredit special interest courses, its image changes in the eyes of both the continuing clientele and the people it seeks to attract. Occasionally this change may pose such a threat that a manager goes to great lengths to avoid it. Thus the proprietor of a specialized correspondence school who adds a new program may pretend to the public that he is creating a separate institution when he is actually only broadening the base of the old one.

The risk of a C-8 situation can be minimized to some degree by developing and testing model programs, each with its own combination of design components. Only when an effective pattern is devised is it put into full-scale operation. Mr. Heylin used this procedure in the Fifth Army program. While the preliminary testing of formats can also be employed in the other categories, it is particularly suited to those in C-8, which offers the opportunity for an institution to provide the shelter and support of its existing resources for the development of the new pattern of work.

C-9: Designing New Activities in Established Formats

Within the established formats of an institution, a constant inventiveness of new program ideas is usually required. For example, a local council on world affairs may have adequate staff and resources to administer about fifteen short courses, three weekend conferences, seven foreign tours, ten luncheon sessions, and fifty meetings with special groups. Some of these can be repeats of earlier offerings, but most of them must be planned afresh each year if the council is to keep up to date with current developments. Other agencies, such as evening schools or community colleges, may be able to build up a large percentage of staples, but each year some of them will lose their power to attract or to serve and must be replaced. The innovations constitute the essential growing edge of the institution's service.

The rapid national growth of adult education in recent years is attributable in large measure to the success of people in C-9 situations in identifying new needs and shaping programs to meet them. Usually the ideas come forward spontaneously and from many sources. The staff of the institution knows that its future depends in part on creativity and therefore keeps on the alert for potential programs. The members of an association put forward their ideas about what should be done. The students of an organization have proposals to make. And the outside community or constituency also presents its requests. Many come in fortuitously, or, as the phrase has it, over the transom. Others result from systematic outside contacts made by the staff and the canvassing of potential funding sources. In fact, the administrators of a successful institution may need to do little creative thinking themselves but merely select the most promising activities that are brought to their attention.

In most cases, however, it is necessary to supplement chance and good fortune by a systematic effort to be creative, using as many approaches as possible to stimulate the ideas of the planners. Among the most frequently used such approaches are those in the four following groups, here cast in the form of questions that such planners might ask themselves. While these questions are most relevant to C-9 situations, many of them can be used (either as they are now phrased or as revised slightly) in each of the other ten program-development categories.

First, some leads to new programs come from within the institution itself. How can the principles that have made it successful in the past be applied in a new time or a new setting? What successful designs can be recast to meet different objectives? What are the logical points of extension of present programs? What institutional objectives are not now being adequately achieved? What topics of interest are being raised in association meetings that are not being adequately dealt with? What information can counselors provide about topics being raised in the interviews they conduct? What requests for service are unmet? What could be learned by questionnaires or systematic interviews of members or clients?

Second, some ideas for programs arise from the availability of a component or components on which a design can be built. What potential leaders, physical facilities, or resources are available but are not being used? Would some medium of public interpretation (such as a newspaper, a ministerial association, or a radio or television station) be interested in helping achieve a community-based goal?

Third, some programs can be borrowed or adapted from other institutions. Are institutions like ours doing interesting things elsewhere? Can we create our own version of a program that is successful in institutions unlike ours? Can we borrow program ideas from other cultures or subcultures? (American, British, and Scandinavian educators of adults have done much borrowing from one another.) Are schools, colleges, and universities maintaining programs for young people that should also be made available to adults? Are there associations of potential students that we should cultivate? Are there other adult educational institutions with which we might cosponsor programs?

Fourth, some sources of innovativeness are to be found within the community or constituency served. Are there special clienteles we should reach and, if so, how? Are there social needs that should be met? Can we discover and get the advice of innovative men and women who generally tend to be ahead of other people in their interests? Are there topics that seem to be of increasing concern in the community? Are there widely discussed issues on which we can base programs before the present interest disappears? Could we learn anything from interviews with community leaders or other informants? Should we have continuing program-finding relationships with consultants, advisers, or advisory committees?

By asking such questions as these, administrators may be stimulated to have many ideas for programs that can be fitted into their service formats. These ideas can then be sifted to see which seem to be the most feasible. In doing so, it is useful to sketch out quickly in advance the way in which the various components might be handled in shaping each proposed design. Some institutions even use planning forms or checklists similar to those mentioned under C-5 in which the pattern of a proposed activity may be quickly outlined. If there are a number of alternatives, the decision can be made as to which potential programs appear on balance to offer the greatest opportunities for fulfilling the institution's objectives.

In C-9 situations, the task of program planning is often divided among the various levels of the administrative hierarchy. Thus the director of an industrial training unit may identify a proposed activity, choose its instructor, and fit it into the scheduling, guidance, financial, and interpretational framework of the institution. The instructor then does the rest of the planning, sometimes alone and sometimes with the advice of the administrator or other staff members. Complex institutions could not be operated without such division of authority, which may be guided by conventional practice or by agreements reached by the parties concerned. As with all divisions of authority, conflicts and misunderstandings occasionally arise, a fact that often makes necessary some revision of plans in the course of their execution.

C-10: Collaborative Institutional Planning

Adult education, unlike earlier schooling, cannot be viewed in terms of the work of a few dominant institutions. Therefore one important effort in creating the total service that should be provided by the field as a whole is the development of collaborative institutional planning. If the argument of this book is correct, the associations and organizations involved use the same fundamental system of program creation and analysis and therefore have much to learn from one another's experience. They all serve the same broad clientele, the men and women of the community, and could provide far better service than at present if they could devise ways of eliminating gaps and duplications of program, reinforcing one another's endeavors, and seeking out and meeting jointly the needs which no single institution can adequately handle. As noted above, Knox (1993) has analyzed 175 such ventures in thirty-two countries; he argues that adult educators can never hope to solve their major problems without synergistic effort.

The problem of coordination is essentially that of bringing independent and often diverse institutions together so that they may interrelate their activities in a harmonious fashion. This task is never easy, as the work of the United Nations demonstrates, but it is capable of being undertaken with some success by those who genuinely seek to develop more comprehensive service than can ever be achieved by piecemeal institutional planning. The social welfare field with its councils of social agencies, its community funds, and its extensive involvement of both professional and citizen leaders has gone further in this respect than other kinds of communitywide service (such as health, culture, recreation, and adult education), though it still has major problems to confront. All such endeavors have essentially the same need to find ways to broaden their scope and coverage of program. This need is particularly strong in adult education since it is so often a partial, peripheral, or supportive function of the institutions that maintain it. But it is equally true that the educators of adults have a special need to establish joint relationships outside their institutions in order to reinforce their work within them.

Collaboration can take countless forms, but they can be analyzed in terms of a few basic dimensions. One of these has to do with the number of parties involved. In multilateral coordination, such as that undertaken by an adult education council, the institutions involved take a general and comprehensive approach, usually governed by an overall parliamentary body that follows the practices of representative democracy. In bilateral coordination, such as that undertaken by the extension divisions of two neighboring universities, there is direct confrontation by each organization of the other in an effort to bring their programs into harmony or to reinforce one another's efforts. In unilateral coordination, such as occurs when a public library undertakes to supply books and other resources for the educational activities of all community agencies, one institution sets itself the task of reinforcing the work of others.

Another dimension has to do with the contribution made by the parties involved. Sometimes institutions facilitate each other's work; they refer students, they promote programs, they support bills in the legislature or representations to government authorities, or they find other ways of offering assistance. Sometimes institutions complement the work of others by blending together dissimilar activities; a community college may provide physical facilities for other institutions and associations, an art museum may create a special display to illustrate the work in art history at a university, and a county agent may circulate books for the regional public library. Sometimes institutions undertake joint sponsorship of activities; several citizen associations may develop a statewide study-action program, two universities may support a leader-training institute, or a number of institutions may support a television channel.

Still another dimension has to do with the complexity of the interaction. Here it is useful to think of a continuum ranging from simple to comprehensive interrelationships between two or more institutions. Thus the public school and public library systems in a city might agree only to hold a meeting at which key staff members of both might learn about each other's programs. At the other extreme, the two systems might work out a wholly coordinated effort from top to bottom, with both the central staffs and the neighborhood schools and libraries in close and continuing contact with one another and with much use of contracts for service, joint appointments, problem-solving committees, liaison officers, or other collaborative mechanisms and practices.

Any form of coordination, no matter what its specific dimensions, may be initiated by the institutions themselves or result from the application of external pressure. Ideally there should be a desire to work together or at least a lack of antagonism toward the idea. In some places, however, long-standing apathy, ancient quarrels, or a spirit of separatist empire building keep apart the people who could work together fruitfully. So long as such conditions prevail, no readily apparent way can be found to reduce indifference or antagonism so as to prepare the ground for positive cooperation. In such cases, the major hope for comprehensive service must rest on some outside development, such as a pressing social need, the demand made by a governmental body, or the rapid rise of a new institution that compels existing ones to rally together for mutual defense.

In all C-10 situations, the individuals or groups involved in planning confront one another in new ways that require them to transcend accustomed habits of work and to rise above parochial loyalties. Each adult educational institution builds its own routines, special language, and procedural dogmas; and this superficial distinctiveness tends to make it feel wholly unique. The difficulties of collaboration can be lessened by the use of a generalized system of program planning. When people move through the decision points of a system such as the one presented in this book, they turn their attention away from themselves and their separateness toward the task they hope to accomplish and the community of interest that they all feel. This approach reinforces the desire to cooperate and thereby strengthens the program that is produced. The representatives of each institution are also provided with a new vantage point for examining and improving its individual efforts.

Administrative considerations influence both the planning and the execution of C-10 situations, particularly when the new interrelationship is a complex one, requiring the working out of many staffing, material, and financial arrangements at several levels of diverse hierarchies. The basic decision to consider collaboration must be made by the policy shapers of each institution, and each one brings to the planning table its own structure and administrative code that set preconditioning frameworks for everything that follows. Thus questions of administration both precede and accompany program planning.

Each of the constituent agencies must usually invest resources in a coordinative program that it would otherwise have available for its own purposes. It is therefore essential that the planning process involve people with sufficient authority to commit their own organizations or associations to the decisions that must be made in sponsoring the new program. Failing such involvement, the planners must have immediate access to the people who can make the necessary decisions. Also, since the staff of each institution is oriented to its specific purposes, the planning group may include people who are not immediately involved with any of the collaborating parties but can focus directly on the program itself as a new endeavor. Lay citizens, acting as spokesmen for the whole community, can often serve very effectively in this role.

C-11: Mass Education

The essential characteristic of any mass educational situation is that the individualities of the learners remain unknown to those who conduct the instruction. This situation is equally true of a lecturer to a large audience, the author of a book, the designer of a radio or television program, the creator of an exhibit, the sponsor of a sequence of videotaped university-level courses, or the team putting together a CD-ROM disk. In most such cases, the program is designed to reach a generalized target audience, though, by the very nature of the communication process used, many other kinds of persons will be reached.

Just as a C-1 situation can be planned and conducted only by learners, so a C-11 situation can be planned and conducted only by educators. They may seek to make their planning cooperative by questioning some members of their target audience. Yet even so, educators must ultimately guess who the learners will turn out to be. Once the activity has begun, its audience is likely to have only limited ways of interacting with the educator. Questions may be asked of a lecturer or telephoned in to a television panel show, and there may be some expression of the opinions of a few participants. But these devices can provide no more than an unscientific sample of the range of response to the program.

Throughout the history of modern adult education, determined efforts have been made to supplement mass instruction by adding activities centered on individual learners. Examples of such efforts are reading circles, radio listening groups, telephone call-in systems, buzz groups, and various approaches collectively called interactive television. Ordinarily such ventures fit better into one of the other categories than they do into C-11. For example, the mass media open up great new resources for independent study (C-1), and reading circles are learning groups (C-3).

In this connection, it should be noted that in some of the other categories program components can become so generalized as to create a C-11 situation. A correspondence course (C-2) can degenerate into a mere series of readings with no interaction between instructor and student. A teacher of a class (C-4) can lose sight of the individuals present and treat them as a group of types, not as real people. Institutional settings are often prone to impersonality of approach, leading those who think about these learners to do so in terms of charts and diagrams. In such cases, the full potentiality for learning inherent in the situation is not realized, and the result is a loss of effectiveness.

So far as periods of learning are concerned, C-11 situations are more often acts than episodes, series, or aggregates. To be sure, radio and television courses, integrated series of readings and lectures, related exhibits, and many other formats are undertaken with the aim of providing more learning than can be accomplished by a single act. Yet realists know that the continuity of contact with learners is almost always far less than the designer of the program hopes it will be for several reasons: the absence of group cohesiveness or discipline, an impersonal relationship between educator and learner, the distractions of the home or work settings in which much mass learning occurs, the tendency of many learners to sample a mass activity with no intention of continuing to do so, and the problems of adjustment required by fixed and demanding schedules. These difficulties are so great that mass educators often try to design each act to be as separately educative as possible, while still linking it to the other acts in the episode or series of which it is a part.

While a C-11 activity is designed in the same way as those of any other category, many of the components must be treated in a special way. In order to overcome the impersonality of the approach and the lack of small-group facilitation, mass programs often mix noneducational with educational goals; efforts are made to amuse, to entertain, or to be topical as well as to stimulate learning. The role of the leader is stylized; even when that person uses an intimate and informal approach, both he or she and the audience know that no actual intimacy of contact exists. The measurement of results is usually gauged by size of audience, warmth of applause, samples of opinion, or ratings that estimate the number of participants. Social reinforcement can be attempted when people are physically present, but it is difficult or impossible to achieve in other situations. Guidance and the fitting of the activity into a total life-style must usually be left to the discretion of the learner, though attention to such matters as scheduling and finance may set an activity at a time when it is thought to be most convenient and least costly. Interpretation both within the activity itself and in its reinforcing public relations may help learners decide whether or not they wish to take part.

New methods of communication have always presented both opportunities and threats to established ways of life, but it appears that the changes occurring in the 1990s will bring challenges of a new order of magnitude. Massive competing plans are being made to redesign communication, using in new ways such devices as telephones, computers, television, laser disks, radio, facsimile transmitters, the almost inconceivable resources of the internet and other instruments not yet perfected, such as computerized systems of virtual reality. These changes will profoundly influence the number and variety of resources for adult learning.

Each innovation must be accepted on its own terms, and one of the major learning tasks for adult educators in the future must be the mastery of new theories of communication and the ways by which they are put into practice. Many of these innovations will be extremely difficult to understand; some of them, despite great early promise, will not be able to meet the challenges of practical operation. The course of a new mass medium is impossible to predict. Some earlier forms presented with great fanfare have not filled their promised potential: the player piano did not greatly enlarge the realm of musical performance; the teaching machine was overtaken by the computer; and the highly anticipated stop-action feature of the educational motion picture was never designed into either machines or films. In other cases, new media reinforce earlier ones, the best example being books. Ever since radio was introduced, each new form of communication has been accompanied by the confident prediction that it would cause reading to decline. Meanwhile the number of published titles has steadily increased, libraries are being built all over the country, and superstores for books are flourishing.

It seems clear that the mastery of the new technology will force adult educators to confront many challenges. But if they continue to define their practical expertise in terms of their ability to apply a system of programmatic decision points—accepting the inherent nature of any innovation but exploring all the possibilities of choice still left open—they will best meet the challenge of shaping a sound new educational system.

Selection and Use of Categories

The eleven categories do not include all the situations in which education can be planned or analyzed, though they do identify those most commonly found in practice. Nor is the differentiation between categories always clear, for some situations lie in shadowy zones where one category merges into another and where arbitrary decision may be necessary for precise placement. But if the definition of the general outline and independent form of the eleven categories is accurate, they provide a basis for decision and action, thereby helping to make concrete the theory and practice of adult education.

It often happens that the designer of a program can work within only one category. Sometimes this limitation is imposed by the goal; the desire to have people learn how to participate in group decision making requires the use of C-3. In other cases, situational factors compel category selection. Learners may have to guide their own education because they can find no tutor, group, or teacher. A television station is required by the dictates of its method to operate in the C-11 category.

Where the possibility of choice exists, the person making the selection must balance the situational factors to see which category is most suitable. The director of an evening college may wish to inform the people of her community about urban problems. Should she use the group-discussion approach (C-3), formal classwork (C-4), a conference (C-5), an all-community effort (C-10), or a lecture series (C-11)? In making her choice, she must take into account how specific goals will be influenced by each of the available categories and also how well her resources permit her to undertake the possible designs.

Many tensions arise when those involved in a program disagree as to its basic category. If a small group plans a program paying chief attention to its own interests (C-3) when it should really be considering those of a larger group (C-5), the resulting activity is almost certain to reveal strains and disagreements. Similarly, if one staff member believes he is suggesting a new activity in an established format (C-9) but his colleagues believe he is proposing a wholly different kind of activity (C-8), conflict is likely to result. It sometimes happens that even when there is surface agreement as to the category being used, its actual practice is subverted by a covert use of another one. The members of a group may feel that its leader, whether she knows it or not, is using the force of her position or personality to manipulate the discussion to reach predetermined decisions and therefore is acting not in a C-3 but in a C-4 fashion. In any of these cases, difficulties can be remediated only by resolving the indecision over which category is dominant. If there is a shift in category (such as when a group becomes a class or vice versa), that fact should also be clear and acceptable to all concerned.

The use of the categories helps to solve one of the most critical conceptual difficulties of adult education. Even those people who have long believed that the field is crucially important to the realization of mankind's potential have realized that its breadth has led to diffuseness of approach. If men and women learn in countless situations in all aspects of their lives, either alone or with some kind of guidance, it becomes hard to grasp the scope of adult education and difficult to guide and direct it. But if the situations in which it occurs can be reduced to a manageable number of prototypes, vagueness and generality of approach can be replaced by a sophisticated conception of form and structure that gives some unity to the field despite its institutional divisions, makes possible distinctions leading toward harmony and away from disagreement, and provides the basis for practical accomplishment. Educators who become aware of the variety of categories in which they can operate have taken a major step toward becoming masters of their fields; learners who understand the options open to them are helped to choose wisely.

5

. . . .

Development of Program Design

The intellectual life of man consists almost wholly in
his substitution of a conceptual order for the perceptual
order in which his experience originally comes. . . .
Had we no concepts we should live simply "getting"
each successive moment of experience, as the sessile
sea-anemone on its rock receives whatever nourishment
the wash of the waves may bring. With concepts we
go in quest of the absent, meet the remote, actively
turn this way or that, bend our experience, and make
it tell us whither it is bound. We change its order,
run it backwards, bring far bits together and separate
near bits, jump about over its surface instead of
plowing through its continuity, string its items on as
many ideal programs as our mind can frame. . . .
We harness perceptual reality in concepts in order to
drive it better to our ends.
—William James, *Some Problems of Philosophy*

The themes explored in this chapter have long been central to the theory and practice of education. Most of the literature concerned with the science and art of pedagogy (and of andragogy, if it be accepted as a separate field of study) is made up of analyses of exquisitely refined topics, each of which is somewhere within the compass of an enormous and complex body of knowledge. This diversification both inhibits and makes necessary some integrating synthesis that can bring coherence to what would otherwise be a shapeless body of facts and principles. The emphasis here therefore is upon the establishment of a symmetry of thought and action, not upon a full treatment of each part of the learning-teaching process.

It is assumed, as was pointed out in Chapter Two, that this symmetry is to be found in the interconnection of coexisting components, none of which is invariably more fundamental than nor prior in time to the others. (It might be useful at this point for the reader to re-examine Figure 2.1.) As in Chapter Two, the series of decision points is here put in the order that experience has shown to be most readily understood. But in either designing or analyzing an educational program, the mind does not proceed in any established sequence but plays back and forth over all aspects of the process. As Robert Oppenheimer has suggested, "The unity of knowledge, long thought of as corresponding to a structure in which the foundation stones imply the whole, has today a very different topology: very much more than a temple, it is a network, as William James foresaw, with no central chamber, no basic truths from which all else will follow, but with a wonderful mutual relevance between its many branches, and with beauty illuminating the growing tips of knowledge, even in the most recondite and unfamiliar branches" (1963, p. 45).

In this chapter, each of the decision points will be considered only in a general way, attention being given primarily to defining terms and showing how components fit together. Those who want for either theoretical or practical reasons to extend their analysis of any one decision point will find it covered amply in the literature reviewed by Houle (1992) or more specifically as part of other general works on programming. Simerly (1990), for example, offers 172 suggestions for programming conferences and workshops. Caffarella (1994), while fitting decision points into a general nonlinear pattern, treats each one separately in a highly practical fashion, using checklists, diagrams, and case examples to illuminate each topic with which she deals. Nowlen (1988), in his study of continuing education for business and the professions, uses the same series of components presented in this book and gives his interpretation of each. And Cervero and Wilson (1994) show how program planners actually undertake the decision-making process.

Identifying Possible Educational Activity

The awareness that a learning activity might occur can arise from many sources and in many ways. It may be an extension of a previous action of the same kind. An experienced tutor talks with a potential client (C-2), a teacher contemplates the resumption of her work during a new term (C-4), or the staff of an institution considers new activities in an established format (C-9). The situation is often such that awareness of a possibility is followed almost automatically by a decision to take action. But, particularly in the education of adults, such an awareness may also arise in a context that makes a negative determination at least as likely and as wise as a positive one.

A potential activity may enter the consciousness of an individual as a result of either internal reflection or response to external events. As people think about themselves, they develop desires, grow dissatisfied with their lives, realize their lack of ability, see disparities between present and desired accomplishments, sense their needs to grow in capacity or usefulness, and distinguish in many other ways between what might be and what is. This self-knowledge may either precede the awareness of a possible learning program or be precipitated by it. Thus a poster describing a music appreciation course may create in a viewer a recognition of ignorance of that subject. External events can create needs, present challenges, or offer opportunities. A man has an accident and finds that a rehabilitation program would help him recover. A marriage fails, and both parties seek to find out why. A woman has an increase in salary that permits her to fulfill a long-standing interest. Almost any event of life, whether it enlarges or limits the range of potential action, can give rise to a recognition of the possibility of learning.

As with individuals, so it is with groups. During a social conversation, in a meeting of a club, at a conference between a worker and supervisor, or in any other form of direct human association, the potentiality of a learning activity may arise from a consideration of the interests and needs of the participants themselves, of some body of potential learners, or of society as a whole. This possibility may grow from an initial suggestion made by one of the persons concerned or may emerge from the interaction and stimulation of a discussion, as several approaches and notions are considered.

People vary greatly in their receptiveness to the idea of education. The threshold of awareness of the value of learning differs from one individual to another. One woman may be so conditioned by past experience that study is an ever-ready option in her mind, while another woman may never consider it for herself or even be aware that it is a possible way of meeting the challenges that confront her. The threshold also varies from one situation to another; thus a businessperson or a farmer may frequently consider education as a way of refining his or her capacity to carry out work while never thinking of it as a way toward a better family, community, or recreational life.

The idea of learning or of teaching may be born with or without marked emotional overtones. Some theories of adult education have been based on a conception of needs or interests that implies the existence of either tension or pleasure. It is true that the facing of a *need* (if that term is understood as a lack of some necessary or desirable good) may have an aura of grim necessity and therefore be unpleasant, whereas the opportunity to engage in an interesting activity may be accompanied by a feeling of keen enjoyment. In either case, emotion can lead to fruitful action. It can also prevent it. Too negative a feeling creates immobility or an inability to learn, even as too positive a feeling prevents the establishment of the discipline usually required by any worthwhile educational activity. But experienced observation suggests that strong emotions are not essential to the undertaking of learning. It is possible to decide coolly and rationally about participation in an educational activity.

Deciding to Proceed

The decision about proceeding with an educational activity may flow directly from the awareness of its existence. A group is formed, a man is asked to join it, and he says yes or no at once. But in other cases, an element of judgment enters in. A choice among alternative programs may require that their relative merits must be weighed. Even when a decision is focused on the acceptance or rejection of a single opportunity, some consideration may need to be given to it if the persons concerned are to avoid either an unrewarding venture or a missed opportunity.

In most of the cases in which a decision is called for, it is negative. Certainly this assertion is true if awareness means simply a casual consideration of a wide range of possible actions such as occurs when someone leafs through a catalog, looks at mailed brochures, or scans announcements or advertisements in the mass media. Similarly a tutor may reject a client, a cluster of people may choose not to form a learning group, and a teacher may decide not to offer a course. Momentary regret may be felt at the negativeness of the decision, but it is usually tempered by the belief that the regret would be greater if the activity were undertaken.

When the decision is positive, later experience sometimes shows that it was unwise. A learner embarks impulsively on a program of self-guided instruction, a student is registered in a course with no counseling as to its relevance for him, or a new institutional program is launched with an inadequate understanding of its potential audience. Rapidity of decision leads to many of the failures of adult education—the insecure, self-guided learners, the low retention rate of students, the waning enthusiasm of groups, the canceled courses and conferences, and the death of institutions. In some such cases, a negative initial decision would have been wise; in others, further thought about possibilities might have created better designs for learning.

The depth of analysis involved in making a decision varies greatly from one situation to another. An opportunity presented to an individual may require her or him only to accept or reject an established program. A man receives an invitation to a conference and, looking it over, sees that all the design components have already been arranged. In such a case, he needs only to consider whether he can accept the announced aims and fit the program into the pattern of his life. But the original decision to sponsor the conference may have required its planners to consider at length whether or not to proceed with it in terms of their knowledge of all the many components that would need to be blended in its design.

It is often necessary to review several alternative programs before a wise choice can be made. Thus when a new educational institution is to be created (C-7), several designs may be constructed so that a determination can be made as to which is best in the situation. Sometimes everything, including the goal itself, may be uncertain. A man may have only a generalized desire to learn and no clear purpose or pattern in his mind. Alone or with such counsel as he can secure, he must map out several possible courses of action and either choose the one that appears to be most appealing or discard the idea of study. Otherwise he will make a blind plunge into some activity and will be fortunate if the results happen to prove rewarding.

In many cases, it is helpful to ask whether a new program is really needed by the proposed learners. Queeney defines a *need* as "a discrepancy between an actual condition or state and a desired standard" (1995, p. 3). An enormous literature has grown up concerning the ways by which needs can be assessed and met; Queeney provides a comprehensive summary and analysis of it. Implicit in her discussion is awareness of the relevance of needs analysis to many of the other elements of the program-planning process.

The decision about proceeding is essentially a matter of subjective judgment, for it is impossible to demonstrate in advance that either a positive or a negative choice will be wise, considered either in its own terms or as the best of alternatives. Those who make the choice must try to consider all aspects of the situation and then on balance decide what to do. Both facts and feelings must usually be considered. Thus in a C-8 situation, the proponents of a new program may present data and arguments in support of their position, but its acceptance or rejection finally reflects the existence of many nuances of interpretation and emotional response apparent only to those aware of the intricacies of the situation.

In the application of judgment, particularly in institutional settings, it may be useful to have policies or principles to use as standards or guidelines. The staff of an agricultural extension service may wish to concentrate on serving commercial farmers, the staff of a general extension division may believe it should offer only work of university-level complexity and rigor, and the staff of a settlement house may choose to work with those people who have the fewest opportunities for progress open to them. Such principles as these may be carried by tradition and precedent, or they may be worked out into a set of codified policies. Their use can never be automatic, however, for discrimination is required in making the judgment as to whether or how a general rule applies in each new case.

Identifying and Refining Objectives

The identification of the objectives to be sought in the learning experience is usually a major step in designing or analyzing it. They have been inherent since it was first contemplated and have usually been somewhat clarified during the process of decision. Indeed, the very act of making a choice may establish the initial goals; for example, a group that decides to study a packaged course has, by that decision, indicated both broad and specific purposes. Usually, however, the planners of an activity must think carefully about what it is designed to achieve.

The shaping or analysis of objectives is never an easy task, since they are always at the heart of an activity, not on its surface.

Whether or not they are stated explicitly, they always give both focus and direction to the program. When put into words, they usually express a desire to achieve some such rational end—to teach illiterates to read and write, to help practicing surgeons acquire a new operating technique, to study modern poetry, or to confer on ways to reduce air pollution. Any learning activity is, however, a force field in which many other purposes than the professed goals are in operation, some leading to harmony, others to conflict.

The classroom, for instance, is a simple form of teaching and learning, but several discernible spheres of influence intersect within it. A teacher has ideals about the mastery of content that may not be achievable with the present class but still serve as guiding stars. She also has a point of view toward teaching that is consciously or unconsciously expressed in her performance, and she has personal purposes and motivations that influence her work. All students accept to some extent the aspiration, the instructional style, and the personal needs of the teacher, but they also have personal requirements and ambitions. Students may come to the classroom because of their ideals or because they want to learn whatever the teacher has to teach. But also they may be present for reasons that may seem extraneous to the formal purposes of instruction but that make participation meaningful for them. The course is also influenced by external forces. It may need to fit within the broader aims of a series of which it is a part, and it may be sponsored by an institution that has an overall purpose. Beyond such formal boundaries are the larger controls and expectations imposed by the sectors of influence in the encompassing society. As all these hopes and intentions blend in the classroom, the group generates and fulfills its pressures toward achievement.

This complexity of goals is present in all educational settings, but it is particularly evident in those designed for adults. Children or young people go to school essentially because it is their expected way of life. Their own feelings and intentions are often not focused on a particular activity but generalized to cover the whole curriculum.

Even their nonschool education may be compulsory, as every piano teacher knows. Some of the learning is specific and voluntary; their clubs, projects, and independent reading programs reflect their own concerns and interests. In society's view, however, such learning is peripheral to the main business of education carried on by schools and colleges. By contrast, adults ordinarily embark on a learning program because it has an immediate and direct meaning for them. Education is usually not their expected way of life; indeed, they may be hard pressed to find time for it. While compulsory or generalized adult educational programs exist (such as those in the armed services, industry, or formal evening schools or colleges), society's root conception of adult education is of specific learning freely undertaken with the intention of achieving clear-cut and definite objectives.

Three terms. In such learning, no matter in what situational category it occurs, three terms should be distinguished from one another. They are *motive, aspiration,* and *objective.* The three are not sharply different; they are sometimes identical, sometimes merged in practice, and always related; but they are analytically separate.

A motive is an inciting cause that helps to determine an individual's choice of an objective and behavior in seeking it. In any learning episode, it is possible to discern many motives, some more strongly held than others. The difference between announced objectives and motives can be demonstrated by asking adults why they take part in various kinds of courses. It would be generally assumed perhaps that enrollment in such groups of subjects as vocational education, religion, English, and practical nursing indicates that the aim in each case is to learn the indicated content, yet a national sampling survey shows that 13 percent of the people who enroll in vocational courses do so in order to meet new people, and 9 percent do so as a means of enjoying their spare time. Of those who take courses in religion, 19 percent do so in order to gain help in their everyday tasks and 17 percent to escape the daily routines of life. English is a highly utilitarian subject; 23 percent of those who enroll do so to prepare for a job, and 45 percent do so to help them with their present jobs. Practical nursing has a broader kind of appeal. Exactly the same number of people (21 percent) take it because they want to meet new people as take it in order to get help on a present job (Johnstone and Rivera, 1965, pp. 146–150). No similar studies have been made of the motives of educators, but observation suggests that they are not wholly concerned with a desire to convey a defined content. In the light of this distinction between announced objectives and motives, a great deal of the content-based discussion of educational aims seems narrow and limited.

An aspiration is a desired perfection or excellence based on an ideal. It exists only as a conception in the mind of either learner or educator. It may arise from such sources as carefully thought out philosophic positions, the expression of basic human needs, internalized cultural patterns of belief, or simple surface values derived from reflection or from interaction with other people.

An objective is an intended result of an educational activity. It does not exist until the decision is made to take action, and it is then the effect sought by that action. It is essentially different from an aspiration. The latter is a theoretical statement of what might or should be, the former is a practical end toward which actions are aimed. An aspiration is in fact two steps away from an objective. An individual, a group, or an institution may have an aspiration but contemplate no action. It may contemplate action but never take it. Or it may take it. Only in the third case does an objective come into being. A hunter sees a whole landscape full of possible targets, and he may consider shooting at several of them. But not until he points his rifle intending to fire does he have an aim. Similarly there are countless things that it might be good to understand, to appreciate, or to do; and one might contemplate learning many of them. Yet not until the process of learning is set in motion is an educational objective created.

Some attributes of objectives. The determination of objectives before, during, or after the learning process is a complex operation, particularly when an objective is defined in its fullest sense as being the actual intended result of learning, not merely the formal expression of that interaction. The task may become more manageable if several interrelated attributes of objectives, which follow from the definitions just given, are made clear.

An objective is essentially rational, being an attempt to impose a logical pattern on some of the activities of life. Only a zealot believes that all life can be reduced to a wholly charted existence. As Pascal said long ago, "The heart has its reasons which reason does not know"; people can never be certain about the wellsprings of their own behavior. Moreover, though planning may be exquisitely refined, it is impossible to devise a set of goals that will take care of all contingencies. Anybody who sets out on a voyage by land, sea, air, or in space identifies an ultimate destination and the way stations that lead to it but expects that events will arise that call for change in plans. Finally, no statement of aims can be completely comprehensive. Usually the planner or analyst of an activity can do no more than identify its major rational guides to action, leaving accepted but unstated the vast sea of motives, aspirations, and specific goals in the lives of those who undertake the educative process.

An objective is practical. It is neither an attempt to describe things as they should be nor an effort to probe to the underlying nature of reality. Such concerns as these are theoretical. In preparing for action, it may be useful to construct ethical, esthetic, or scientific systems, to define the nature of broad concepts, or to describe ideal patterns. An objective comes into being, however, only when a plan of action is devised to achieve some concretely defined change in a specific person or persons. The ultimate test of an objective is not validity but achievability.

Objectives lie at the end of actions designed to lead to them. Many good things in life are achieved by serendipity, but an objective is not merely the attainment of a fortunate outcome. It is the result of effort designed to bring it about and is always inextricably related to such effort in both theory and practice.

Objectives are usually pluralistic and require the use of judgment to provide a proper balance in their accomplishment. To learn a foreign language, for example, it is necessary to build vocabulary, to perfect pronunciation, and to understand and use grammatical construction. The teacher employs the limited time available to seek to achieve all three goals, allocating to each its proper share of emphasis. Sometimes objectives impose limits on one another. Thus a major American industrial firm has defined the goals of its training department as "the improvement of our business and the personal development of our people." The great majority of the company's educational activities can lead toward both ends. But in some cases, they may run counter to one another in their application. In any such case, the acceptance or rejection of a specific course of action can only be determined by the use of judgment.

Objectives are hierarchical. A broad educational purpose is made concrete by the provision of subordinate purposes that in turn are made even more definite by specific goals. It is possible to build an ordered statement of aims that runs from the broadest relevant purpose of an educational series to the specific and detailed identification of what is to be achieved in each minute of each act. The folklore of curriculum analysis contains accounts of such earnest young teachers as the one who prepared an outline of 2,728 objectives for the first semester of seventh-grade English. Ordinarily the identification of goals in this detail is not only wearisome but also uses up time better spent in learning or teaching. In practice, it is customary to identify the major purposes of an activity at two or three levels of analysis, leaving to the good sense of the participants the continuing determination of more specific goals.

Objectives are discriminative. By indicating one course of action, they rule out others. A public library staff that says that its function is to help people improve themselves can make such a statement meaningful only by making some further decisions. For example, it can have a "comprehensive" book-purchasing policy with the result that its coverage is so thin that nobody is served with any depth, or it can emphasize some areas of knowledge, thereby scanting others. Since means are almost always limited, the selection of one choice inhibits or denies the selection of others. In determining objectives it is therefore necessary to go beyond an identification of all the possible aspirations that might apply in the situation. The next and crucial step is to decide which ones will be operative in guiding further action. If selection is not made at the start, it will have to be done later by choice or default.

Objectives change during the learning process. In all situational categories, the beginning of action makes concrete what was formerly only potential. A young woman deciding to learn to play the violin begins with a romanticized view of her eventual level of accomplishment; her experienced tutor will have a different conception of what can be achieved. The hopes of both may change at the very first lesson and continue to do so as time goes on. The teacher in a classroom often has a carefully worked out set of objectives whose accomplishment can be measured by observable behavior and may hold fast to them to the very end of the course. Nevertheless they are only a skeletal framework of what is to be achieved, one representing neither the full range of possible goals nor the varied measure of achievement of the students. Practically speaking, the educator or learner thus needs to make an initial judgment about what the objectives should be but then be prepared to abandon some, add others, and change the emphasis of those retained.

Refinement of objectives. Now that objectives have been defined and described in detail, it is time to inquire how they may be chosen or identified in specific situations. In introducing this topic, it is useful to begin with some examples.

1.   The dean of a university evening college decides that his institution should try to improve directly the conditions of life in his city. Where is he to start? The topic of urban development broadens to include the major elements of modern culture and narrows to involve such persistent problems as the billowing smoke from factory chimneys, the crying child in the jungle of the slum,

and the sharp conflict at the frontier of racial expansion. In this milieu, many individuals and groups need education, but the dean's attention finally focuses on one target audience—the members of the various boards and commissions that control and manage the public and private health, welfare, recreational, and cultural agencies of the city. Such people learn whatever they know about discharging their functions only by the slow process of trial and error. But the dean knows that there are books on board structure and function and that a professor of social welfare at the university has specialized in this content. Both dean and professor believe deeply in the need for responsible citizenship, a view shared to varying degrees by the board members. So a new program of service is developed in which lectures, reading, and discussion are intermingled. Before very long, the professor discovers something she might well have known before but did not. Many of her students are present for other reasons than because they want to be of greater service to the city or to gain mastery of the content. They hope among other things to take part in a highly publicized community activity, to learn skills that will win the respect of others, to identify promising new members for boards that need them, or to become known to leaders who might choose them for such boards. Without ever identifying these motives openly, the professor shifts her procedures to allow them to be more fully achieved by the activities of the course. Some of the learners note meanwhile that the professor seems deferential to her more prominent students and make some judgments of their own about her motives.

The objectives of the course are therefore defined by the simultaneous interaction of six factors. The beginning point was the *milieu*, the city itself in its full social and physical context. The nature of the specific *learners* was identified next. The *content* existed; a body of developed knowledge was available and could be taught, and a *design* for teaching it could be devised. The *aspiration* was the achievement of responsible participation by citizen leaders, and the *motives* were the personal desires and hopes that led both learners and educators to take part. A change in any one of these key ingredients would have altered the goals of the program as well as its format.

These same factors determine the objectives of every adult educational program. The planner or the analyst may begin with any of them but employs each of the others in refining eventual goals. It may be useful to see how this process works by taking each one of the five latter factors as a beginning point for the following examples.

2.   The president of a club says, "When I retired from my job, I went through the usual period of disorientation, but it ended when I found some other fellows—professional men and managers—like myself who didn't know what to do with themselves. Some of us got together and set up this little club. We're all reasonably well fixed, and we live in the same part of town; we all belong to the country club. We decided that we didn't want to be a golden age club or a senior citizens' group or engage in artsy-craftsy kinds of things. We wanted challenge—to our minds and to our sense of independence. So we have a weekly lunch and afternoon at the club. Sure, we have fun and games in the late afternoon, but earlier there's always a serious part. Our program committee brings in a speaker who talks on something really serious; then we go after him and each other in a hammer-and-tongs discussion. It has worked out rather well. We have to make allowances for some of our members who aren't as serious as the rest of us, and some fellows are more interested than others in a given subject or lecturer. But taken by and large, we get along very well."

3.   At a sensitivity workshop, the director of a local welfare council becomes convinced that the use of a new theory of interpersonal relationship would vitalize the overly formal programs of the member agencies. With a grant from a local foundation, a series of residential weekends is set up at a vacation retreat with good food and recreational facilities, and a trainer from a nearby university is engaged. The staff members of the agencies are invited to apply, but a final selection is made on the basis of who seems to have the most

influence in the various programs. After the first weekend, the director has to suggest to the trainer that he play down his apparent desire to become a paid consultant to the agencies represented. As the
series proceeds, some of the more "practical" members of the group
have difficulty in understanding that the content of the course lies
in the acquisition of interpersonal skills rather than of a body of
knowledge. But each successive conference is better accepted by its
participants than the one before.

4.   A wealthy man dies, leaving his country estate and funds to
maintain it to a private university, with the sole stipulation that it
be turned into a residential conference center. Before accepting the
bequest, the university board asks the president to appoint a committee of faculty members and administrators to deal with the following questions: What would it cost to put the mansion in proper
condition to serve as an educational center? How many conferences
could be held there each year? What purposes should they serve?
Why should people want to come to them rather than taking regular courses in the evening? What faculty members and other
resource people would be available and interested in taking part in
the center's program? What conference topics would interest the
faculty? What kinds of people would attend? What could the university hope to achieve by operating such a center?

5.   "The ultimate best hope of mankind lies in building a better
understanding among the peoples of the world," concluded the
speaker at the annual Chamber of Commerce luncheon in a flourish of rhetoric. The unspoken response of most of his hearers was
that he had not uttered a highly original thought; but one listener,
the new president of the Chamber, took the idea seriously. The city
had an increasing number of companies engaged in foreign trade,
most of it in the European Community. What about setting up a
study group led by several industrial, commercial, and financial
experts who could go to Europe and observe matters firsthand, each
company paying the cost of its own representatives? The members
selected for the tour should be women and men who had an endur-

ing stake in the city's economic life and who would accept the responsibility to study and learn, though naturally a trip to Europe would lend spice to the idea for everyone. Would such a tour work out well? Why not try it to see?

6.   The West End Community Center, located in a markedly deprived neighborhood, had had some success in reaching children and older adults. Yet almost nobody between the ages of twenty-two and forty ever entered its doors. What are such people interested in? the director asked herself. Her answer was finding jobs, making a home, raising children, and getting established in the community. What could she do to help these young people become more fully participating citizens? Well, perhaps she could begin by persuading other community agencies to use the settlement's facilities. Would the Board of Education provide a literacy teacher? Would the Department of Health offer a well-baby clinic? Could a vocational counselor be found to teach young men and women how to present themselves more effectively to prospective employers? Should there be a family-planning center? Some of the activities suggested by these questions are inherently educative; others are facilitative services that might lead to education. Several approaches would need to be made simultaneously. The kinds of people to be reached are highly resistant to influence, and nobody knows what will appeal to them. So the director scheduled a series of exploratory meetings with the heads of other agencies.

In each of these six cases, the beginning point was different. In succession, it was a milieu, a group of learners, a body of content, a resource that required a certain kind of educational design, an aspiration, and a cluster of motives. But in each case, the initial factor was insufficient to establish the objectives; for that purpose, the other five were needed. In practice, it often happens that a statement of objectives is the expression of only one factor, most often an aspiration ("to achieve better interracial understanding"), a body of content ("to convey an appreciation of modern poetry"), or some component of an educational design ("to use the expertise of the university's faculty to help solve urban problems"). The making of such a statement assumes that others will know what he or she is trying to achieve. But in the absence of further information, they cannot know—and it sometimes turns out that the person also does not know. Before objectives can fully emerge as guides to action, it is necessary to consider how the six factors mesh together.

The process by which this result is brought about can to some extent be observed and to a lesser extent be made systematic. Essentially, however, the meshing is a creative process, having to do with the capacity of individuals and groups to weigh and evaluate available information and to establish priorities based on the assessment of present and future conditions. Beginning educators or learners must ordinarily think their way laboriously through the process of identifying and stating objectives. Gradually, as a result of experience, their capacity to make decisions in particular cases is improved, so that they can simultaneously take account of all the factors and make them mesh together smoothly.

Statement of objectives. Objectives may be implicit and undefined, but often they are stated in oral or written form for any of a number of reasons, among them: to help shape a format, to restrict the sphere of action, to provide a brief description of the activity, to clarify the thought of planners or analysts, to create a sense of unity, or to serve as a basis for public relations. The actual form of the statement varies; it may be conveyed in oral discourse, in a syllabus, in a promotional brochure, in an annual report or catalog, in a law, or in other ways.

The educative process is usually facilitated by the clear expression of purpose. Even in the very simple situations, as when a man maps out a course of reading for himself or a tutor guides a learner, the statement of aims may help to raise the eventual level of accomplishment. Such statements are even more necessary in formal and complex situations in which individuals play differing roles or when many people are involved. An institution achieves unity through its sense of purpose and therefore tends to suffer if that purpose is not clear.

Any effort to state objectives must begin with the realization that they are the actual guides to action embodied in the learning program and express the hopes of those who take part in it. A first essential is to make written or orally expressed objectives conform as closely as possible to reality, taking account of the factors in the situation, making judgments about them, and fitting the results together to shape those specific and tangible goals at which the learning process may most profitably aim. Otherwise the statement may be essentially a relic of the past, an embodiment of fantasy, or an effort to attract attention and support.

However refined a statement of objectives may be, it can never be more than a notation in abstract terms of the goals that are actually sought. "To gain an understanding and appreciation of Shakespeare's plays" is an announced aim that shows a clear direction. It can be the apex of an extensively outlined hierarchy of statements of skills, knowledge, and attitudes, worked out with elegant precision according to the best canons of curriculum making. Yet a sensitive understanding of Shakespeare's plays as it is realized fully in the minds of learners has a richness, depth, variety, and scope related to the formal definition of the various levels of goals as a mountain is related to the cross-hatched lines on a map that symbolize it. Some writers on education have failed to make this distinction and have treated the statement of a goal as though it were the goal itself; they study the map, not the terrain. A cartographer uses an essential and highly developed art and so does a writer of formal statements of objectives, but both work with abstractions, not with the realities that they describe.

Educational objectives may be stated in terms of the desired accomplishments of the learners. They are to become different people because they have gained the knowledge, ability, or sensitiveness the experience is designed to provide. The measurement of change requires observation of their behavior. Do they, for example, voluntarily read and reread the works of Shakespeare, cite these works in conversation, get a high score on written examinations on the author, and in other ways demonstrate both mastery and enjoyment? To help answer such questions, goals are sometimes stated in relation to the actions that would demonstrate their accomplishment. But unless care is taken to distinguish between the developed power of a human being and its exercise in specified ways, the latter itself becomes the goal, not merely the means of measuring achievement. The path of a subatomic particle is traced by the chain of droplets its passage leaves in a cloud chamber, but the particle and the evidence of its behavior are clearly different from one another. Similarly growth in the ability of a man may be measured by evidence of his actions, but the measurement is not the ability.

Educational objectives may also be stated in terms of the actions that are likely to achieve the desired changes in the learner. A teacher planning a class in human relationships may wish to proceed through a process of individual and group self-discovery; she might say, as one educator did, "I aim to (1) excite the student's curiosity about aspects of behavior which he has hitherto overlooked, taken for granted, or considered insignificant, (2) motivate him to discover his own insights, and (3) help him to absorb these insights in a personal-emotional way rather than merely to accumulate them as so many psychological facts" (Malamud, 1955, p. 1). Such a teacher is aware of the depth of insight of master psychologists and of the existence of established concepts, but he is skeptical that the accumulation of psychological facts will be significant for most learners. He believes that they will be profoundly changed only if they are stirred by the process of self-analysis and the excitement of self-discovery. He therefore states his goals in terms of principles, not accomplishments.

The understanding and acceptance of educational objectives will usually be advanced if they are developed cooperatively. A person who has had a share in deciding what is to be done will understand it better and be more interested in doing it than she who must accept a goal developed by someone else. This principle can be applied in only an analogical fashion in C-1 and C-11 situations—the independent student may hypothesize an educator, and the mass educator may hypothesize the nature of the students. In the other categories, this principle can be made to work in varying ways through the mutual effort and thought of the individuals and groups concerned. Thus the teacher (C-4) plans with certain kinds of potential students in mind, then adjusts those plans with the help of the actual students when they appear. In a C-5 situation, representatives of the potential learning group may from the beginning be members of the planning committee.

An objective should be stated clearly enough to indicate to all rational minds exactly what is intended. Otherwise it will give rise to countless interpretations, many of which contradict one another, thereby fostering confusion rather than comprehension. Goals are sometimes stated in single words or brief phrases ("brotherhood" or "a higher standard of living") that do not provide an adequate understanding of what is being aimed at. It may be argued that ambiguity of this sort is desirable since it allows the maximum subsequent freedom. But since an objective exists to provide shape and focus for action, obscurity in its wording leads to formlessness. After the activity begins, changes will occur in its goals, but revisions can be made most intelligently only if the original statement is clear enough so that any change in purpose can be understood.

In many teaching and learning situations, but particularly in those sponsored by institutions, objectives can be stated in terms not only of the outcomes of education but also of changes in the design components that will presumably make those outcomes better. These facilitative objectives have to do with such matters as the acquisition of learning resources, the improved training of leaders, the establishment of more efficient counseling procedures, and the discovery of new sources of revenue. Thus the board of a cooperative grocery store may wish to strengthen its work in consumer education and therefore set as an objective the hiring of a full-time specialist in that field (an accomplishment goal) or the provision of more product information by all staff members (a principle goal). Either is a facilitative rather than an educational purpose, and yet here as elsewhere the two kinds of objectives are intimately interrelated and sometimes hard to distinguish from one another.

A threat to learning arises when facilitative objectives crowd out educational objectives. It is relatively easy to identify the former and to measure their accomplishment. An administrator expresses the need for more money, better methods, increased resources, and more effective public relations. And as a result of his efforts, the budget is increased, the techniques used are diversified, more books and visual aids become available, and additional students are enrolled. The facilitative goals have been achieved, but what of the educational ones? Are desired changes being brought about in the learners served? As long as an answer to that question seems important, educational objectives remain; however, to the extent that it ceases to be significant or even relevant, the program becomes bureaucratized as the improvement of process proceeds without proper attention to the results it is intended to achieve.

As a designer or an analyst of an educational program refines both educational and facilitative objectives, he must engage in creative thought as he makes judgments about how the six factors are meshed together in the situation with which he is concerned. It is true that many prefabricated adult educational programs already exist or can be quickly devised. In a rough-and-ready sort of way, they are applicable to a variety of situations and thereby give some aid to learners, just as a pair of eyeglasses bought in a variety store can sometimes provide help to those who need to correct their visual deficiencies. But most discerning people would prefer to have an ophthalmologist use advanced skills of diagnosis and prescription in analyzing their individual needs rather than to rely on the untrained assistance of a clerk to choose the right pair of lenses from a limited supply. A really good educational program requires careful attention to the unique nature of the situation and skill identifying the objectives uniquely appropriate to it.

Developing Format

During the time that a decision to proceed with a program is being made and later when objectives are refined, the mind of the planner is constantly darting ahead to consider the components of the proposed design. As just noted, objectives are determined at least in part by a foreknowledge of the availability of certain elements in the format, but at some point it is usually necessary to consider whether all of them are adequately cared for. Otherwise important deficiencies may subsequently appear. Some elements (such as the method of measuring progress or of making the program pattern clear) may be overlooked entirely. Others may be only narrowly applied. For instance, the dictates of program scheduling and of budget may require a television station to offer twenty-six-week courses and to use only lecture and demonstration methods. Even so, within that apparently rigid framework, creative thought about leadership, resources, and sequencing may greatly enhance the effect of the activity. Moreover, while the selection of objectives limits the range of choice as far as various elements are concerned, some freedom to decide among alternatives remains. One who wishes to learn to swim can make relatively little use of either the lecture or the discussion method, but he or she may still choose to hire a tutor, join a class, or try to learn alone by using a manual.

A format blends together the various elements, each interacting with the others. For example, decisions about roles and relationships influence decisions about leadership or social reinforcement and vice versa. There is no invariable order in the determination of the elements. Often several of them are inherent in the situation; then others are decided; and at the end of the format-designing process, the whole pattern is reviewed and revised until the necessary harmony is achieved. After the episode begins, adjustments are usually required. If it is repeated, still further alterations may be made. In the army case reported in Chapter Three, the best overall pattern of instruction did not emerge until the fifth episode in the series.

The acceptance of education as a cooperative art is particularly important in designing the format. In C-2, C-3, and C-5 situations, decisions about the various elements can be made collaboratively. In others, such as C-4 situations, the probable needs and desires of the learners can be estimated in advance and taken more fully into account after the episode begins. In every category, the elements of a format are evident and important to all who share in the educational process. They may have difficulty grappling with the intangibles of objectives, which in many cases are not completely clear to learners until the entire educational process has been completed. Nevertheless everybody has an immediate reaction to such matters as the books, visual aids, leadership, and social reinforcement used in the format. All participants usually want, in one way or another, to help make decisions about the elements and fit them together into an acceptable pattern.

In analyzing an educational activity, either during its progress or after its completion, judgments about its relative success often center on one or more of the format elements, such as scheduling, individualization, or sequence. By reflecting over their experiences, planners come to realize that they must be aware of all the elements of the format if they are to have the greatest possible measure of success. Eventually they may become so accomplished in designing a harmonious pattern that they scarcely need to think about each of the elements in turn; when they have a failure, as even the most experienced planners sometimes do, they usually realize that they have either overlooked an element or handled it badly.

Selecting learning resources. A *resource* is here defined broadly as any object, person, or other aspect of the environment that can be used for support or help in an educational activity. Resources may be categorized in any number of ways as materials, instruments, media, facilities, and so on. While a resource exists independently of any usage, it gains its educational meaning from its application to learning in a particular situation. Thus the shell of a chambered nautilus may be handled and admired as an object, but it may also be used as an instructional resource in marine biology, art, architecture, cultural history, American literature, the study of submarine design, and psychology and as an illustration of the diversity of educational uses to which a single object may be put.

Ordinarily the resources used in a program, taken collectively, make up one of the two chief means by which content is conveyed, the other being leadership. (As already noted in Chapter Two, leaders can be viewed as resources, but ordinarily their active role in guiding instruction makes such a classification inappropriate.) In some cases, other elements become important in conveying content, as method does in any program in which a heightened awareness of interpersonal relationships is a goal. Even then, resources usually play an important though secondary part. Thus in sensitivity training, the physical setting may greatly facilitate or hinder the interactive process whose understanding provides the content.

While resources and methods are always interrelated, they can usually be distinguished for planning or analytical purposes. In some cases, the existence of a resource implies the method by which it is used—the book and reading, the film and its showing, or the art museum and the tour of its paintings. In other cases, as noted in the preceding paragraph, the resource supports the method. But the proper design of an educative experience requires that the two be thought of separately, for the selection of resources and the choice of methods are essentially independent processes. The question "What books will be used?" is thus different from the question "How will the books be used?"

Because resources are so important in conveying content, they have often been considered the heart of the educational format. Some institutions, such as libraries, audiovisual centers, and industrial displays, are based on the collection and use of resources. For centuries, the college curriculum was defined as the mastery of certain books; in adult education, the coordinated course, the farmers' bulletin, or the display of a museum's treasures has sometimes provided the focus of instruction. But resources cannot be educative unless they are used, and the manner of that use does much to determine their effect. Thus if a film is well introduced before it is shown and is then discussed afterward, it has a greater impact on its viewers than if it is merely screened. Maximum learning occurs only when resources are effectively combined not merely with method but also with all the other elements in the format.

Resources vary greatly in availability. Some are absolutely nonexistent; no book or other piece of material exists that can teach mankind how to cure cancer, control genetic coding, create life in the laboratory, or travel to the distant reaches of space. Most resources are limited in their distribution. Primitive parts of the world have a great scarcity of instructional materials (most people now alive cannot use a book and may never have even seen one), whereas complex, urban, industrial societies have them in profusion. But even where either scarcity or glut generally prevails, variation still exists. An underdeveloped country may have a university as a sanctuary for learning, and an advanced society may have places of cultural impoverishment.

The greatest variance in adequacy of resources, however, has been over time. In earlier eras, learning materials were so limited in quantity that they could be used by only a very few people, usually those in a monastery or a royal court. To the man who chiseled out inscriptions in stone or who laboriously copied a manuscript, the printing press came as a new instrument full of promise as it offered enlightenment to more people, or full of danger as it threatened to open the sacred mysteries of learning to vulgar eyes. The spread of print has had both effects, and so have the other media of communication that followed it. A transformation has also occurred in the availability and attractiveness of physical facilities. The first history of adult education, published in 1851, says of the mechanics institutes of that day that "their Parnassus is reached from a back street by a narrow intricate stair, dimly lighted on winter evenings" (Hudson, 1851, p. 44). In the modern city, facilities for learning, such as universities, evening schools, proprietary institutions, libraries, museums, and residential centers, abound and are located on main thoroughfares.

The growth of such resources has brought about both quantitative and qualitative differences in education. A lecturer's ideas used to be available only to those within the sound of his voice at the time he expressed them; now they can be sent throughout the world by satellite and captured for posterity by book, record, videotape, and CD-ROM. The development of high-fidelity auditory systems enables countless people to study music who would earlier have been denied that opportunity. The growth of new communications materials has expanded not only the reach but also the scope of learning. As André Malraux pointed out, the reproduction of pictures makes possible new dimensions in the understanding of art since it enables the student to place side by side the representations of works that are actually far away from one another and thereby to make detailed comparisons and contrasts hitherto denied even the greatest authorities. The same kinds of results have flowed from the computer and from other new media and instruments and are likely to continue to do so from communications inventions not yet perfected or even contemplated.

So it has come about that while the scarcity of learning resources is still the major problem for most people in the world, for others the central difficulty is one of choice. Decisions must be made not merely about which materials are best to achieve a given goal but also about which goal is best among the many made possible by the existence of profuse resources. In making either kind of choice, the central point of reference is the situation itself. At a specific time and place and with a known audience, which of the available resources will be most useful as it is combined with the other elements of the format to achieve the desired goal? Or if many resources are at hand, which of them should be chosen and combined with other factors? In answering such questions, the designer must rely on experience and an intuitive grasp of what is immediately important. She or he also has available an impressive and growing body of knowledge about the assessment of learning resources. Much is known about such matters as readability, the display of exhibited material, the way to arrange items of content so that they are maximally educative, and the best use of various resource categories. Here, as with the other components, both the practical wisdom that comes from experience and the principles derived by research can be used to enhance the outcomes of learning activity.

Choosing leaders. As already noted in Chapter Two, those who take part in any educational activity tend to occupy one of two major roles—the educator or the learner. The first role is a broad one and includes professional program planners, curriculum specialists, administrators, and supervisors, as well as those who are here called *leaders,* the people who directly assist learners to achieve their objectives. A leader works in various ways and in all categories from C-2 through C-11. Even in self-guided learning, the person concerned may consciously separate two ways of behavior, sometimes planning as a leader might do and sometimes carrying out the plans she or he has made.

The source of a leader's influence is often crucial in determining the nature or the results of an educational activity. If leaders are presumed to be masters of content or process, they must demonstrate their capacity clearly to their students. If leaders have been chosen only because some aspect of the situation confers status or responsibility upon them, they must be careful not to claim any special knowledge of the educational content or process; a presiding officer may need to make it clear that he or she is not an authority on the subject being discussed. Sometimes a mixture of two or more kinds of influence is required. It may inhere in a single leader, as when an industrial supervisor uses both special knowledge and institutional authority to guide a worker, or it may require the complementary service of several people, as when a conference has speakers, discussion leaders, and chairmen. Also a group may rotate leadership, or a conference may follow a procedure in which participants serve as leaders on some occasions and as learners on others. At any given moment, it is usually apparent who is occupying each of the two roles and the authority of the leader is accepted as long as he or she exercises it well.

Leadership in adult education is far more fluid and fluctuating than it is in the schooling of children and young people. With adults, the authority of the leader is usually restricted to the situation itself and does not broaden to create a caste system as it tends to do in schools and colleges. Furthermore, while some people devote their careers to adult education, far larger numbers undertake it as a part-time or occasional activity. This fluidity has saved the field from the sterility of a rigid professionalism, but it has occasionally diminished the caliber of leadership and thereby made the outcomes of learning less significant than they might have been.

Insofar as a profession of adult education exists, its structure does not resemble that of any of the other educational professions. They tend to be oriented to institutions and are designated as school teachers, school administrators, college professors, university administrators, or librarians. The highly trained adult educator, like the physician, lawyer, architect, social worker, or nurse has an expertise that is applied in any of a number of settings, each of which may be central to that person's own work but not to that of the whole profession. Moreover, full-time career adult educators see themselves as part of a network of other people whose service they may guide or direct but from whom they do not separate their own work sharply since they regard them as colleagues essential to their own endeavors. For example, a university extension division may have only fifty full-time staff members but may plan for and direct the activities of two hundred faculty members who teach adults on a part-time basis, three hundred nonfaculty members who are engaged occasionally to teach, and a hundred lay citizens who serve as volunteers in various capacities. (Knox, 1994, p. 128, estimates that "full time adult education practitioners constitute less than twenty percent of people working in the adult education field.") This broadly based pattern of leadership is likely to continue and to set limits to any tendency to establish a separate adult educational caste.

The selection and use of leaders in an adult educational program is usually not a task of filling well-defined slots in a table of organization with people already trained for their work, but of considering and acting upon a conception of format in which the relevant elements (including leadership) are meshed to achieve a defined goal in a specific setting. It often happens that the planner of a program intends to become its leader, as when a teacher organizes a class. In such a case, this element becomes the starting point in constructing the format, influencing from the beginning all other aspects of the design, including the objectives. In other cases, the designer must take account of the requirements of the intended activity to determine what functions its leaders should perform. He or she must then find the people with the desired qualities of personality and the specific competence required and reinforce the efforts of such people in any way necessary.

Such reinforcement is often essential because most adult educational activities cannot be based on a teaching profession whose members have been trained for their work and whose competence is certified by some authority. Even when the members of an educational profession can be used, they often need special training for their work with adults. Thus an elementary school teacher accustomed to working with preadolescent children may require help in adjusting her outlook and procedures when she undertakes a literacy class for adults.

Leadership training directly geared to the situation is often essential, particularly when new institutions or institutional activities are created. If Congress establishes a program to train the unemployed, its staff must be recruited from available manpower, but then it must be prepared for its work. When a settlement house launches a nutrition program for welfare mothers using other women on welfare as aides, the latter group requires preparatory education in both content and method. This preservice preparation must usually be supplemented by in-service training by means of supervision, manuals, the stimulation of reading and attendance at conferences, staff seminars, and the fostering of advanced study. The leaders of adult education promote the continued learning of others and therefore believe in it for themselves.

Selecting and using methods. A *method* is an established and systematic way of work used to achieve an educational objective. In traditional schooling, it is exemplified by lecturing, discussion, recitation, laboratory work, and coaching. In recent years, many methods have been created or expanded in usage, such as the case method, programmed instruction, role playing, psychodrama, simulation games, and Link trainers. In the situations in which adults learn, the range of methods broadens from these well-established procedures to include other aspects of life deliberately manipulated to increase their educative effect. A self-directed learner may choose certain experiences because he knows they will help him, a tutor may try to become a role model for her student, and a group may diversify its membership to achieve a broader viewpoint. Activities not centrally educative may also use instructional methods: a television program designed for entertainment may introduce serious content; a manager may handle problem-solving processes so that they yield maximum learning for staff members; and recreational activities may be conducted to build character and interpersonal skills.

Throughout the twentieth century, American educators have been preoccupied with method; as a result, the term itself has acquired countless shades of meaning. It has been narrowed to signify a specific way of conducting an act of learning, such as the use of mnemonics or drills. In a broader view, it includes all of the aspects of learning or teaching here identified collectively as elements in a format. In the most sweeping sense, as in the work of Dewey and his followers, method encompasses the entire educative process, erasing customary distinctions between ends and means. The term and its synonym *technique* are used, as just noted, in a pragmatic sense to mean an identifiable and generally recognized procedure, sometimes overlapping others but distinguishable from them, that is used by a learner or educator to achieve certain objectives.

Every method has its own rules of excellence that must be learned if it is to be performed well. To give a lecture, lead a discussion, or conduct a panel is an art that can be greatly improved by experience, study, and the conscious effort to excel. Some people have natural talent and learn to use a method more swiftly and effectively than do others, but it may be doubted whether any natural-born teachers exist. Individuals so designated have usually put themselves through a process of self-guided instruction to gain their mastery, and the height of their art lies in its concealment. When a method has been truly learned, it is so absorbed into the personality of its user that other people may not be aware that a technique is being employed. The twin enemies of method are self-consciousness and obviousness of use.

In designing a program, a major consideration in choosing methods is therefore the capacity of leaders to use them. Other considerations also come into play. The method may itself be the beginning point in the design of a format, as is the case with a television program or a correspondence course. Other aspects of the situation that influence the selection of method are the amount of time available, the number of people involved, the resources at hand, the level of sophistication of the learners, their personal preferences, the cost, the sequence, and the schedule.

The definition of objectives limits the range of alternative techniques. If the goal of a program is to teach a physical skill, appropriate methods might be drill, coaching, demonstration, and guided experience; other techniques such as role playing, panel discussion, field trips, debates, and buzz groups would be less useful. The relationship also works in reverse, for goals are usually implied by method. For instance, anyone who admires the discussion method usually indicates by that fact a high regard for the discovery of truth by personal interaction.

Most activities need to use several methods. For example, the teaching of a complex skill ordinarily requires several complementary approaches—presentation of theory by reading, lecture, and other means; demonstration by a master performer; practice by the learner; and continued coaching by the instructor. The use of several methods instead of a reliance on one has other values as well; it broadens the range of achievable objectives, stimulates the interest of both leaders and learners, encourages participation, and takes account of the differential response of individuals to various approaches.

It follows from these comments that no method is inherently and universally superior to all others. Again and again during the last half-century, some technique or cluster of techniques has been advanced as having such supremacy in adult education. The case for discussion, for example, has been advanced on the lines that adults have had more experience than children, that the essential element of adult education is the sharing of experience, that the best way for minds to interact is by discussion, and that therefore discussion is the best method to use in all circumstances. New methods sometimes seem to have such limitless horizons that their advocates believe they will replace all other techniques. Claims of this sort have been made for the use of audiovisual materials, group dynamics, nondirective leadership, programmed learning, and computer-based instruction; other such claims will doubtless be made for techniques not yet invented. But experience demonstrates that a method has limitations as well as advantages, and eventually it takes its proper place in the inventory of techniques available for choice and use.

For a long time, instruction has been offered by correspondence. As new electronic media (such as the telephone, radio, and television) have been perfected, they have been adapted for use in programs in which teachers taught specific learners but were not in face-to-face contact with them. In the latter part of the twentieth century, such instruction has come to be called *distance education*, and both theoretical and practical books on the subject have been produced in many countries. Two such works of particular value in program planning are those by Perraton (1982) and Moore (1990).

A rapid expansion of learning opportunities based on perfected new techniques is likely to occur in the years ahead if educators can discover how to use them, both separately and in combinations. Kurshan and Lenk have sketched what the future may bring:

> Today, the technologies commonly found in homes, schools, and other learning environments such as the workplace, museums, or day-care centers include television, VCRs, personal computers, video games, videodiscs, CD-ROM, modems, faxes, cable television, and satellite dishes. Networks that connect technologies into integrated information processing facilities that can link several computers in a school to worldwide telecommunications are increasingly commonplace. Critically, more children and adults than ever before regularly use one or more of these computer-connected media for learning. For the future, there is a wealth of technological innovation on the horizon such as improved CD-ROM technology, interactive television, and hand-held computers that will expand the access, use, and potential of computer-based technologies beyond what can currently be imagined [1994, p. 110].

Making a time schedule. A schedule is the timetable of an educational activity. It may be simple, as when a group decides to meet on ten successive Wednesday afternoons from 3:00 to 5:00. It may be complex, as when a five-day conference of four thousand people has plenary sessions, simultaneous sectional meetings, group discussions, dinner and luncheon programs, and opportunities for counseling. It may be rigid, as when an activity must be fitted into a college semester or a television season. It may be flexible, as when correspondence course students proceed at their own pace. Scheduling has several aspects that must be considered simultaneously: the total elapsed time; the various kinds of sessions required; their frequency and duration; and their placement in the day, the week, the month, the year, or other period of time. Proper choice among these aspects becomes harder as the time frame grows more complex. It is more difficult to determine the timing of an episode than of an act, and scheduling a series or an aggregate is even harder.

Scheduling has been less extensively studied than other format elements, perhaps because schools and colleges (the chief foci of educational research) have well-established patterns governing the timing of their activities. In recent years, many ideas about the diversification and rearrangement of schedules have been tried. Unfortunately objective studies of the value of such innovations are scarce, and the conventional system resists change. Research on such generalized topics as the relative value of spaced or concentrated practice has chiefly been done under laboratory conditions, and its results have more relevance to educational acts than to episodes or series of episodes.

Despite the scarcity of studies on adult educational scheduling, the topic has great practical importance. Adults lead complex and varied lives and are widely distributed in space. Finding the timing for an educational activity that will best fit into the life patterns of participants is often crucial to its success. More general problems also arise. In the worlds of business and government, when should a course be offered on company time and when on personal time? How long can a session last or a series of sessions be maintained without encountering diminishing returns? How can a complex activity be designed to provide sustained variety and interest? How can the adult educational use of an essential resource, such as a computer or a laboratory, be best accommodated to its other uses? Such questions constantly accompany the designing of new educational activities and the operation of ongoing ones.

Most present decisions about scheduling are determined by tradition, necessity, the best available judgment, or an arbitrary choice among alternatives. Many institutions have a standard format or policy. The courses in an evening school may run for a set number of weeks on a fixed pattern of hours, or an industry may follow the principle that all its education must be on company time. In any such case, the schedule becomes a beginning point for planning. Where greater freedom to develop a schedule is possible, choice must be made in terms of the objectives, the other elements in the format, or the adjustment of the activity to the participants' life-styles. Judgment about scheduling tends to be improved by experience as planners learn how to take these diverse influences into account. Learners too become habituated to established schedules. For example, they have grown used to having school and college begin in the autumn; it seems appropriate to them for adult educational activities to do so as well.

Devising a sequence. Sequence has to do with the order in which content is learned. It may itself have an inherent structure (geometry moves from axioms to postulates to an ordered series of theorems; history is chronological) that establishes a pattern of progression. But in education, the requirements of the content and the needs of the learner must be kept in balance. One must start with people where they are, as the old saying has it, and where they are at any given time determines the next step they must take to get where they want to be. It is equally wrong for a teacher to be so true to content that she ignores the abilities and desires of her students and for her to be so concerned with their wishes and feelings that she forgets or denies content.

In the last quarter-century, perhaps no other aspect of education has had more lay or professional attention than sequencing. Debate has been continuous about the proper way to teach reading. New national curricula in mathematics and science have radically revised the ordering of topics. Programmed instruction that seeks to elevate sequencing to a science has become a permanent part of education, and its earlier application in teaching machines and self-instruction manuals is being supplemented by the use of computers that take account of the varied approaches of different individuals to the learning task.

This variance among learners is particularly important in adult education. As previously noted, men and women have had more experience than children and have had kinds of experience that no children can have. The pathways of maturity are much more diverse than those of childhood. These facts have many implications for the selection and presentation of content. Since the time of the ancient Greeks, it has been recognized that some bodies of knowledge cannot be fully understood until adulthood. As Aristotle observed, "One may enquire why a boy, though he may be a mathematician, cannot be a philosopher. Perhaps the answer is that mathematics deals with abstractions whereas the first principles of philosophy are derived from experience: the young can only repeat them without conviction of their truth, whereas the definitions of mathematics are easily understood" (*Nichomachean Ethics*, Book VI, Chapter 8). When adults learn an exact science, the sequence they therefore follow may be very like that used by a child; but when they wish to gain broader, less precise kinds of knowledge, their starting point and their continuing pathway are influenced by the depth and breadth of their own experiences and those of fellow learners.

Sequence is also influenced by the fact that adult learning ventures usually arise from specific needs or desires. The generalized social reinforcement of education characteristic of childhood does not apply. Adults must have a continuing sense of tangible accomplishment, or they will abandon their efforts to learn. The designing of instruction must incorporate rewards or interest-maintaining features to ensure continuity of effort. Thus a literacy teacher may establish certain accomplishments—such as writing one's name or a simple letter—that his students can use in daily life, even though these evidences of progress are not inherently necessary in achieving the ability to write.

A desirable sequence is most readily accomplished in C-2 or C-4 situations where the teacher has a grasp of content and an opportunity to interpret it to a specific group of students with known capacities and concerns. The task of sequencing is particularly difficult in programs that have no content leader, especially in self-directed study where the learner may never know where next to turn. In each of the other categories, the arrangement of the subject matter has special aspects and problems. In C-11 situations, for instance, where the nature of the students can only be guessed, the sequence is determined by the planner's estimate of what is appropriate for a hypothesized audience.

Providing social reinforcement of learning. Learning almost always occurs in a social context. Even self-guided students usually reach out for help in informing or reinforcing their efforts. In each of the other categories, individuals are brought together into some established or improvised form of intercommunication. One motive for doing so is economy; a teacher can handle thirty students in a classroom much more quickly and inexpensively than if she served as a tutor to each of them separately. But in modern educational theory, the resulting loss of individualized attention is usually thought to be balanced or outweighed by the gain in social reinforcement in which each learner is helped by interaction with the others. This situation is particularly true in a mass society in which learning activities have become the surrogates for waning forms of collective action, such as those provided by religion, farm, and village life, and of the extended and interdependent family. As a result, the socializing possibilities of organized education have become more and more important to both learners and educators.

When people work together to achieve a purpose, an ethos is created by the interactions of individuals with one another, but it is far more than a blending of personalities. Before long, idiosyncrasies are savored, group-originated anecdotes are enjoyed, special terms and shadings of meaning are established, differentiated roles are developed and performed, and subgroups with congenial interests appear. Incorporating but transcending these behavioral patterns is a community spirit and a desire for its preservation. This ethos can be planned, fostered, or analyzed to discover its subtle blend of awareness, acceptance, cooperation, and challenge.

A special question must be asked, however, about the collective spirit of an educational entity: how can it reinforce the desired changes in the nature of its members? Put another way, how can the behavior of everyone stimulate the learning of each one? The easy answer is that the higher the morale, the greater the amount of learning that will occur. In a sense, this answer is usually true. A warm, positive, and inviting social climate within the activity helps to offset the ill-at-ease feeling of many adults when they enter a new learning experience, particularly when they have little support from their customary associates for doing so. Yet too great an attention to building a social spirit may eventually lead to a reversal of ends and means. Learning objectives can be lost because the members of the social entity become so concerned with its preservation that they forget the task it was intended to accomplish.

The proper balance is most likely to be struck if the cooperative nature of education is manifest at every stage in the planning and execution of a learning design. In the short run, warmth of personal relationships is rewarding and valuable. Yet in the long run, the chief cause of high morale is a sense of social reinforcement that is directed not merely at the maintenance of the group or institution but at the accomplishment of its goals. If the members share in refining objectives and choosing the means of their accomplishment, they are likely to remain task oriented, not letting the creation of a positive social climate outweigh the other elements of the format.

The designers of programs have many ways to foster social reinforcement. Physical arrangements have an influence; when a group can sit around a table, each member having direct eye contact with the others and sharing the physical and psychological support provided by the table itself, the sense of community is likely to be stronger than when the group sits in rows of chairs facing the same way. There should not be so many people as to create facelessness, nor so few as to lead to tedium. The people concerned should be neither too similar nor too heterogeneous. Leaders can display attitudes of acceptance and support and use techniques that create good rapport, such as the careful introduction of each participant to the others, the fostering of discussion, and the use of wit and vivid illustration. The experiences of the individual members can illuminate and enlarge the comprehension of the content. An activity should last long enough so that the people involved come to know one another but not so long that they grow bored with each other. And wise planners realize that some of the most rewarding learning occurs between sessions, not during them. For example, experienced conference planners insert what they call white space between their work sessions to give time for reflection, the reassertion of individuality, and the rebuilding of a zest for assembly.

Each of the categories imposes its own requirements. The foregoing comments have been most relevant to C-2 through C-6. As suggested, independent learners may seek support from other people. In a C-11 situation, a speaker to a large audience can use the arts of the lecturer to build a powerful social reinforcement, but the author of a book can do relatively little in this respect. Institutionalized programs have many ways of providing social reinforcement. Some are obvious though often ignored. A public library can appear to be warm and inviting, or it can seem to be a fortress protecting its riches. An evening college can make its physical plant attractive and conducive to informal gatherings, build student councils and advisory panels, schedule all-college social activities, and select administrators, counselors, secretaries, and other staff members who are open and friendly. Other institutional supports are less obvious. With the best intentions in the world, a director of a center may streamline registration, abolish attendance records, and discontinue the awarding of grades and certificates, only to discover that the adult students like to talk over their programs with counselors, want to establish their presence at class, and feel a need for evaluation and a record of accomplishment. Such feelings are not merely a holdover from outmoded patterns of schooling. Learning, particularly in adulthood, is enhanced by social reinforcement, and anything that provides it and does not negate some other element is worth introducing into the educational format.

Adjusting to the nature of each learner. The central component of all education is the learner; the effect of the educational process can be most directly measured by its changes in that individual. The planner of a program must try to design and conduct it so that the growth of each participant is fostered. Occasionally it is enough to consider how learners vary idiographically in terms of some trait crucial to the instruction. Thus the teacher of a simple motor skill may give selective assistance to students only as it is required by their varying physiological aptitude. Since most education is complex, however, each learner should usually be considered nomothetically in terms of the whole personality, not some defined dimension of it.

It is never easy to keep the path of progress open for each individual. The wide range among adults of ability, experience, interest, sense of need, previous education, and other personality dimensions means that any effort to take account of all such factors in providing individual attention is costly in terms of time and resources. Sometimes the brevity of the activity, the size of the group, the desire of the learners for privacy, or other reasons prevent any substantial effort to incorporate this element into the design. But, as far as possible, the effort should be made.

In every form of education, the learner considers personal desires and needs, particularly when, as an adult, she or he is required to accept responsibility for each act of learning. This fact is the essence of the C-1 situation. In other cases, the responsibility is shared as in C-2, by the tutor; in C-3, by the other members of the group; in C-4, by the teacher; in C-5, by the planning committee and the leaders they choose; and so on. In institutional situations, individualization may occur not only in the learning itself but also from such administrative reinforcements as testing and personal counseling. Even in C-11 situations, efforts may be made to individualize by paying attention to a few selected learners, though this practice sometimes hampers the leader's capacity to influence the entire audience.

Clarifying roles and relationships. A *role* may be defined as the characteristic behavior expected of individuals in a situation as perceived by either themselves or others. Though they are unique human beings, their attitudes and actions are influenced by what they think it right to do or what they believe is expected of them. This role expectation helps to define their relationships to other people. A woman can be a teacher of one group, a presiding officer in another, and a student in a third. Each role differs from the others and so does the way by which she relates herself to the members of the group. In educational settings, roles and relationships may never be stated, but they are usually deeply felt; and the planner or analyst of a program needs to take account of them. As already noted, though the primary role distinction is that between the educator and the learner, there are countless other complexities of formalized relationships in educational settings, particularly those in which many people are involved.

Even the minimum social relationship, the dyad, is remarkably complex. For example, county agricultural extension agents are usually responsible to district supervisors, each of whom oversees a geographic area within a state. The county agent is an officer of local government, a representative of the state land-grant university, and a part of a nationwide federally supported endeavor. The district supervisor represents only one of these sources of power and influence, the university, and therefore is not the boss of the county agent in any simple sense. In a study of this relationship, Durfee (1956) identified three kinds of role performance. The supervisor is simultaneously a superior officer with authority to require certain actions, a stimulator who takes the initiative to influence the county agent, and a consultant who stands ready to furnish help and advice on demand. Durfee discovered ninety-six topics with which the dyad might concern itself, including items in such areas as budgeting, the building of morale, the maintenance of relationships with other people in the county, in-service training, and evaluation. He then asked a large number of county agents and their supervisors to identify which of the three roles the supervisor should play with respect to each topic and was able to draw up a detailed analysis of both roles and relationships as a result. He also demonstrated that the most satisfactory dyads were those that had the greatest similarity between the expectations of the county agent and those of the agent's supervisor.

A research investigation of this sort is too complex to serve in most program building, but it does suggest the importance of defining the roles and relationships of any situation as far as is practically possible. Particularly in C-7, C-8, and C-9 situations, it is often necessary to consider very carefully how a new institution is to be organized, how a new program is to be added to an existing framework of service, or how new activities can be provided in an existing format. The need for adequate definition is even more crucial in C-6 and C-10 situations where no overarching structure of authority exists and the activity can be maintained only if roles and relationships are clearly understood and agreed upon.

Complete freedom of choice seldom exists in any of the eleven situations. Tradition is usually important, since people tend to behave in accepted though often unexamined ways. In large institutions, the need for hierarchy and structure may create a complex bureaucracy that establishes firmly set roles and relationships among its members. When well-established professions are involved, they impose standardized patterns of behavior; the doctor, the nurse, the lawyer, or the clergyman expect (and are expected) to behave in ways appropriate to their callings. And always personality breaks through, giving uniqueness to the performance of even the most well-established role.

Sometimes the potential service of an institution of adult education is limited because no satisfactory way can be found for establishing a new educative role. In public libraries, an effort was made in the 1920s and 1930s to create the position of reader's adviser, a person who could help patrons learn by using books and other resources. This attempt proved to be unsuccessful, and no other helping relationship of an adult educational sort has been defined and widely adopted. As a result, though the public library remains an invaluable educational resource, it has only limited significance as far as the guidance of adult learners is concerned.

Other institutions perform several functions and must define adult educational roles in the light of that fact. In a university, a community college, or a public school system, young people (often significantly called regular students) occupy the center of attention. In museums, industrial concerns, labor unions, and voluntary associations, education is paralleled by such other functions as research, economic production, and the fostering of fraternal feeling. In all such cases, those who are concerned with the education of adults may have a feeling of marginality that pervades their performance and the continuing relationships they have with other people both inside and outside the institution. This feeling can be either inhibiting or challenging. In the latter case, it may give rise to determined efforts to make the roles more significant in the prestige system of the institution or to redraw the lines on the organizational chart so that adult education has a more exalted place in the hierarchy than before. In the long run, neither effort is likely to succeed unless it is accompanied by a greater capacity to design and execute programs and by the demonstration of that capacity in the performance of the role.

Identifying criteria for evaluation. From the start of an educational activity, it should be clear what standards, rules, or tests will be used to judge relative success or failure. Criteria of evaluation are suggested by the objectives; some people would argue that the two are interchangeable. But "to learn the basic principles of economics" is related to but different from "to learn the content of a specified textbook on economics." The second establishes a criterion for the decision as to how well the first has been accomplished since it sets the framework for the construction of tests of the learners' knowledge.

Many kinds of criteria are available to the designer of an educational format. Some measure the accomplishment of defined skills, content, or appreciation. Others have to do with the principles of action by which desired changes may be brought about, measuring, for example, group interaction and cohesiveness, the satisfaction of the learner with the process of learning, the growth of problem-solving ability, or the heightened self-awareness of an individual. Some criteria are easy to apply and understand, whereas others are difficult to use, requiring elaborate interpretation and inference.

An awareness of the criteria to be applied in measuring the extent of learning gives concreteness and definition to an educational activity. A goal may be clear ("to learn to play the organ," "to understand statistics," or "to be sensitive to group processes") and yet lead the learner on forever, since he or she would never achieve full mastery. When precise levels of accomplishment or exact principles of action are defined, they structure the whole endeavor. Both educator and learner know what is expected by the end of the activity and can have the gratification of assessing concrete accomplishment. It is the lack of clear criteria that gives to many adult educational activities (particularly those in the C-1, C-3, C-6, C-10, and C-11 categories) a sense of vagueness and lack of significance.

The criteria used in adult education are broader in scope and less sharply defined and developed than those of childhood and youth education. In the latter, heavy reliance is placed on formal achievement tests, many of which have been standardized and have well-established norms. Sometimes these tests can be adapted for use by adults; less often, tests specifically devised for them have been developed. For the most part, however, pencil-and-paper tests for adults are prepared by teachers or are used as inherent parts of the instructional rather than the evaluative process. Adults enjoy taking self-evaluative tests, as both magazine editors and the arrangers of museum displays have discovered; and this fact has been extensively used in the construction of self-directed instructional materials.

Most of the criteria now used in adult education are inferential, such as those based on the belief that the higher the participants rate their enjoyment of a program, the more they are learning from it. Some of the most frequently used inferential measures are those of enrollment, attendance, number of meetings held, number of registrants, extent of circulation of books or other materials, and cost indices. Alternatively learners or educators may feel that if they use an established process, the proper results are bound to occur; they judge their success by the rigor with which they follow procedures. (One is reminded of the oriental hunter who, while returning from a fruitless day in the field, asked his gun bearer what had gone wrong, to which the quick-witted servant responded, "Master, you shot divinely, but Allah was merciful to the birds.") While inferential criteria have some values (measures of volume of service seem to have a particular appeal to financing authorities), they do not directly measure growth in relation to the accomplishment of objectives and therefore cannot meet the basic test of evaluation.

In many cases, however, that test can better be met by adult educational activities than by those provided for children and youth. The success of the latter may not be measurable until many years after the learners have left school, but much of the education undertaken by men and women is designed to make an immediate change in their life patterns. They want a promotion or a better job, an increased or improved productivity in a vocation or avocation, a capacity to handle a family problem, or the ability to adjust to a physiological handicap such as a stroke or diabetes. Or an educator may have social goals, such as the reduction of disease or illiteracy, the improvement of economic life, or the acceptance of a new governmental policy, whose accomplishment can be measured by community statistics or other tangible evidences of success.

As an activity proceeds, original criteria may change, some being altered or abandoned and others added. Thus an association formed to study a social problem may initially measure its success in terms of growth of resources and membership and maintenance of a high morale. As time goes on, its leaders may realize that its actions are having an effect on society and that the measurement of that effect constitutes evidence of the educative impact of the association. But while criteria are often altered in this way so that eventual judgments are different from those forecast at the start, the original design will lack both definition and the capacity to measure movement if it does not include a statement of the criteria that from the beginning seem to offer the best available indications of success.

Explaining the design. When any program is initiated, those who take part in it should understand so far as possible both its objectives and its format. As learning proceeds, any change in goals or processes should also be made clear. These observations are truisms, but they are frequently violated in practice. It is often said of an educational activity that its purposes or design are not clear to its participants. The planner may know so exactly what is to be undertaken that he or she assumes that other people share that awareness; the planner thus does not take the apparently minor but actually crucial step of informing them. They know neither what they are supposed to accomplish nor the principles they are being asked to follow. As a result, they grope in the dark, sometimes developing such a sense of frustration that they abandon the program or even the quest for knowledge.

The need for providing as much clarity as possible (particularly for the learners) is made all the more important because the nature of education as a change-inducing process makes a complete awareness of either goals or format impossible until the changes have actually been brought about and the activity completed. The ability to operate a lathe, the knowledge of the essentials of cultural anthropology, or the possession of insight into the wellsprings of behavior can be stated as abstractions but are never fully grasped until they have been mastered by the learner. Similarly one may understand the general format of a program's activities but fail to absorb the actual nature of the experiences to be undertaken. A mariner's chart suggests what a traveler may encounter, but only the person who has actually lived through the voyage knows what it is really like. But while learners can never understand everything at the start, they should be as aware as possible of the eventual goal and of the paths necessary to get there. Otherwise they are likely to feel they are wandering through a trackless territory toward an unknown destination.

Fitting the Program into Life Patterns

The need to find a way of fitting adult education into the customary patterns of adult life has been a powerful impetus for many programs. This fact is particularly evident in remedial education for men and women who somehow missed in childhood the instruction customarily provided then. The GED test was developed in the late 1940s as a way of measuring the completion of secondary school studies; special instruction to prepare for the test could then replace the tedious years of night school instruction that had been the only previous way of securing a high school diploma. Similarly the non-traditional higher education movement that began in the early 1970s aimed at the reconstruction of collegiate and university formats to make them more responsive to adult patterns of individual, group, and institutional life.

Successful innovation is sometimes brought about by the examination of aspects of adult life to see how they can provide the basis for new formats. In 1975, the creators of Elderhostel saw that empty college dormitories and classrooms, faculty members available to teach in the summertime, and the greater ease of travel at that time of year could be fitted together into inexpensive one-week residential courses for older adults interested in cultural studies. This basic pattern proved to be so successful that by 1995 Elderhostel services blanketed the United States and were offered in forty-five other countries. Many other institutions are providing similar programs.

Those who plan or conduct programs of adult education must sometimes confront the fact that the cultural or institutional climates in which they operate are indifferent or hostile. The literature on public school or university activities in this field is filled with complaints of the marginality of such ventures. Marsick and Watkins (1990) suggest that much of the learning in the workplace must be informal and incidental. Campbell (1978) shows vividly how prison authorities obstruct educational programs even though rehabilitation is presumed to be a major purpose of the institution. It sometimes happens, to be sure, that ventures in learning aim to challenge or change the prevailing social order. One such example is the Highlander School in Tennessee, which has been described by Glen (1988) and Horton (1989).

These examples highlight the significance of placing education within adult life patterns; the need to do so is universal. At every stage in the shaping and operation of a program, its developer must consider how it can best fit into the customary pursuits of the learners, the leaders, and the sponsoring institutions, if any. In a strictly logical sequence of program planning, a format might first be devised and then announced to its potential constituencies; however, this rational order is seldom followed in practice, particularly when programs are first introduced. While such elements of a format as resources, leadership, or scheduling are being considered, decisions concerning them are partially made in terms of the ways by which the proposed activity is to be incorporated into the lives of the persons concerned. Once the activity is under way, it must often be altered to accommodate unexpected conditions or events.

There are at least three prime foci of attention in making such decisions. In all situations except those in C-1, learners confront an activity that they may have helped to plan but that is essentially external to them. They must therefore consider how they are to accommodate themselves to the new venture. The educator who plans a program must think of its influence on his or her own life and on that of the learners, making a proper allocation of time and resources in both respects. And an institution that sponsors a program must provide reinforcing supports for it. Specialized personnel, such as administrators, supervisors, counselors, financial officers, public relations specialists, and clerks, may be required to bring harmony to the design of the whole institution and to reinforce each of its separate programs.

An illustration may help to make clear the need to consider the situation from these three focal points—the learner, educator, and institution. The principal of a suburban adult education center may invite a teacher to offer a course on the culture of the new African nations. The format itself may be left completely in the hands of the teacher with such guides and restrictions as general institutional policy requires. He must also give some thought to how he will fit this new activity into his present work pattern, what kinds of students will most profit from the course, how he can keep the cost reasonable, and how he can help to interpret its objectives to the community. All potential students will consider such matters as the influence of the course on their customary pattern of life, whether they have the financial resources to undertake it, whether they understand what it will require, and whether they prefer it to some other course they might take. But the heaviest responsibility for accommodating the activity to the lives of the people of the suburbs will fall on the staff of the evening school, who must underwrite the program's financing, interpret it to the public, fit it into the overall schedule of courses, and counsel students into or out of it. The course merges into the aggregate of activities undertaken by the institution and benefits or suffers by the competence with which such matters are handled.

In the adaptation of educational designs to the general circumstances of life, four kinds of adjustments are so commonly found that they have become the bases of generalized discussion and research. Each will here be considered separately, though in practice they overlap.

Guiding learners into or out of the program. A question often asked about an educational program is who should be included, who excluded? It sometimes happens that this query arises at the time a decision is made about proceeding with the activity, when the matching of suitably qualified and interested learners with appropriate formats may be an important factor in the decision. (In C-1 or C-2 situations, the decision is crucial; the activity cannot be undertaken if the judgment is negative.) The same issue continues to arise even after the activity has begun. A learner may ask himself from time to time whether it is appropriate for him, and the educator may often consider whether or not a specific learner should be encouraged to drop out.

In many cases, guidance poses no severe problems. A group chooses and retains the people its members regard as congenial. A teacher identifies the nature and level of competence required in a course and excludes overqualified, underqualified, or aberrant applicants. In institutional settings, formal or informal methods help potential learners decide whether they wish to take part; it often happens that such efforts, even simple ones, work well enough in selecting and retaining participants that the activity survives. Even those learners who might have been excluded if there had been rigorous admission procedures may finally profit from their study, particularly if the leader can individualize the instruction.

But it would be wrong to take for granted, as many educators do, either that adults know what they want or that they would resent any effort to guide them into or out of learning activities. While both assumptions are sometimes valid, it often happens that men and women have only vague and ill-defined feelings about how to improve themselves. They may come to an educational activity with strongly negative feelings: they have a sharp sense of need or deprivation; their memories of the repressiveness of early schooling haunts them; they encounter resistance to study at home or work; they feel inadequate about their ability to learn; or they are unfamiliar with the program patterns of adult education. This last problem is particularly prevalent in institutions, where the array of courses or other learning opportunities, the interlocking requirements, and the complexities of scheduling seem formidable to those unfamiliar with them.

The initial need for guidance continues throughout the learning process. Within a program, effective individualization helps achieve objectives, but learners may require help in fitting one activity to another or in adjusting to their general pattern of education. It is not easy for adults to become so fully oriented to the organized learning process that they can pursue it in a normal, natural fashion, without occasional self-consciousness, frustration, or depression. In every situation, attention should therefore be given to providing the appropriate kind and amount of guidance. Realistic assessment may indicate that no help can be given. Even in such cases, some explanatory material about an activity may be offered to help people who want guidance—a summary of a library's services and service points, a map of a museum that indicates the location of its chief collections, or a description of a lecture or television program that identifies its central theme, its level, and its target audience. Though only a few people are reached by these or other devices, they help establish the fact that the institution cares about the people it serves.

The failure to provide guidance for adults has important consequences, the most obvious one being a low retention rate. Many men and women enter activities in which they are not fundamentally interested, that require more work than they originally contemplated, or that are not designed to achieve the purposes they want to accomplish. As a result, such people drop out. A chain reaction may then set in. Those who remain begin to wonder whether the decline in attendance is an indication that the program is faulty; perhaps they should leave too. Some of them do. The leader grows uneasy and shows it. More people leave. The program limps along or is abandoned. A second consequence of failure to provide guidance is the loss of one of the most fruitful ways of improving programs, since unmet needs or desires of individuals are often discovered in counseling interviews. A third consequence is a failure of recruitment, for the guidance process draws people's attention to programs they might otherwise overlook or misunderstand.

One major difficulty with providing guidance for adults, particularly in institutions that require special staffs to perform the function, is the establishment of an appropriate interpersonal relationship between counselor and client. The counselor must go beyond the provision of information about requirements, fees, and schedules to take a sincere interest in the individual or group being helped. Many men and women turn to education out of a sense of need and frustration and with the belief that they are inadequate to life's tasks; they need sympathetic reinforcement. Yet counselors are not psychotherapists and should not allow themselves to adopt that role. Other adults turn to education with an almost religious spirit; they want to undergo a spiritual or humanistic rebirth or to have their values reordered by someone or something beyond themselves. Some educators, both religious and secular, are ready to try to provide that service. Others have different aims that their counselors must explain to those who would otherwise expect something more exalted than they will actually find.

Various approaches are used to establish the right framework for guiding adults into or out of educational programs. The most customary way of handling the matter is simply to provide necessary information with a warm and accepting manner. A second way is to adapt some psychotherapeutic or psychometric approach, such as nondirective counseling, the interpretation of tests, or group encounter. A third way is to use a pragmatic, common-sense approach, giving information but also trying to discover a client's deeper, rather than more apparent, needs and desires and quickly terminating any interview that seems likely to lead to problems with which the counselors feel they should not try to cope. This last approach may be the most useful one at the present time, since no systematic and sophisticated theory of adult educational counseling has yet won widespread acceptance.

Modifying life-styles. As previously stated, an adult educational program must always be fitted into the life pattern of those who undertake it. In childhood and youth, schooling takes precedence over most other affairs. In adulthood, by contrast, the individual must find the time and place for study; must spend money for this purpose rather than another; must alter associations with family, fellow workers, and friends; and must give education a high enough priority so that it will not be neglected. Education is never simply added to the actions of a life; it replaces something else. And that replacement must be carefully considered both when an activity is planned and throughout its duration.

In a C-1 situation, this reorientation must be enforced by the individuals themselves. They can be as flexible in fitting study into their lives as they like but must also be ready to make changes later on and to be resolute in carrying out plans. In other categories, educators must adjust activities to help learners fit them into their patterns of life. Some attention is usually given this matter at the start, particularly in terms of scheduling; but a format may need to be reexamined periodically to be sure that it conforms to the life patterns and resources of the learners.

Most activities also require alteration in the previously established patterns or routines of the educator. The tutor, the leader, and the teacher must fit the student, the group, or the class into their schedules, and the institution must reshape its ways of work since its aggregate of activities is changed. This adjustment is particularly essential in C-6 and C-10 situations, where groups or institutions must be prepared to alter their existing programs to conform to the requirements of the collaborative venture.

Arranging financing. To learners, the question of finance varies greatly. They may be paid to go to school, their required outlay may be nonexistent or negligible, or their cost may be high and include tuition charges, incidental expenses (such as payment for transportation, lodging, meals, and child care), and the sacrifice of income. Thus they adjust their learning patterns to the resources available.

Adult education is usually financed by taxation; student fees; grants from government, foundations, or other sources; income from endowment; or allocations from the general funds of such sponsoring institutions as universities, voluntary associations, or industrial corporations. Much of the real cost, however, is indirect and comes from contributed service, physical facilities, or other resources.

Adult education, like other community functions, makes extensive use of volunteers, and other workers receive compensation substantially below their customary levels. For example, a college professor who teaches an overload class of adults usually gets only a fraction of what would ordinarily be paid for a similar class of regular students. The task of financing an activity requires the use of all of the available resources in the best fashion possible to achieve the desired results.

The field of adult education has traditionally had three major fiscal problems. The most familiar is inadequacy of funds, which prevents an activity from coming into being, restricts its effectiveness, and limits participation to those who can afford it. An equally serious though less frequent problem occurs when too much money must be spent too rapidly. It sometimes happens that a government bureau or a philanthropist cannot or will not allow time to shape and perfect a new pattern of service but requires that it be created at once and spread immediately to large numbers of people. In such cases, early optimism is usually followed by disillusionment. A third problem arises when an institution or activity has unstable resources; feast and famine alternate, no capital accumulation is built up to assure a steady flow of income, and the program leads a precarious life.

One question perennially considered in one form or another by program planners is whether people appreciate education more if they have to pay for it. Folk wisdom and common sense suggest that the answer is yes, and that view is often supported by anecdotal evidence offering examples of how high-priced activities succeed while low-priced activities do not. However, at least as many examples can be given to support a negative answer. Free public libraries have not been driven out of existence by rental libraries; the imposition of a fee by an evening school or a museum often limits attendance; and American agriculture has been revolutionized by the essentially free assistance provided to farmers by the Cooperative Extension Service. Moreover, it is seldom suggested that a high fee can by itself save an activity whose other aspects are poor. The issue must be regarded as unresolved. No objective studies have isolated fee payment as one component of design and assessed its relative influence on various kinds of adult education. Whether or not this form of financing is used depends on the judgment of the planner and the necessities the situation imposes.

Interpreting the activity. Those who plan an adult educational activity must usually try to win support, approval, or acceptance for it from outside persons or publics. A wife wants her husband to agree to her absence from home for several weekend conferences. A high school teacher of literature feels he should explain to other teachers why he offers a class at night. An administrator hopes to increase enrollment in the activities of her institution. The need for interpretation arises from such simple and direct desires as these.

Learners may encounter no such need if they live within an enclave of associates who accept the value of education or alternatively if their temperaments are so autonomous that they feel no need for social reinforcement. Many individuals believe their families and other intimates oppose their desire to learn. A study of young mothers in homemaking clubs showed that only 55 percent of them thought their husbands approved of their participation, only 63 percent thought their mothers approved, and only 60 percent believed that their best friends approved (Goble, 1964, p. 72). Such figures as these, even for a simple, practically rewarding, and easily interpreted activity, suggest why so many adult learners feel they must either hide their participation or find ways of explaining it if they can.

The educator who designs a program usually tries to present it in a way that will win public support. In a tribal, peasant, or small-town culture, education may threaten powerful mores and folkways. It must be introduced with great care, or it will be summarily rejected. Even in more sophisticated societies, attention must be paid to accepted values. Occupational advancement, getting to know the "right" people in town, or the achievement of a college degree may be socially accepted; a course of study that may not be centrally concerned with any of these objectives may need to be presented in terms of its possible contribution to one of them. In complex societies, competition for attention is so great that the designer of a program must often find some special way of heightening or expressing its appeal if it is to attract learners away from other forms of activity, including other adult education programs.

The desire for effective public relations must not endanger the integrity of the program itself. Most adults have been subjected to a lifelong barrage of promotional efforts and easily recognize overselling or deceitful promotion. Even if initially impressed, they do not remain so very long. A celebrity may be chosen as a leader because her name will attract enrollments, but the novelty of her presence will quickly wear off. If she does not perform effectively, the participants will soon grow disillusioned. An advertising campaign may create widespread attention, but if the activity itself is not a good one, word of mouth soon negates the paid promotion. When people are asked why they enrolled in a program, the most common answer is that it was recommended to them by some person who had already taken it or who knew of its reputation. The frequency of this response suggests that, at least in the long run, the most effective way to interpret a program is to have a good one.

General institutional interpretation can provide powerful support for the specific activities that an association or organization sponsors. As soon as it establishes itself in the public consciousness, it commands a ready-made audience for its entire offering. Thus an institution must define the image that it wishes to create and then establish and reinforce it by interpretational strategies and techniques, symbols, and the use of other means available to it. It will then have greater power to recruit students, increase its resources, win community support, and demonstrate its accountability to society.

As a program or institution continues, its interpretive needs are likely to change. A place may have been won in the community's consciousness, but the resulting conception may be so constricting that it limits any growth that is not in accordance with the accepted pattern. This problem was touched on in Chapter Four in the description of the C-8 category. When an institution tries to introduce a wholly new format, it may have great difficulty in interpreting its wish not merely to its desired new public but also to the established clienteles who may feel betrayed by the change.

As the foregoing paragraphs suggest, no widespread generalized climate of opinion now supports and reinforces all adult educational efforts and minimizes the need for constant interpretation and reinterpretation of them. Despite the enormous recent growth of the field, those who engage in it use a fragmented approach in which the several parts do not add up to a coherent whole. In such comparable areas of concern as welfare, health, conservation, or recreation, it is generally accepted that a broad social function can be performed in many ways and by many institutions, each playing its distinctive role but all orchestrating their efforts to reinforce one another. No comparable recognition of adult education exists, a fact that greatly impedes the growth of the field. The most immediate consequence is that every new learning activity must be separately interpreted to the publics influenced by it with little reinforcement from a general social understanding of the human need to continue education to the end of life.

Putting the Plan into Effect

In a customary time sequence, such as that followed by most forms of schooling for both adults and children, a learning design is first devised and then carried out. It is usually expected that however well laid the original plans may be, they will almost at once require changes, since even the most experienced educator or learner working within a well-established framework can never foresee all of the contingencies that must be cared for. She or he may have ignored crucial elements, made wrong decisions concerning others, or find that the situation actually encountered is different in some way from the contemplated one. In every such case, the abstractness of the plan must be altered in terms of the concreteness of reality confronted.

In other cases, a complete design is not possible until after the activity begins. A residential conference may be sketched out only in broad outlines, so that the participants can help determine its pattern. In other forms of learning, particularly those having to do with problem solving, original inquiry, or sensitivity training, only a few general guidelines can be set at the start; everything else must be developed after the program is under way. A community development worker may plan to help citizens learn how to work collectively but does so by using the difficulties they identify. The elements in the evolving educational design will emerge only during the activity itself and may not be fully identifiable until it has been completed.

The time period of an educational activity helps determine how faithfully it adheres to original plans. In an act, changes must be accomplished quickly or not at all; if reality differs significantly from the plan, the activity may have to be abandoned, as when an announced lecturer fails to appear. In an episode, greater latitude for variation is possible. In a series of episodes, planning and action alternate and may even overlap, so that gradual improvement in execution is possible. The accounts of the Fifth Army program and that of the 528 Club in Chapter Three suggest how this process occurs. In an aggregate of simultaneous episodes, each process may reinforce the others, as a teacher or a learner discovers how to improve one episode by the experience of what is occurring in another.

In sum, the execution of a program is never merely the working out of a design already made in preparation for an evaluation that will come later. It is a time of both the accomplishment of plans and their constant readjustment.

Measuring and Appraising Results

While a program is under way, its quality is constantly being appraised by its participants. After it has been completed, they all make a summative judgment of how good it has been. When the members of a group, class, or conference disperse, never to be reassembled, when the spirit and harmony of their community of interest disappear, when the final speeches have been made and the good-byes said, what values remain? Has it all been worthwhile?

The answer to this question is provided by the use of a dual process. The first is *measurement*, the determination by objective means of the extent to which learners have achieved the criteria of evaluation. The second part is *appraisal*, a subjective judgment of how well educational objectives have been achieved. Appraisal may incorporate the data provided by measurement, but it goes beyond them to sum them up, to reflect on their meaning, and to make a culminating assessment of the value of the activity. A simple illustration of the interworking of these two processes is given in this project report prepared by a county home adviser:

> The standard set for completion of our project on the reduction of obesity (which we called *Lines and Figures*) was that each of the 100 rural women included should attend at least half the lessons and actually reduce her weight. By the first standard, there was a 60 percent finish. In terms of the second, the women averaged losing one pound per week. When final classes were held, a total of 601 pounds had come off. The most anyone lost was twenty-four pounds. I believe that this project has resulted in more changed habits and practices than any other project attempted in the last two or three years. The changes recommended were very basic and self-discipline not easy. The success of the sixty finishing members was gratifying but 60 percent is not enough to satisfy me.

As noted earlier, the establishment of criteria for evaluation is one element of a format. Wherever possible, data relevant to them should be collected from the beginning of the educational activity, and information on progress should be reported and interpreted. While it is useful to have many kinds of evidence to provide the basis for a balanced appraisal, only as much measurement should be undertaken as the situation allows. Otherwise evaluation becomes an end in itself, which may be appropriate in research investigations but which distorts its proper purpose in most educational activities. Sometimes too the concept of an exquisitely refined assessment of achievement is so daunting that it keeps educators from doing any evaluation at all.

The science of measurement has grown apace in recent years, but relatively little is known about how its results can be harmoniously combined into a balanced appraisal. Education has to do with the human mind, body, and spirit, all highly resistant to mechanistic formulations. The precise refinement either of objectives or of measurement instruments is itself a sustained exercise in the making of choices. The effort to be completely objective can lead to a tendency to seek only those goals whose accomplishments are readily measurable and to forget the rest. It may be easy, for example, to test the skill of a worker but hard to assess the sense of craftsmanship; the first may therefore be stressed at the expense of the second. Even making a distinction between physical skills and values calls for the exercise of judgment; putting together the lines of evidence that blend them requires an even greater subjectivity of approach.

The learner or the educator must therefore examine all available evidence and make an appraisal of how much the educational program has accomplished in terms of her or his sense of the realities of the situation. The basic questions to be asked are simple and direct. How well was each objective achieved? If I did better than expected, why? Was the goal too high, or was the design poorly planned and executed? If the latter, what specifics were wrong? If the objective was reached, would I have done better if I had set higher levels of accomplishment? If goals changed during the course of learning, should they have? What additional criteria of evaluation should have been used? Can I make an estimate of how well I would have done on them? Such questions call for judgmental answers but are the only kinds on which appraisal can be made and the process of evaluation completed.

Repeating the Educational Cycle

Even as appraisal looks backward to judge the past, it should also look ahead to help shape the future. The questions asked in an appraisal can be recast to give this forward orientation. In a C-4 situation, for example, a teacher can consider such matters as these as she thinks about repeating a course for a new group of students: Should the original goals be used? Should there be additional ones, or should any of the previous ones be deleted? Should new criteria be employed? Should standards on the criteria be the same or made higher or lower? What elements in the format or in its accommodation to life-styles should be changed? Such questions can only be guides to subjective thought. Yet it is only by trying to answer them fully and honestly that improvement is likely to occur. The military program described by Mr. Heylin in Chapter Three shows how he revised each successive offering in the sequence he was administering.

If learning is to be lifelong, new acts and episodes will constantly occur; and both learners and educators should gain through contemplative practice an increasing understanding and mastery of educational design. In Figure 2.1 of Chapter Two, a line connects the final step of measurement and appraisal in one activity with the first step of the next one. The learner or the educator has completed one cycle and is now in a new phase in which he or she is ready to identify a possible new activity, to decide whether to proceed, and, if the decision is affirmative, to embark upon a new process of educational development using the same steps as before.

Afterthoughts

The length of this chapter may serve to defeat its purpose if it has caused the central unity of good educational design to be obscured by the consideration of each of its components. Some people may treat the system mechanically at first, as a series of formal steps. Nevertheless, even as they use it in this fashion, they will come to see that its parts have interconnections not solely determined by time. Whatever people may learn about each component can be incorporated into the overall system without destroying its unity. With increased practice, they can move forward more and more confidently because they will need to think less and less about the several decision points. Finally, as in the mastery of any other complex process, they will achieve that highest form of art in which they seem not to be using any art at all.

. . . .

6

Mastering a Personal System of Practice

The unexamined life is not worth living.
—Plato, *Apology*

The theme of this final chapter has been foreshadowed throughout the book. Practitioners of adult education become more proficient specialists (such as directors of human resource development, museum curators, operators of conference centers, or county extension agents) by reflecting over their own experience and that of other people and using it to refine their patterns of operation. Sometimes the occupants of these or other like positions realize that they are working in a broader field than they had realized and that by becoming generalists in adult education they can both improve their present practice and open up new career opportunities for themselves. To do so, they must deeply understand one or more general programming models that they can integrate into their thoughts by analyzing many educational episodes and that they can apply by incorporating what they learn into their own practice. This chapter is devoted to a description of how this mastery can be achieved.

A general plan of operation is usually involved. (1) The first step is to choose the program model that seems most relevant and useful. For the sake of convenience, it will here be assumed that the model chosen is the one described in this book, but other models could serve as beginning points. (2) An overall though necessarily superficial understanding of the model should be gained from a study of its theoretical statement. (3) A first case, drawn from the literature or from personal experience, should be given thorough study. If a lack of congruity seems to exist between any part of the model and the case, it should be noted for later reexamination. (4) Further cases should be analyzed; they may be found from introspection over past or present experience, from program planning currently under way, or from accounts found in the literature. (5) Each of the elements of the model and their interaction with one another should be reviewed. (6) Another model should be examined closely, first independently and then in comparison with the first one. (7) Several cases should be assessed in terms of both models. (8) The ongoing practice of adult education should be continually modified in terms of what seems to work out best pragmatically and in relation to how the model is refined in the mind of the practitioner.

The desired outcome of this process is the mastery of a way of work drawn from one or many models and ultimately unique to each individual. It is relatively easy to gain an overall view of a pattern of programming. The essence of the model presented in this book is contained in Table 2.1 and Figure 2.1. A leader can quickly make them clear to learners by going over each element of the design, using anecdotes to illustrate unclear points, and responding to questions. In an hour or less, an individual, a group, or an audience can be brought to a surface comprehension of the basic design of the model. But subsequently the listeners will not be able to use it (nor even remember it) unless they study rigorously its application in practice; they will not master it unless they use it many times to guide their own learning or that they provide to others. It may well take years to reach a satisfactory and well-established level of competence in which all the separate components of good practice have been so synthesized that the practitioner can proceed with confidence—as learner, educator, or both—with no need any longer to move laboriously through the specific steps of the model unless poor or mediocre results require a return to fundamentals. To cite a parallel case, an airline pilot, after first checking each of his instruments, flies his plane in any kind of weather in terms of his understanding of the total system he is operating. Similarly, an internist in medicine sees her patients as whole people with highly complicated and interrelated physiological components that can act with or against one another in influencing the complaint that has necessitated a visit to the doctor. In like fashion, the adult educator needs to act from an awareness of the complex interrelationships present in any episode of learning; but she or he cannot do so without first understanding each of the elements of the situation and how they fit together and then using that understanding in practice.

Praxis

As this chapter's epigraph suggests, the value of the self-examined life has ancient roots in philosophy. Many modern writers, most notably Apps (1985 and 1994), have built their proposals for the improvement of adult education on the idea that the practitioner should constantly speculate about the relationship between theory and practice. In furthering this idea, the word *praxis* has been used by Freire and others to indicate actions guided by theory. The Oxford English Dictionary (OED) notes that this term has many meanings. In the seventeenth century and later, it was an antonym for *theory* and denoted habitual action, accepted practice, or, as one writer put it, "the crystallization of custom." Karl Marx reversed this usage and used praxis to mean (in the OED's words) "the willed action by which a theory or philosophy becomes a social actuality." The term has now broadened to have general usage and is linked only historically with Marxism.

Praxis is relevant to many aspects of adult educators' lives, but attention here is focused solely on how a theory of program-building can be put into effect to become the central and distinctive element of educators' competence. They also need to examine other parts of their practice so that they can apply theory there as well. They need, for example, to study their personal values to see where they want to place their emphasis in their work. They must know the distinctive elements of their service as teacher, group leader, counselor, facilitator, or administrator. Some writers go beyond these specifics to suggest that anything people do to examine and improve themselves or their actions will improve their ability to undertake their work; a better and more fully realized human being brings to every situation an increased capacity for inspiration or service. These other uses of praxis are all accepted here as valid ways to improve the quality of adult education, but they lie beyond the scope of this book.

It is not precisely clear how praxis works. Vella (1994, p. 11) calls it "a beautiful dance of inductive and deductive forms of learning. As we know, inductive learning proceeds from the particular to the general whereas deductive learning moves from the general principle to the particular situation." As this analysis suggests, praxis is not simple trial and error; it is not problem solving; it is not speculation or contemplation or introspection; it is not inspiration; and it is not transcendental meditation—valuable though all such processes may be. It is the active and focused examination of one or more minds comparing theory to practice and vice versa—and then using the results of that examination.

Cases

Most of those who use cases to give concreteness to a theoretical model will already have in mind experiences and anecdotes of their own drawn from memory, from observation or participation in present activities, from proposals for future action, or from hearing or reading accounts of what has happened at other times and places. Everyone also begins with some awareness of what at least a few of the elements of any model look like in real life. Such components as objectives or teaching methods or guidance will be at least superficially clear, while others, such as sequence or clarity of design or life-style, may have little meaning. All components of a model will eventually require a great deal of study in order to be understood in depth, but they should be seen from the beginning in terms of their interrelationship. That is why it is important early in the process of analysis to look carefully at cases.

Often a problem is at once presented: case reports almost never include all the relevant information needed to test a model, and they almost never present their data in terms of the elements present in the model. In cases drawing from personal experience, it may be possible to discover missing facts by engaging in inquiry or further introspection. However, cases drawn from the literature must be accepted as they are presented by an author primarily interested in accurate description or in illustrating a point not related to any model. Sometimes, as in Mr. Heylin's account of education in the army presented in Chapter Three, the design category and framework of action are stated or can be easily inferred. The cases in the Hobo School require more interpretation, but they are so simple that the task of analyzing them is not hard. The patterns of learning in the other three cases of the chapter are varied and complex; the analyst must use much conjecture to understand how they take account of all aspects of program design.

After a first case is fairly well understood, the learner needs to examine others. In the references at the end of this work, certain books are noted as being rich in their provision of cases. The examination of a number of them will help develop a more comprehensive view of the model by showing how it varies when applied to different settings. The learner needs to bring an inquiring and synthesizing mind to this analysis. For example, a design component covered fully in one case may not be mentioned in another. The effort to decide whether it was overlooked, not considered important, or merely not mentioned is an important part of the learning process, as is the effort to understand any other apparent inconsistencies between theory and practice.

The true usefulness of the case method comes when it is applied to ongoing practice; it is here that praxis comes into its own since it becomes the way by which, to quote the OED, "a theory or philosophy becomes a social actuality." Let us assume that the staff of an adult educational agency is meeting to plan its program for the next year. Each proposed new activity is presented and discussed in terms of the category into which it fits and the way its program elements will be designed. This way of proceeding gives focus to the discussion and highlights points that need resolution or further thought. During the ensuing year, each activity receives an ongoing formative evaluation. Ultimately a summation is made both in respect to the desired outcome and to a judgment as to how various components might be revised to bring about a better result if the activity should be repeated. Subsequently, throughout all the years of practice, those who shape and guide learning become more proficient in doing so.

Situational Categories

Those who seek to master a general programming model tend to use one or more of the first four categories of design identified in Chapter Two and more fully described in Chapter Four. An individual creates an activity for herself (C-1), works with one or more mentors (C-2), belongs to a group that designs its own activities (C-3), or takes a class (C-4). The other seven categories can be used to create opportunities for the mastery of a program model: for example, this book was prepared as a resource for a mass audience and therefore falls into C-11. The other six (C-5 through C-10) do not present general challenges or opportunities that need to be considered in this chapter.

Each of the four most often used situations will now be discussed separately. To avoid duplication, general points made in earlier descriptions will not be repeated in later ones.

An individual designs an activity for herself (C-1). Examples: a person with no previous experience in adult education is appointed to the staff of a program in this field; a volunteer in a community agency decides to prepare for a paid job in it; and a person experienced in only one kind of adult education wants to enlarge her career opportunities by gaining broader competence in the field.

Such a person, going it alone, might use one or many kinds of resources, getting help from wherever it can be found. If she were to turn to this book as a primary source of information and guidance, she might read it straight through, scan it quickly, or dip into it as she sees interesting bits. But she might like to follow the general plan of operation suggested in the second paragraph of this chapter. To follow this design, the independent learner should begin by reading the part of Chapter Two starting with the heading "A Two-Part System." She should then read the case on military education by Heylin in Chapter Three and follow that reading by a close comparison of the program and the model, first establishing the situational category or categories and then checking each of the component decision points. When this task is completed, she should reverse the analysis and inquire whether Mr. Heylin dealt with any fundamental matters not found in the model. At some point but preferably after her own analysis, she should read mine to see how it compares with her own. She should then read the other four cases in Chapter Three, thus strengthening an awareness of the breadth of the field. And following that reading, she should examine each case in terms of the model, contrasting her analysis with mine.

Periodically during the foregoing process, she should look to her own present or past episodes of learning or teaching to see how they relate to the model, though never trying to force practice to fit theory or the reverse. At any point where the match between the two seems absent or imperfect, her effort to reconcile them is likely to lead to the growth of a personal and individualized style. At some point along the way, she should read the first half of the second chapter of this book to see how well she agrees with the nine assumptions on which my model is based.

It will then be time to test this first model against others. She should read the first chapter to gain perspective on the history of model making and choose from among the systems mentioned there or elsewhere the one that seems most compatible with her own views. Three recent books presenting broadly comprehensive models and rich in illustrations, anecdotes, and case accounts are Caffarella (1994), Knowles and Associates (1984), and Vella (1994). Any of these three is sure to be helpful by giving insights into practice, broadening the understanding of the whole field, and providing a model that can be contrasted with mine, both directly and in terms of their relevance to the cases our learner has studied.

By this time, the independent learner will have acquired a way of thinking about adult education that is essentially based on books and theoretical in character. This thinking will need to be refined and enlarged by practical experience or by interaction with other minds. In real life, she may well have moved into another learning situation in which she has found a mentor, a discussion group, or a class. She may also have started into a new phase of her career that enables her to examine and be introspective about the practical realities of her work.

An individual or a group designs an activity for another individual (C-2). Examples: a graduate student in adult education takes an individual study course with a professor; a new staff member of an adult educational agency is guided by a senior staff member with the occasional help of his colleagues; and a retired administrator serves as adviser to somebody still in service. The profound difference between such examples and independent study is that they put the direction of learning in the hands of people (here called mentors) who, ideally at least, understand deeply a programming model and its applications, are aware of the learner's experience and ability, take the tasks of guidance seriously, and are able in a face-to-face collaboration to enliven and enrich a continuing relationship.

A mentor may very well follow the general plan of operation suggested at the start of this chapter or even the specific application of it using the process outlined in this book as a possible procedure for an independent learner. Whatever sequence is chosen, the process is controlled by the specifics of the situation and unwinds from beginning to end as immediate circumstances dictate.

Let us hypothesize that a young man, Jack, is hired as an executive assistant to the director of the Office of Educational Development (OED), a twenty-six-person unit in the Department of Human Resources of a factory. Jack likes the setting very much, does his job well, and asks for consideration for more responsible employment. The director agrees but only if Jack will prepare himself for a broader assignment. The two agree on a plan in which Jack will review with the director of the OED all of its subunits, making some firsthand observations in each. The director then helps Jack understand the developmental nature of the OED's work, particularly how perceived needs in the factory are identified and met by educational programs. The flow chart of new ventures on the director's office wall shows the decision points by which general ideas are given concrete reality. The segments of the flow chart suggest that all successful adult educational ventures have the same basic components. Jack is asked to study and report on three existing programs that on the surface are very different from one another. Do all three follow the same model? If not, how does it differ in the three cases? As he discusses each of the three with the director, his perception of practice sharpens, and his misunderstandings are cleared up. He sits in on the sessions of planning committees and talks with their leaders about what he has witnessed. In time, he is given small projects of his own to work out and is monitored in their execution by the director, whose critiques cover every aspect of operation but stress the ways basic components have been handled. Not long after that, a vacancy occurs in the senior staff, and Jack is appointed to the position. The director gets a new assistant.

Most of the people who work in adult education enter it as casually as Jack did but are forced to learn only by trial and error. Any mentoring they receive has to do only with the immediate knowledge required to get by on a daily basis. Since their initial mastery of their craft is not centered on a model or indeed on any theory of programming, their experience at work tends to become routine and does not help build a sounder mastery of present assignments or create the basis for a broader career. Many people have no mentors available: they occupy one-person slots in museums, social welfare agencies, foundations, or retirement communities. To get personal guidance into program theory, they must usually register for a tutorial course at a university or find a master practitioner with the time to help them. In such an eventuality, the relationship between mentor and learner will be profoundly influenced by the absence of a common work environment. An external mentor may have a broader view of the field than a program director, but her case material may have to be drawn from the literature and therefore be one step away from reality. Also the follow-through that tests the mastery of the model by the learner may have to be self-evaluated.

In the case of an independent learner, relatively few decision points exist. (It may help here to review Figure 2.1.) When social interaction is introduced, as it is with mentoring, many of the components of the design may need to be considered to be sure that the procedures to be followed are the best available. Only "individualization" by definition does not apply. Those acting as mentors, whether single or multiple, confront the learner directly. Success or failure in the endeavor is measured wholly in terms of its influence on one person; that fact is inherent in the relationship itself.

A group (with or without a continuing leader) designs an activity for itself. Examples: several staff members of a moribund adult educational institution conclude that it can be brought back to a vigorous life only if they collectively study the rules of sound programming; an organization that has been very successful with its first endeavor wants to broaden the base of its service, and its senior staff members themselves constitute a study group to decide how to do so; and a group of students in a nontraditional graduate program in adult education develop a seminar on programming.

Group activity has at least initially an attractive spontaneity of approach that arises from the mutual acceptance of the members and a sense of shared responsibility. In mastering a program model, a group has at least two advantages not present in the situations already described. First, the range of cases that can be discussed is greater because of the diverse experiences of the members of the group. Second, any proposed model is likely to be strongly tested by the expression of different points of view. Consensus often comes only after vigorous debate has clarified definitions and issues, thus making the members more vividly aware of all aspects of the theory with which they are dealing. The existence of alternatives also encourages the members of the group to develop distinctive models appropriate to their own practice.

A group activity developed for the purpose of mastering a model is itself an adult educational activity. To be successful, it must be well designed. A review of the decision points summarized in Figure 2.1 shows that they all apply. A group that studies a model needs a leader; if this person is not appointed at the start, she or he will emerge later. The group must have human or other resources to provide content for its discussion. All of the other components must eventually be cared for. Perhaps none is more important than being clear about the criteria of evaluation. Some task may have been required or may emerge: a report to be written, a meeting to be planned, or a governing document to be drafted. The need to fulfill this requirement may cause the group to pay insufficient attention to the growth of competence by the group members.

A teacher or group of teachers designs an activity for, and often with, a group of students. Examples: a university offers a graduate course; a specialist employed by a national voluntary association offers an intensive course in a residential center for the chairmen of the educational committees of some of its state and local affiliates; and several highly skilled programmers offer a four-weekend course for faculty members of a nontraditional baccalaureate program.

This situation differs from those already mentioned in that it is designed and conducted by one or more people who have a deep knowledge of adult educational design and are masters of its practice.

Sometimes they are deeply committed to a specific model but even so can handle expertly the strengths and weaknesses of several approaches to programming. The abilities of the instructors are usually further enriched by the literature they make available. Particularly this situation is true when the course is held at a university, and the learners have access not only to the literature of adult education but also to all of its allied theoretical and professional subjects. The latter are particularly useful to those students whose earlier preparation has been in nursing, law, librarianship, social work, religion, or other service-related fields. Such students can often locate cases for analysis from these other disciplines.

A wide range of techniques is also available in a teacher-designed activity. A graduate course may include presentations by the professor geared to the abilities of the students; group discussion; collective analyses of cases furnished by the instructor or presented by the students; readings in the literature of programming; and term reports by the students dealing with such subjects as the close examination of a model and its components, comparative analyses of two or more models, the presentation of examples of all program development situations, or any other related topic. Usually the instructor has already conducted similar courses and can profit from that experience both in handling the content and also in designing the new venture to make it more educative. Such a course has an advantage in offering an in-depth experience, but it may have the disadvantage of being unrelated to a work setting. Therefore complete mastery is impossible to achieve in the course itself but must be gained by the student in some other fashion.

A Summing Up

Adult education will emerge as a full-fledged and well-regarded field of work only when its master practitioners (by the foregoing methods or any other) achieve the ability to use fundamental educational designs, choosing in each case the one that best meets the requirements of the situation. The need for a large number of people to build careers in this field has been created by the astonishingly rapid spread of participation in learning by men and women throughout the world. The idea that education should enrich life throughout its whole duration is not new. Yet only in this century has it been seriously believed that such an idea was possible for most people and perhaps eventually for everyone. Meanwhile many personal and social ills can be remedied only by widespread or universal education, and it takes disciplined intelligence of a very high order to devise the programs required to deal with them. In the future even more than in the past, the meeting of needs and the satisfaction of desires will necessitate creativeness, the expenditure of great individual and social effort, and the use of sophisticated thought about the design of education.

Glossary

> *He who lets the world or his own portion of it,*
> *choose his plan of life for him has no need of any*
> *other faculty than the apelike one of imitation.*
> *He who chooses his plan for himself employs all his*
> *faculties. He must use observation to see, reasoning*
> *and judgment to foresee, activity to gather materials*
> *for decision, discrimination to decide, and when he*
> *has decided, firmness and self-control to hold to his*
> *deliberate decision.*
>
> —John Stuart Mill, *On Liberty*

This glossary will be presented in two forms. The first is a summary of the book's content in which key terms (which are italicized when first mentioned) are in context. The second is a listing and definition of the same terms in alphabetical order. To avoid excessive elaboration, only one form of a word is given, the variant forms being implied. Thus the term *measurement* is given but not such terms as *measure* (as a noun or a verb), *measured*, or *measuring*. Some words (such as *objective*, *resource*, or *schedule*) that have many general meanings are defined only as used in educational terminology. The definitions are not intended to reflect or to provide standard meanings but to indicate how terms are used in this book.

Summary

Adult education (and perhaps all *education*) is considered to be a *cooperative* (not an *operative*) art designed to increase *skill* (or *ability*), *knowledge* (or *information*), or *sensitiveness*. As a *process*, it becomes operationalized when some segment of human experience that is lived within a complex personal or social *milieu* (or *setting*) is separated out for examination by a *learner*, an *educator*, or an *analyst*. This segment is called a *situation*. Situations are always unique, but they can be classified into eleven *categories* (designated in this book numerically from C-1 to C-11). These categories may be broadly divided into those that occur on an *individual*, a *group*, an *institutional*, or a *mass* basis. Two basic institutional forms are identified, the *association* and the *organization*.

In a situation, an educational *activity* may be planned but not come to fruition, or it may actually occur either by chance or by intent. Both planning and analysis usually occur in terms of a time *period* (*act*, *episode*, *series* of episodes, or *aggregate* of simultaneous episodes) or a combination of such periods. The planning or analysis requires two reciprocal actions that, taken together, make up the total *system* suggested here. The first one of these actions is the determination of the category in which the situation falls. The second action is the application to this situation of a *framework* (or *model*) of planning or analysis that includes a number of interrelated *components* of which the chief groups are

1.   The *objectives* (or *aims*, *ends*, *goals*, or *purposes*). The factors that determine objectives are the milieu, the nature of the learners, the *aspirations*, the *motives*, the *content*, and the framework itself. Objectives may be stated either as *accomplishments* or as *principles*.

2.   The *elements* that combine together into an educational *format*. These elements include *resources*, *leaders*, *methods* (or *techniques*), *schedule*, *sequence*, *social reinforcement*, *individualization*, *roles* and *relationships*, *criteria of evaluation*, and *clarity of design*.

3.   The *adjustments* required in fitting the format into the milieu. These adjustments include *guidance*, introduction of the program into the *life-style* of the participants, *finance*, and *interpretation*.

4.   The *measurement* and *appraisal* of results that, taken together, are called *evaluation*.

The actual application of this framework to a situation, often as a result of a *need* or an *interest*, results in a *design* (or *program*) that takes account of all the components relevant to the situational category involved. The process of application is always unique to the situation because the components are not related to one another in any invariable order. A design may begin with any of them and proceed in any fashion. In both planning and analysis, however, it is often useful to review the components as they occur logically in a time flow, requiring the use of several *decision points* from the time when a possible educational activity is identified until its results are evaluated.

If there is a series of episodes, the experience gained in each should be used to improve the subsequent ones in a steady process of *revision* of the design.

The proposed system is compared to a number of other approaches to process that have evolved during the recent history of organized *adult* education. Some of these are simple *credos*. Others are complex systems based on the thought of John Dewey, Ralph W. Tyler, Kurt Lewin, and Malcolm Knowles. Lewin's followers have devised two systems, *group dynamics* and *change theory*. Knowles's pattern of analysis is generally known as *andragogy*. Other complex approaches are those based on *community development*, on *systems analysis*, and on *transformative learning*. In recent years, many other models have been proposed. In some cases, *functions* related to but different from adult education have been the source for systems that have been inappropriately applied to it; among such functions are *public relations*, *service*, *recreation*, *esthetic appreciation*, *fraternization*, *welfare*, and *therapy*.

List of Terms

ability   See *skill*.

accomplishment   A discernible achievement, here used to indicate one of the two major ways of stating objectives, the other being *principle*.

act   A specific and relatively brief learning or teaching event.

activity   A specific educational action or succession of actions occurring in a situation.

adjustment   A way of harmonizing an educational format with the milieu in which it is to occur or with the lives of the learners or educators involved; usually requires some change in either the format or the milieu.

adult   A person (man or woman) who has achieved full physical development and who expects to have the right to participate as a responsible homemaker, worker, and member of society.

adult education   The process by which men and women (alone, in groups, or in institutional settings) seek to improve themselves or their society by increasing their skill, their knowledge, or their sensitiveness. Any process by which individuals, groups, or institutions try to help men and women improve in these ways.

aggregate   A cluster of educational activities (either related or unrelated to one another) occurring in the same span of time in the life of an individual, a group, or an institution.

aim   See *objective*.

analyst   One who tries to understand the nature of an educational activity by examining its parts or basic principles. An analyst may be a learner, an educator, or an independent observer. The term is most frequently used here to signify the observer.

andragogy   A system of program design centrally based on the nature, wishes, and participation of the learner or learners, particularly those who are adult.

appraisal   A subjective judgment of how well educational objectives have been achieved, often based in part on the results of measurement and akin to measurement as a part of evaluation.

aspiration   A desired perfection or excellence based on an ideal. It can exist in the absence of a plan of activity, or it can establish the broad value inherent in an objective.

association   A structured body of members who join together, more or less freely, because of a shared interest, activity, or purpose and who, by the act of joining, assume the same basic powers and responsibilities held by other members. The collective membership elects its officers, giving them temporary authority. An association usually has its own members as its beneficiaries. It is distinguished from a group largely by size and complexity and may in fact be a constellation of groups.

category   A set of similar situations in which educational activities occur.

change theory   A system of individual, group, institutional, or community improvement. It involves a relationship in which a change agent enters into a helping role with a client or client system and by various means (some of them educational) seeks to alter performance and stabilize it at a new level.

clarity of design   The degree of understanding of an activity by those taking part in it or analyzing it.

community development   Any organized effort by which those sharing a defined territorial area (as a base for carrying out a major share of their activities) can work collectively to try to solve a common problem.

component   An essential constituent part of the educational framework; includes objectives, elements of the format, adjustments, and measurement and appraisal of results.

content   Anything taught or learned in an educational activity, including knowledge, skill, or sensitiveness.

cooperative art   A system of principles and methods used to create a product or a performance when such an outcome is achieved by guiding and directing a natural entity or process. See also *operative art*.

credo   A statement of belief that is not part of any larger system of ideas or conceptions.

criteria of evaluation   Standards, rules, or tests used for measurement and on which an appraisal can be based.

decision point   One of the places in the application of a system at which a program planner or analyst uses his or her judgment in creating a design.

design   The plan developed to guide educational activity in a situation or the plan that can be inferred by an analyst of that activity. Synonym: *program*.

education   The process by which human beings (alone, in groups, or in institutional settings) seek to improve themselves or their society by increasing their skill, their knowledge, or their sensitiveness. Any process by which individuals, groups, or institutions try to help human beings improve in these ways.

educator   One who seeks to improve other individuals or society by increasing their skill, their knowledge, or their sensitiveness. The term implies that the educator exerts purposeful effort to achieve such objectives, though the people influenced may or may not intend to achieve them.

element   An essential and separately definable part of an educational format.

end   See *objective*.

episode   A related succession of acts making up a coherent educational whole.

esthetic appreciation   The enjoyment of the beautiful in any of its varied forms.

evaluation   The determination of the extent to which an educational objective has been accomplished. Evaluation includes the two closely related processes of measurement and appraisal.

finance   The direct and indirect cost of an educational activity.

format   The pattern of interrelated elements used in an educational design as an immediate and direct way of achieving objectives.

framework   The fundamental theoretical construct used in a situation to plan or analyze an educational design. Synonym: *model*.

fraternization   Association with other people in a brotherly or congenial way.

function   A generalized form of human activity differentiated from others by the intended result. Education, recreation, welfare, and therapy are distinguishable human functions.

goal   See *objective*.

group   A collection of human beings that has a common purpose and among whom interaction occurs.

group dynamics   The study of the nature of small groups and the way they influence the thoughts and actions of their members; also the planned use of such knowledge to aid learning processes.

guidance The direction, advice, or assistance that one individual provides to another, usually by reason of the former's greater experience or knowledge. Often used here specifically to mean the special assistance given to those who are deciding whether or not to undertake a given educational activity or who need help in adjusting it to its milieu.

individual A single human being.

individualization The adaptation of a process to meet the requirements of each of the persons that it is intended to serve.

information See *knowledge*.

institution A comparatively stable, formally, and often intricately structured body of persons that carries out common purposes or advances common causes and whose members share a standardized and complex system of habits, attitudes, and material facilities. Institutions tend to be either associations or organizations, though each of these two forms usually incorporates certain elements of the other.

interest A feeling of curiosity, fascination, or absorption in an object or activity often leading to experiences with it that give rise to satisfaction and enjoyment.

interpretation The clarification of meaning, often with the intent of winning acceptance. Usually used here to signify the interpretation of an educational activity to some person or public external to it.

knowledge A cognitive or intellective mental component acquired and retained through education or experience. Here taken to be one of the three major kinds of interrelated educational accomplishments, the others being sensitiveness and skill. Synonym: *information*.

leader A person who guides or directs another or others toward the achievement of objectives. Here usually used to refer to persons who exercise their influence because of their mastery of either content or process but who may also be chosen because of their personality or status.

learner   One who increases her or his skills, knowledge, or sensitiveness. This result may be brought about because of purposeful educational effort on the part of the learner, purposeful educational effort on the part of an educator, or as a byproduct of a random activity or one designed to achieve essentially noneducational purposes.

life-style   The general pattern of behavior of an individual, a group, or some other body of people.

mass   A large number of persons who share an educational experience but who are so numerous or so dispersed that the individuals and groups included can be treated only in general and nonspecific ways.

measurement   The determination by objective means of the extent to which learners have achieved the criteria of evaluation; closely related to appraisal as part of evaluation.

method   An established and systematic way of learning or teaching. Examples are reading, discussion, or laboratory work. Synonym: *technique*.

milieu   Broadly speaking, the total social and physical environment surrounding a situation at a given time and place. More specifically (and with defining adjectives), some set of circumstances that is related to the institution in a meaningful way—for instance, the institutional milieu (the pattern of structure and action in the institution of which the situation is a part) or the social milieu (the pattern of culture in which the situation occurs). Synonym: *setting*.

model   See *framework*.

motive   An inciting cause that helps to determine an individual's choice of an objective and behavior in seeking it. A motive may be comprehended or unconscious.

need   A condition or situation in which something necessary or desirable is required or wanted. Often used to express the deficiencies of an individual or some category of people either generally or in some set of circumstances. A need may be perceived by the person or persons possessing it (when it may be called a felt need) or by some observer (when it may be called an ascribed need).

objective   An intended result of an educational activity or a guiding policy intended to achieve such a result. Objectives may be stated either as desired accomplishments or as principles. An objective may be known prior to the activity, emerge while it is occurring, or be perceived subsequently. Synonyms: *aim, end, goal,* and *purpose*.

operative art   A system of principles and methods used to create a product or a performance when such an outcome is controlled by the person using the system. Compare *cooperative art*.

organization   A body of people who work together to achieve a common purpose and whose internal structure is characterized by a hierarchical flow of authority and responsibility from the top downward with relatively permanent (rather than periodically rotating) occupants of the seats of power; when replaced, these occupants are ordinarily designated from above rather than from below. Organizations ordinarily exist to benefit their owners, a defined clientele outside their own employees, or the public at large.

period   An interval chosen by an educator, a learner, or an analyst as a time boundary for the planning or analysis of an educational activity.

principle   A basic policy or mode of action. Here used to indicate one of the two major ways of stating objectives, the other being *accomplishment*.

process   A series of related actions undertaken to bring about an educational result.

program See *design*.

public relations The methods or activities employed to promote a favorable relationship with the general population or with some part or parts of it.

purpose See *objective*.

recreation A pleasurable or diverting activity of either mind or body.

relationship The formal or informal interaction of two or more people. See also *role*.

resource Any object, person, or other aspect of the environment that can be used for support or help in an educational activity.

revision A change or modification of a design. Here used chiefly to mean the normal process of altering the design of an episode when it is repeated. Such alteration usually arises from the appraisal of past accomplishment. Contrasted with reconstruction.

role The characteristic behavior expected of an individual in a situation as perceived by that person or by others. The definition of roles and the establishment of relationships are here considered two aspects of the same element in the format of an educational program.

schedule The timetable of an educational activity.

sensitiveness A capacity to feel or perceive, to make discriminations, or to have insight into some aspect of life, often accompanied by some ethical value. Here taken to be one of the three major kinds of interrelated educational accomplishments, the others being knowledge and skill.

sequence The order in which content is presented in an educational activity.

series A succession of related educational episodes.

service The provision of assistance or benefit to another or others.

setting See *milieu*.

situation The specific and unique combination of circumstances in which an educational activity occurs.

skill The capacity to perform some mental or physical act, whether it be easy and simple or difficult and complex. Here taken to be one of the three major kinds of interrelated educational accomplishments, the others being knowledge and sensitiveness. Synonym: *ability*.

social reinforcement The facilitation of the educational process in a collective activity by the creation or maintenance of an emotional tone that may be characterized either by positive and supportive feeling or by a sense of challenge.

system A body of interdependent factors that form a collective entity. Here most commonly used in two senses: as the way of planning or analyzing educational designs proposed in this book or as the way of achieving the same end proposed by someone else.

systems analysis The conceptualization of a general process, usually in a diagram, by which the making of judgments and the taking of actions can be put into an orderly and established flow of work.

technique See *method*.

therapy The treatment of illness or disability.

transformative learning An adult educational program intended to change a basic orientation or system of belief of the learner.

welfare The provision of help or comfort for people who have been deprived of the goods or services thought to be essential in the society in which they live.

References

The art of progress is to preserve order amid change,
and to preserve change amid order.
—Whitehead, *Process and Reality*

In 1992, I published a book called *The Literature of Adult Education: A Bibliographic Essay* (Jossey-Bass) which identifies and categorizes over a thousand books whose authors intended to make a contribution to the literature of adult education or one of its component institutions or concerns. This review of the writing in the field deals so fully with all aspects of program design, development, and execution that the comprehensive bibliography that was a feature of the first edition of this book seems unnecessary here.

In testing to see whether the design here presented is relevant to all adult education, it was necessary to gain a grasp of the nature, structure, and operation of that field. One such description had been derived inductively from the study of the literature for the 1992 volume. Four other recent analyses were also of major help in my effort to gain a comprehensive viewpoint. They are Knox (1993); Merriam and Cunningham (1989); Peters, Jarvis, and Associates (1991); and Titmus (1989).

The case-study approach to program analysis and development has been stressed in the foregoing pages. A number of the references included here describe cases that might be useful for individual or group study. Some are book-length descriptions of specific programs; others are collections of cases. All are marked with the notation CS. Many additional references include case studies to illustrate their presentations.

The remaining works included in this listing of references are the sources of citations made in previous pages, works that have special reference to topics considered, and outstanding books on program development published since my 1992 bibliographic essay.

Addams, J. *Twenty Years at Hull-House*. New York: Macmillan, 1910. CS

American Psychological Association, Education and Training Board. "Education for Research in Psychology." *American Psychologist*, 1959, *14*, 169.

Andersen, B. D., and Andersen, K. *Prisoners of the Deep*. New York: Harper-Collins, 1984. CS

Apps, J. W. *Improving Practice in Continuing Education: Modern Approaches for Understanding the Field and Determining Priorities*. San Francisco: Jossey-Bass, 1985.

Apps, J. W. *Leadership for the Emerging Age: Transforming Practice in Adult and Continuing Education*. San Francisco: Jossey-Bass, 1994.

Argyris, C. *Increasing Leadership Effectiveness*. New York: Wiley, 1976.

Beals, R. A., and Brody, L. *The Literature of Adult Education*. New York: American Association for Adult Education, 1941.

Bennett, N. L., and Fox, R. D. "Challenges for Continuing Professional Education." In L. Curry, J. F. Wergin, and Associates, *Educating Professionals: Responding to New Expectations for Competence and Accountability*. San Francisco: Jossey-Bass, 1993.

Berridge, R. I., Stark, S. L., and West, P. T. *Training the Community Educator: A Case-Study Approach*. Midland, Mich.: Pendell, 1977. CS

Boone, E. J. *Developing Programs in Adult Education*. Englewood Cliffs, N.J.: Prentice-Hall, 1985.

Boyle, P. G. *Planning Better Programs*. New York: McGraw-Hill, 1981.

Bradford, L. "Report of the Division of Adult Education Services of the National Education Association." *Adult Education Bulletin*, 1947, pp. 167–170.

Brookfield, S. *The Skillful Teacher: On Technique, Trust, and Responsiveness in the Classroom*. San Francisco: Jossey-Bass, 1990.

Brooks, J. S., and Reich, D. L. *The Public Library in Non-Traditional Education*. Homewood, Ill.: ETC Publications, 1974. CS

Brown, C. *Literacy in 30 Hours: Paulo Freire's Process in North East Brazil.* London: Writers and Readers Publishing Cooperative, 1975.

Brunner, E. deS. *Community Organization and Adult Education.* Chapel Hill: University of North Carolina Press, 1942. CS

Buber, M. *Between Man and Man.* (R. G. Smith, trans.) London: Routledge and Kegan Paul, 1947.

Buck, P. S. *Tell the People.* New York: Day, 1945. CS

Burrell, J. A. *A History of Adult Education at Columbia University: University Extension and the School of General Studies.* New York: Columbia University Press, 1954. CS

Caffarella, R. S. *Program Development and Evaluation Resource Book for Trainers.* New York: Wiley, 1988.

Caffarella, R. S. *Planning Programs for Adult Learners: A Practical Guide for Educators, Trainers, and Staff Developers.* San Francisco: Jossey-Bass, 1994. CS

Campbell, W. R. *Dead Men Walking: Teaching in a Maximum-Security Prison.* New York: Marek, 1978. CS

Candy, P. C. *Self-Direction for Lifelong Learning: A Comprehensive Guide to Theory and Practice.* San Francisco: Jossey-Bass, 1991.

Casner-Lotto, J., and Associates. *Successful Training Strategies: Twenty-Six Innovative Corporate Models.* San Francisco: Jossey-Bass, 1988. CS

Cavanaugh, S. H. "Connecting Education and Practice." In L. Curry, J. F. Wergin, and Associates, *Educating Professionals: Responding to New Expectations for Competence and Accountability.* San Francisco: Jossey-Bass, 1993.

Cervero, R. M., and Wilson, A. L. *Planning Responsibly for Adult Education: A Guide to Negotiating Power and Interests.* San Francisco: Jossey-Bass, 1994.

Chancellor, J. (ed.). *Helping Adults to Learn: The Library in Action.* Chicago: American Library Association, 1939. CS

Churchill, W. *My Early Life.* London: Thornton Butterworth, 1930.

Clapp, E. R. *Community Schools in Action.* New York: Viking Penguin, 1940. CS

Clark, B. R. *Adult Education in Transition: A Study of Institutional Insecurity.* Berkeley: University of California Press, 1968. CS

Clark, R. J., and Rooth, S. J. *Case Studies in Australian Adult Education.* Armidale, Australia: Department of Continuing Education, University of New England, and New South Wales Board of Adult Education, 1988. CS

Coady, M. M. *Masters of Their Own Destiny: The Story of the Antigonish Movement of Adult Education Through Economic Cooperation.* New York: HarperCollins, 1939. CS

Cooley, W. W., and Glaser, R. "The Computer and Individualized Instruction." *Science,* 1969, *174,* 574–575.

Cranton, P. *Understanding and Promoting Transformative Learning: A Guide for Educators of Adults.* San Francisco: Jossey-Bass, 1994.

Curry, L., Wergin, J. F., and Associates. *Educating Professionals: Responding to New Expectations for Competence and Accountability.* San Francisco: Jossey-Bass, 1993.

Daloz, L. A. *Effective Teaching and Mentoring: Realizing the Transformational Power of Adult Learning Experiences.* San Francisco: Jossey-Bass, 1986. CS

Darkenwald, G., and Merriam, S. B. *Adult Education: Foundations of Practice.* New York: HarperCollins, 1982.

Davies, J. H., and Thomas, J. E. (eds.). *A Select Bibliography of Adult Continuing Education.* (5th ed.) Leicester, England: National Institute of Adult Continuing Education (England and Wales), 1988.

Davis, L. N., and McCallon, E. *Planning, Conducting, Evaluating Workshops.* Austin, Tex.: Learning Concepts, 1974.

Dewey, J. *Experience and Education.* New York: Macmillan, 1938.

Durfee, A. A. "Expectations Held Toward the Extension Supervisor's Role." Unpublished doctoral dissertation, University of Chicago, August 1956.

Elias, J. L. *The Foundations and Practice of Adult Religious Education.* Malabar, Fla.: Krieger, 1982.

Ely, M. L. (ed.). *Adult Education in Action.* New York: American Association for Adult Education, 1936. CS

English, M. E. *College in the Country.* Athens: University of Georgia Press, 1959. CS

Flexner, J. M., and Edge, S. A. *A Readers' Advisory Service.* New York: American Association for Adult Education, 1934. CS

Fordham, P., Poulton, G., and Randle, L. *Learning Networks in Adult Education.* New York: Routledge & Kegan Paul, 1979. CS

Fostering the Growing Need to Learn: Monographs and Annotated Bibliography on Continuing Education and Health Manpower. DHEW Publication no. (HRA) 74–3112. Washington, D.C.: Division of Regional Medical Programs, Bureau of Health Resources Development, Department of Health, Education, and Welfare, 1974.

Glen, J. M. *Highlander: No Ordinary School, 1932–1962.* Lexington: University Press of Kentucky, 1988. CS

Goble, E. L. "Participation of the Young Homemaker in Group Learning Activities." Unpublished doctoral dissertation, University of Chicago, 1964.

Graham, S. *College of One.* New York: Viking Penguin, 1967. CS

Green, L. W., and others. *Health Education Planning: A Diagnostic Approach.* Palo Alto, Calif.: Mayfield, 1980. CS

Griffith, W. S. "Implications for Administrators in the Changing Adult Education Agency." *Adult Education,* 1965, *15,* 139–142.

Hartley, H. J. "Limitations of Systems Analysis." *Phi Delta Kappan*, May 1969, p. 516.

Hawkins, G. *Educational Experiments in Social Settlements*. Studies in the Social Significance of Adult Education in the United States, no. 5. New York: American Association for Adult Education, 1937. CS.

Hawkins, G. *Education for Social Understanding: Programs of Case Work and Group Work Agencies*. Studies in the Social Significance of Adult Education in the United States, no. 22. New York: American Association for Adult Education, 1940. CS

Heim, K. M., and Wallace, D. (eds.). *Adult Services: An Enduring Focus for Public Libraries*. Chicago: American Library Association, 1990. CS

Heimlich, J. E., and Norland, E. *Developing Teaching Style in Adult Education*. San Francisco: Jossey-Bass, 1994.

Hesser, F. E. *Village Literacy Programming in Pakistan: A Comparative ABE Study with Guidelines*. Vancouver: Centre for Continuing Education, University of British Columbia, 1978. CS

Hodgkin, T. *Nationalism in Colonial Africa*. London: Frederick Muller, 1956.

Horton, A. I. *The Highlander Folk School: A History of Its Major Programs, 1932–1961*. Brooklyn, N.Y.: Carlson, 1989. CS

Houle, C. O. "The Relevance of Research to the Preparation of Professional Adult Educators." *Adult Leadership*, 1972, 20(8), 305–308.

Houle, C. O. *The Literature of Adult Education: A Bibliographic Essay*. San Francisco: Jossey-Bass, 1992.

Hudson, J. W. *The History of Adult Education*. London: Longman, Brown, Green, and Longmans, 1851.

Hudson, R. H. *Radburn: A Plan of Living*. New York: American Association for Adult Education, 1934. CS

Hutchinson, E., and Hutchinson, E. *Learning Later: Fresh Horizons in English Adult Education*. New York: Routledge & Kegan Paul, 1978. CS

Johnson, L. S. (ed.). *Reading and the Adult Learner*. Newark, Del.: International Reading Association, 1980. CS

Johnstone, W. C., and Rivera, R. J. *Volunteers for Learning*. Chicago: Aldine, 1965.

King, D. *Training Within the Organization*. London: Tavistock, 1968. CS

Knowles, M. S. *Informal Adult Education*. New York: Association Press, 1950.

Knowles, M. S. "Andragogy, Not Pedagogy." *Adult Leadership*, April 1968, 16, 350–386.

Knowles, M. S. *The Modern Practice of Adult Education: From Pedagogy to Andragogy*. (Rev. ed.) Chicago: Follett, 1980.

Knowles, M. S. *The Adult Learner: A Neglected Species*. (4th ed.) Houston, Tex.: Gulf, 1990. CS

Knowles, M. S., and Associates. *Andragogy in Action: Applying Modern Principles of Adult Learning.* San Francisco: Jossey-Bass, 1984. CS

Knox, A. B. "Educational Leadership and Program Administration." In J. M. Peters, P. Jarvis, and Associates, *Adult Education: Evolution and Achievements in a Developing Field of Study.* San Francisco: Jossey-Bass, 1991.

Knox, A. B. *Strengthening Adult and Continuing Education: A Global Perspective on Synergistic Leadership.* San Francisco: Jossey-Bass, 1993. CS

Knox, A. B. "Recent Adult Education Trends in the United States." In W. Lenz, *Modernisierung der Erwachsenenbildung.* Vienna, Austria: Bohlau Verlag, 1994.

Knox, A. B., and Associates. *Developing, Administering, and Evaluating Adult Education.* San Francisco: Jossey-Bass, 1980.

Kotinsky, R. *Adult Education and the Social Scene.* New York: Appleton-Century-Crofts, 1933.

Kurshan, B., and Lenk, C. "The Technology of Learning." In Institute for Information Studies, *Crossroads on the Information Highway: Convergence and Diversity in Communications Technologies.* Nashville, Tenn.: 1994.

Langenbach, M. *Curriculum Models in Adult Education.* Malabar, Fla.: Krieger, 1988.

Learning Behind Bars: Selected Educational Programs from Juvenile, Jail, and Prison Facilities. Pittsburgh, Penn.: QED Communications, 1989. CS

Lindeman, E. C. *The Meaning of Adult Education.* New York: New Republic, 1926.

Lovett, T. *Adult Education, Community Development, and the Working Class.* London: Lock, 1975. CS

McLagan, P. A. *Helping Others Learn: Designing Programs for Adults.* Reading, Mass.: Addison-Wesley, 1978.

Magill, S. B., and Monaghan, J. E. "Job Instruction." In R. L. Craig and L. R. Bittel, eds., *Training and Development Handbook.* New York: McGraw-Hill, 1967.

Malamud, D. I. *Teaching a Human Relations Workshop.* Chicago: Center for the Study of Liberal Education for Adults, 1955.

Malcolm X. *The Autobiography of Malcolm X.* New York: Grove Press, 1964.

Marrow, A. J. *The Practical Theorist: The Life and Works of Kurt Lewin.* New York: Basic Books, 1969.

Marsick, V. J., and Watkins, K. E. *Informal and Incidental Learning in the Workplace.* London: Routledge, 1990. CS

Mathews, A. *Library Programs: Library Literacy Program, Abstracts of Funded Programs, 1986.* Washington, D.C.: U.S. Department of Education, 1987. CS

Merriam, S. (ed.). *Linking Philosophy and Practice*. New Directions for Continuing Education, no. 15. San Francisco: Jossey-Bass, 1982. CS

Merriam, S. B., and Cunningham, P. M. *Handbook of Adult and Continuing Education*. San Francisco: Jossey-Bass, 1989.

Mezirow, J. *Dynamics of Community Development*. Metuchen, N.J.: Scarecrow Press, 1963. CS

Mezirow, J. *Transformative Dimensions of Adult Learning*. San Francisco: Jossey-Bass, 1991.

Mezirow, J., and Associates. *Fostering Critical Reflection in Adulthood: A Guide to Transformative and Emancipatory Learning*. San Francisco: Jossey-Bass, 1990.

Miklas, S. (ed.). *Principles and Problems of Catholic Adult Education*. Washington, D.C.: Catholic University of America Press, 1959. CS

Mill, J. S. *Autobiography*. New York: Columbia University Press, 1944.

Miller, V. *Between Struggle and Hope: The Nicaraguan Literacy Crusade*. Boulder, Colo.: Westview Press, 1985. CS

Monroe, M. E. *Library Adult Education: The Biography of an Idea*. Metuchen, N.J.: Scarecrow Press, 1963. CS

Moore, M. *The Effects of Distance Learning: A Summary of the Literature*. University Park: American Center for the Study of Distance Education, Pennsylvania State University, 1990.

Morrison, T. *Chautauqua: A Center for Education, Religion, and the Arts in America*. Chicago: University of Chicago Press, 1974. CS

Nadler, L. *Designing Training Programs: The Critical Events Model*. Reading, Mass.: Addison-Wesley, 1982.

Nelson, T. H. *Ventures in Informal Adult Education*. New York: Association Press, 1933. CS

Newman, J. H. *The Idea of a University*. White Plains, N.Y.: Longmans, Green, 1910.

Newsom, B. Y., and Silver, A. Z. (eds.) *The Art Museum as Educator: A Collection of Studies as Guides to Practice and Policy*. Berkeley: University of California Press, 1978. CS

Nowlen, P. M. *A New Approach to Continuing Education and the Professions*. New York: National University Continuing Education Association, American Council on Education, and Macmillan, 1988. CS

Ogden, J., and Ogden, J. *Small Communities in Action*. New York: HarperCollins, 1946. CS

Ogden, J., and Ogden, J. *These Things We Tried*. Charlottesville: University of Virginia Extension, 1947. CS

Oppenheimer, R. "The Added Cubit." *Encounter*, 1963, *12*, 45.

Paulston, R. G. *Other Dreams, Other Schools: Folk Colleges in Social and Ethnic Movements*. Pittsburgh, Penn.: University Center for International Studies, University of Pittsburgh, 1980. CS

Perraton, H. (ed.). *Alternative Routes to Formal Education: Distance Teaching for School Equivalency*. Baltimore, Md.: Johns Hopkins University Press, 1982. CS

Perry, W. *The Open University: History and Evaluation of a Dynamic Innovation in Higher Education*. San Francisco: Jossey-Bass, 1977. CS

Peters, J. M., Jarvis, P., and Associates. *Adult Education: Evolution and Achievements in a Developing Field of Study*. San Francisco: Jossey-Bass, 1991.

Phinney, E. *Library Adult Education in Action*. Chicago: American Library Association, 1956. CS

Poston, R. W. *Democracy Is You: A Guide to Citizen Action*. New York: Harper-Collins, 1950. CS

Poston, R. W. "The Relation of Community Development to Adult Education." *Adult Education*, 1954, 4, 194.

Powell, J. W. *School for Americans: An Essay in Adult Education*. New York: American Association for Adult Education, 1942.

Powell, J. W. *Education for Maturity*. New York: Hermitage House, 1949. CS

Queeney, D. S. *Assessing Needs in Continuing Education: An Essential Tool for Community Improvement*. San Francisco: Jossey-Bass, 1995.

Reigeluth, C. M. (ed.). *Instructional Design Theories and Models*. Hillsdale, N.J.: Erlbaum, 1983.

Reischmann, J. (ed.). *Adult Education in West Germany in Case Studies*. New York: Verlag Peter Lang, 1988. CS

Rogers, C. *On Becoming a Person*. Boston: Houghton Mifflin, 1961.

Rosentreter, F. M. *The Boundaries of the Campus: A History of the University of Wisconsin Extension Division, 1885–1945*. Madison: University of Wisconsin Press, 1957. CS

Rumble, G., and Harry, K. (eds.). *The Distance Teaching Universities*. London: Croom Helm, 1982. CS

Schon, D. A. *The Reflective Practitioner*. New York: Basic Books, 1983.

Seashore, M., and others. *Prison Education: Project NewGate and Other College Programs*. New York: Praeger, 1976. CS

Simerly, R. G. *Planning and Marketing Conferences and Workshops: Tips, Tools, and Techniques*. San Francisco: Jossey-Bass, 1990. CS

Simerly, R. G., and Associates. *Strategic Planning and Leadership in Continuing Education: Enhancing Organizational Vitality, Responsiveness, and Identity*. San Francisco: Jossey-Bass, 1987. CS

Simpson, E. L. *Faculty Renewal in Higher Education*. Malabar, Fla.: Krieger, 1990. CS

Sork, T. J., and Buskey, J. H. "A Descriptive and Evaluative Analysis of Program Planning Literature, 1950–1983." *Adult Education Quarterly*, 1986, *36*, 86–96.

Sork, T. J., and Caffarella, R. S. "Planning Programs for Adults." In S. B. Merriam and P. M. Cunningham (eds.), *Handbook of Adult and Continuing Education*. San Francisco: Jossey-Bass, 1989.

Squires, G. D. *The Learning Exchange: An Alternative in Adult Education*. East Lansing: Institute for Community Development and Services, Michigan State University, 1975. CS

Stewart, C. W. *Moonlight Schools for the Emancipation of Adult Illiterates*. New York: Dutton, 1922. CS

Stocks, M. *The Workers' Educational Association: The First Fifty Years*. London: Allen & Unwin, 1953. CS

Strauss, A. L. *Mirrors and Masks*. Glencoe, Ill.: Free Press, 1959.

Strother, G. B., and Klus, J. P. *Administration of Continuing Education*. Belmont, Calif.: Wadsworth, 1982.

Stubblefield, H. W., and Keane, P. *Adult Education in the American Experience: From the Colonial Period to the Present*. San Francisco: Jossey-Bass, 1994.

Studebaker, J. W. *The American Way*. New York: McGraw-Hill, 1935. CS

Tennant, M., and Pogson, P. *Learning and Change in the Adult Years: A Developmental Perspective*. San Francisco: Jossey-Bass, 1995.

Titmus, C. J. (ed.). *Lifelong Education for Adults: An International Handbook*. Elmsford, N.Y.: Pergamon Press, 1989.

Torbert, J. K. *The Establishment of an Adult School*. New York: Macmillan, 1936. CS

Tough, A. M. "The Teaching Tasks Performed by Adult Self-Teachers." Unpublished Ph.D. dissertation, Department of Education, University of Chicago, September 1965.

Tyler, R. W. *Basic Principles of Curriculum and Instruction*. Chicago: University of Chicago Press, 1950.

Vella, J. *Learning to Listen, Learning to Teach: The Power of Dialogue in Educating Adults*. San Francisco: Jossey-Bass, 1994. CS

Verner, C. "Definition of Terms." In G. Jensen, A. A. Liveright, and W. Hallenbeck (eds.), *Adult Education, Outlines of an Emerging Field of University Study*. Washington D.C.: Adult Education Association, 1964.

Walshok, M. L. *Knowledge Without Boundaries: What America's Research Universities Can Do for the Economy, the Workplace, and the Community*. San Francisco: Jossey-Bass, 1995.

Weeks, E. *The Lowells and Their Institute*. Boston: Little, Brown, 1966. CS

Welch, E. *The Peripatetic University: Cambridge Local Lectures, 1873–1973*. Cambridge, England: Cambridge University Press, 1973. CS

Wolff, K. H., trans. and ed. *The Sociology of Georg Simmel*. Glencoe, Ill.: Free Press, 1950.

Name Index

• •

Subject Index

A

A Distance Education Consortium (A*DEC), 85

Act, concept of, 47, 254

Actions, objectives related to, 192

Activity identification: in Army program, 102; in framework, 61–62, 175–177; in health education, 120–121

Adaptation credo, 7

Adult education: in Army, 87–104; assumptions in, 41–53; attention to process in, 3–4; background on, 1–2; categories of educational situations in, 125–171; in community improvement programs, 104–113; credos and systems for, 1–39; defined, 20, 41, 254; for destitute persons, 75–81; as field of study, 2–6; fiscal problems in, 227; fundamental system for, 41–73; glossary for, 251–261; for health, 113–122; institution-centered, 4, 149–165; literature on, 263; personal mastery in, 237–249; program design in, 173–235; rationale in, 15–16; rural program for, 81–87; summaries on, 248–249, 252–253

Adult Education Committee (United Kingdom), 6

Adult educators: aspects of personal mastery for, 237–249; background on, 237–239; case method for, 240–242; concerns of, 5; judging, 44; as leaders, 201–202; praxis for, 239–240, 241–242; situational categories for, 242–248; summary on, 248–249; task of, 6–7

Africa: and community development, 24; independent study in, 127; learning groups in, 139, 141

Aggregate, concept of, 47–48, 254

Aim. See Objectives

American Psychological Association, 49–50

Analyst: concept of, 254; role of, 48

Andragogy: concept of, 255; systems based on, 26–30

Andrews University, and continuing nursing education, 117

Appraisal: concept of, 232, 255; evidence for, 233; of Hobo School, 81

Appraising results, in framework, 69–70, 231–233

Aspiration, concept of, 182, 255

Association, concept of, 149–150, 255

B

Boston University, and andragogy, 27